Material Culture and People's Art Among the Norwegians in America

Edited by *Marion John Nelson*

1994
The Norwegian-American Historical Association
Northfield, Minnesota

Preface

MATERIAL CULTURE and artistic expression plays a significant part in defining ethnicity and national identity. Objects from the everyday environment of average people in addition become documents of history. In these two regards, the material record provides a unique entrance into the past as well as the contemporary experience of Norwegian Americans. The sensitive and observant student will discover the subtle ways in which national symbols and cultural expressions are altered to interpret and to reflect upon an immigrant reality within an American matrix, and how a collective historical memory evolves and is preserved in profane structures and sacred edifices, in pictorial art and religious icons, in festive as well as everyday dress, and in decorative objects and public monuments.

In its earlier publications the Association has unfortunately been unable to take full advantage of the historical evidence that the material record represents. The Association is indebted to Marion John Nelson for making it possible to publish this well illustrated and carefully assembled collection of articles, *Material Culture and People's Art Among the Norwegians in America*, which goes a long way in correcting past neglect, although, to be sure, there remains much more to be done. The contributed essays amply illustrate the richness of the sources and the possibilities that exist for continued investigation of them. The volume will hopefully serve as an incentive to the scholarly community to produce additional books treating Norwegian-American material culture and popular art.

Finally, it is my pleasure, as in past volumes, to acknowledge with much gratitude the professional services of Mary R. Hove, my competent and genial assistant in the editorial work.

Odd S. Lovoll
St. Olaf College

Foreword

IN NORWAY'S native culture, material things had great importance. It was in such things that the creativity of the people found its highest expression. In storytelling and music the tradition was also strong but perhaps not stronger than that of many other peoples in Europe, primarily the Germans and the Irish. In the richness of its material culture, however, Norway is almost unique. One must turn east and to the far south—to the Baltic, Slavic, Balkan, and Mediterranean countries—to find the nearest counterparts, and even there the comparison is more in abundance and brilliance than in historical, social, and expressive richness.

The people of rural Norway both retained their traditions in material culture from medieval times and freely absorbed into them the new impulses that through the centuries reached them from outside. Even the native material culture of neighboring Sweden does not have the same exuberance and historical complexity. The geographic and political isolation of Norway, a remote and often neglected province under Danish rule through most of its modern history, may account in part for its retaining more than most countries of Europe that fascination and reverence for objects and images characteristic of primitive cultures.

In spite of the role played by material things in native Norwegian life and the tendency of the Norwegians not completely to reject the past when coming under the influence of the new, little has appeared in print about material culture among Norwegian Americans. The importance of objects to them is revealed by their exceptional collecting and preservation activities, a subject dealt with extensively in the first essay of this volume, but little of the collected and preserved material has been investigated in a way that has brought it to print. The following essays are an initial attempt to rectify that situation.

Since shelter was one of the first needs of the immigrants that required a material solution, two essays on immigrant architecture appear early in the volume. Reidar Bakken reveals how immigrant building in Coon Valley, Wisconsin, continues Norwegian traditions beneath a surface of Americanization. Houses that have the L shape and surface decoration of American farmhouses of the time prove upon investigation to consist of several units each of which has the three-room plan of traditional rural dwellings in Norway. Farmsteads that appear to have the loose arrangement of buildings typical on American farms prove when studied to reflect the divided farmyard characteristic of Gudbrandsdalen, the region in Norway from which most of the immigrants in the area came. Kenneth Breisch, who presents early Norwegian immigrant architecture in Bosque county, Texas, finds continuity not only in the floor plans of units within the houses but in the longitudinal way houses were enlarged. This is true even where a lack of timber led to a shift in building material from log to stone. Breisch also detects an affinity among Norwegian immigrants for American house types that are near in basic character to traditional Norwegian types.

Immigrant answers to an even more immediate material need, clothing, are considered by Carol Colburn. Fashionable dress, which had become standard American dress, was fairly international by the time of mass emigration from Norway in the latter half of the nineteenth century. It had by then even in Norway begun working its way out from the cities into the rural areas from which most of the immigrants came. They were, therefore, somewhat prepared for the dress they encountered on arriving in America. As in architecture, however, certain characteristics from traditional dress tended to affect choices. Something in dress without a significant counterpart in architecture of the early immigrant period was a tendency to retain some obvious symbols of Norwegian tradition, primarily in such accessories as jewelry, with clothing that was otherwise completely American. One manifestation of this clinging to traditional accessories is presented in the essay by M. A. Madson, who shows that the number of vinaigrettes, small vessels for carrying salts or perfume, brought to America and retained by Norwegian women far exceeds that brought by immigrants from Denmark, where the practice of carrying them appears to have been even more established.

Carlin Hibbard and Kristin Anderson demonstrate in separate essays how the lack of fine artists on the western plains together with the tradition in Norway of allowing artistic expression among the common people made it possible for Norwegian immigrants with little or no academic training to function for the community in artistic capacities generally reserved for professionals in America. Hibbard gives a detailed presentation of S. O. Lund, who with modest rural Gudbrandsdalen origins and no training outside the vicinity of Eau Claire, Wisconsin, became for several decades that community's major source of paintings for homes, churches, and secular public buildings. Anderson reveals how the Norwegian Lutheran practice of adorning the church with a painted or carved altarpiece allowed artists of the people for a time to carry out major works for the church as they had done in the rural areas of Norway. When professional artists became available, however, they soon put pressure on congregations to abandon the use of local talent. The irony of this is that the work of the local artists without professional status is now receiving much more attention in the art world than that of those with academic credentials.

The volume is a sampling which merely suggests the possibilities for further study in Norwegian-American material culture and people's art. Such subjects as the local production of handcrafted furniture in immigrant communities, the psychological role played by objects from Norway in the immigrant home, or the motivation for the extensive and spirited revival of Norwegian arts and crafts among the immigrants after World War II have scarcely been touched on. Much is also left to be said about dress, a category of material culture to which every immigrant made a unique contribution. Local artists like S. O. Lund with little or no formal training, who supplied the artistic needs of their own communities, existed throughout Norwegian America but have received little or no attention. The early architecture of only two relatively small settlements has been covered here, leaving a vast field for study in that area alone. Since all objects perish and the information about them has a way of disappearing even before the objects themselves, there is some urgency in continuing investigations of the kind presented in this volume.

Marion J. Nelson
University of Minnesota

Contents

Material Culture and People's Art
Among the Norwegians in America

Material Culture and Ethnicity:
Collecting and Preserving Norwegian
Americana before World War II

by Marion John Nelson

*Preservation and the
Norwegian Folkways*

THE FIGURE in Norwegian folk tales most commonly associated with Norwegian national character is Askeladden, the "ash lad" who gets his name from sitting dreaming by the fire and making marks in the ashes. In one of the best known stories he and his two older brothers are headed for the palace to test their wits in the competition for the princess.[1] Askeladden stops and puts in his satchel the old things he finds along the way, a dead magpie, an old wooden loop for making a rope sling, a broken dish, two ram's horns, a wedge for splitting logs, and the worn-out sole of a shoe. Each time his brothers make fun of him and each time he responds, "I have such things to do; I have such things to carry; I might as well take this one." It turns out to be precisely these objects that get him through the test his brothers have failed and that win for him the princess and half the kingdom.

There are numerous indications in Norwegian folk culture of respect for even the simplest things and of veneration for that which has acquired exceptional age. A quite ordinary ale bowl at Vesterheim, the Norwegian-American Museum, has the inscription "I have now been around for seven generations. The eighth restored me. Long may he live."[2] Many such objects are dated as if the maker recognized their ultimate significance as documents of a specific time. But the most direct reflection of the Askeladden mentality in Norwegian folk practice is the tendency to keep anything that has for whatever reason entered one's life. When one storehouse is full, build another.

The wealth of antiquated and therefore dispensable objects of everyday or festive use on Norwegian farms is documented by the overwhelming collection of ethnographic materials assembled in rural Norway by Artur Hazelius and his staff at the Nordic Museum in Stockholm during a comparatively short period in the 1870s and 1880s.[3] Just after him came Anders Sandvig, who single-handedly and primarily in Gudbrandsdalen assembled the mammoth collections of Norwegian ethnographic materials at the Maihaugen Museum in Lillehammer.[4]

In spite of the above and the collecting activities of the Norwegian Folk Museum in Oslo, local museums, and private collectors, farms still remain with the accumulated material culture of several centuries stored in outbuildings and extra rooms in the house. Three instances are known, undoubtedly out of many, in which the inventory of such farms was inherited in its entirety by members of the family who had immigrated to America. The heirs in two of these cases had lost their Askeladden mentality and sold most of what came to them. [5] Askeladden's brothers too were Norwegian. In the third case, the Askeladden characteristic survived the Atlantic crossing. The material was from the Svidal farm in Jølster, Sogn, which was inherited by the children of the last owner's sister, who had emigrated to North Dakota. Personal property included seven handwoven coverlets and three early bench covers representing at least three or four generations of weaving on the farm and well over a ton of wood and metal household and agricultural objects covering about the same span of time. Eight trunks on the farm, several from the eighteenth century, were used as crates for the shipment, as were several other pieces of early furniture. What could not be easily transported was left for the purchaser of the farm or given to the local museum. The objects that came to America were systematically divided among seven children, and they can literally not be bought with love nor money (Vesterheim, the Norwegian-American Museum, Decorah, Iowa, tried). To the family members, now scattered throughout the United States, they are treasured links to the past that function much as they did in a less self-conscious way when taking the form of an accumulation from ancestors on the family farm.[6]

Askeladden's respect for old and apparently useless things is encountered among individual immigrants from the beginning. By the 1890s, the Askeladden mentality was already finding institutional expression. Efforts to preserve architecture related to the immigrant past occurs almost simultaneously with efforts to preserve smaller objects. The institutions that led the way were two branches of the immigrant church: the United Lutheran Church with its stronghold at Luther Seminary in St. Paul, Minnesota, and the Norwegian Synod with its cultural center at Luther College in Decorah. They did not long remain competitive in preservation efforts. Even before theological matters were settled between them in the merger of 1917, an unwritten understanding appears to have been arrived at which left major responsibility for the preservation of material documenting immigrant history with the Synod. Luther College remained the nucleus of all preservation activity until the process of segregating these efforts from the church began with the founding of the Norwegian-American Historical Association in 1925.[7]

A number of circumstances other than the Askeladden characteristics of Norwegians contributed to the exceptional achievements of Norwegian Americans in preserving the material record of their past. Two have just been referred to, the early role of institutions in the effort, which gave it official status as well as continuity, and the early acceptance of centralization. The latter minimized internal conflict or competition. The pioneering position of Scandinavia in the preservation of material culture also gave the immigrants a model on which to build. Finally, the period during which the Norwegians left their country was one of intense nationalism, and nationalism is generally accompanied by a search of the past for deeds that might foster pride and for symbols of identity.

Even the emphasis on the material culture of the common man, which becomes an identifying characteristic of Norwegian-American preservation efforts, relates to historical circumstances. The lack of sovereignty and therefore of an indigenous ruling class in Norway made the history of the country the history of the "common people," mostly farmers and fishermen. Among them the written record was sparse but the material record rich. This situation was recognized by Norwegian scholars already in the late nineteenth century and led to methods and directions in historical research and presentation that were part of the heritage on which Norwegian-American scholars built.

It is not surprising that one of the first preservation projects to be carried out by the Norwegians in America involved a church. The preservation mentality is rooted in the same recesses of human psychology as that which led to the veneration of relics in the Middle Ages. The latter simply gave a mystic dimension to something which for us today is more pragmatic. An element of faith, however, must lie behind all the preservation of objects that no longer serve a practical purpose or have special æsthetic value. There has to be the belief that this is somehow for the good because it is often hard to justify rationally. Believers therefore tend to defend their positions simply with quotations such as Santayana's "Those who cannot remember the past are condemned to repeat it" or Ivar Aasen's "Lat oss inkje Forfederne gløyma" (We must not forget our forbears). That Askeladden's brothers laughed at him is completely understandable. His actions did not make sense but were based on a faith that ultimately brought him victory.

For immigrants in general and for the immigrant church in particular the preservation of objects from the past had an immediate but not easily definable purpose somewhat distinct from a belief in its ultimate good. This was establishing legitimacy and identity, proving, in other words, that they had roots. The matter of legitimacy and roots presented a special problem for the Norwegian Lutheran church in America because it was not a part of the church of Norway as the Catholic Church was of the church in Rome. The several Norwegian-American Lutheran church bodies, in spite of their spiritual

Old Muskego.
An Icon for the
Immigrant Church

Ill. 1. Muskego church as it
appears on the grounds of
Luther Seminary in
St. Paul, where it was
reconstructed in 1904.
*Courtesy of Luther North-
western Theological Semi-
nary Archives*

lineage, were merely seedlings from the mother church left to establish themselves on new ground. They were caught in the dilemma of representing
divine authority and yet, as institutions, having brought themselves into
being.[8]

The first major effort of the Norwegian Americans to preserve a historic
immigrant artifact was the moving of the Muskego church from near Milwaukee, Wisconsin, to the grounds of Luther Seminary, St. Paul, Minnesota, in
1904 (Ill. 1).[9] This early structure had been replaced by a new building in
1869 and moved to a neighboring farm. According to the Reverend Rasmus
Anderson, pastor of Our Savior's Lutheran Church in Brooklyn, New York
(not to be confused with Professor Rasmus B. Anderson), the idea of preserving the church had been taken up with him by the Reverend Gjermund
Hoyme, president of the United Lutheran Church, in 1894.[10] By 1900 the
building, which was then being used as a pig house by the owner Hans Jacobson, had been purchased for the United Church through the efforts of the
Reverend Gerhard Rasmussen and President Hoyme.[11] Two years later, at the
annual meeting of the United Lutheran Church, a resolution was passed urg-
ing pastors to collect money for the church and making Rasmussen chairman
of a Muskego church committee.[12] In another two years, by December, 1904,
the logs were on the grounds of Luther Seminary.

C.L. Jacobson, who knew the original church from when his father was the
sexton there, was in charge of the restoration.[13] The fact that he was brought
from Wisconsin for the task reveals the committee's concern for authenticity
in preserving this venerable structure from the formative period of the Norwegian Lutheran church in America. Someone with knowledge of the original

building was essential for the restoration because Hans Jacobson had sold the walnut pews and the pulpit (which was an integral part of the altar) to a furniture maker in Milwaukee.[14] At least these portions of the interior, if not more, had to be reconstructed from memory at the time of the restoration.

Why Muskego? The text which was read in the 1930s and 1940s at the annual memorial services at the church for the seminary students asks the same question and answers it with a quotation from Isaiah 51:1, "Look unto the rock whence we were hewn, and to the hole of the pit whence we were digged." The same text includes the underlined statement *This is the first building erected exclusively for a church by Norwegians in America*."[15]

The emphasis given the above assertion may have been necessary to assure its acceptance because the facts are not completely clear. Even the author of the text safeguards himself by admitting that "Elling Eielsen's meetinghouse in Norway, Fox River, Illinois, was earlier, but it was a combination dwelling and meetinghouse without altar or pulpit." This building does not seriously challenge the assertion. The two churches at Koshkonong are another matter. The author again safeguards himself by making an honest admission of the facts. The Muskego church, he says, "was finished late in the winter of 1844 and dedicated March 13, 1845. The two churches at Koshkonong were dedicated December 19, 1844, and January 31, 1845. Nothing remains of the Koshkonong churches." Then to be sure that the figures have not misled the listener, we are simply told, "The Muskego Church was built and finished first."

The Muskego church has, indeed, generally been recognized as the first building constructed exclusively for church purposes by the Norwegians in America. An important issue at the turn of the century was which of the several church bodies that were organized later had greatest claim to the "rock whence we were hewn" and "the pit whence we were digged". Hoyme from the United Church had clearly taken the lead in having it preserved, but the Synod, with its stronghold in Decorah, also had a certain historic claim to it in that both bodies had grown out of the formative activities in the Muskego colony. Representatives of the Norwegian Synod had apparently shown interest in the church at a comparatively early date. The Reverend Wilhelm Rasmussen, who served Muskego from 1892 to 1901, wrote in *Lutheraneren*, September 7, 1904, "I do wish to mention in this connection that the United Lutheran Church was close to losing the old church and the Norwegian Synod getting it. In that case it would not be lying where it is now, it would have been rebuilt at Luther College in Decorah, Iowa, which was the idea."[16]

The Synod had known the circumstances of the church and been aware of its significance for some time before the matter of obtaining it for restoration became an issue. An early accessions book of the Luther College Museum lists the hinges and other parts of the church door as a donation from the owner himself, Hans J. Jacobson, on March 10, 1898. This gift would most likely have been solicited. The Synod was apparently not at that time ready to make a commitment on the entire building. However, after President Hoyme and Gerhard Rasmussen had given Jacobson an informal offer for it on behalf of the United Church, an envoy from the Synod came to Jacobson with a counter-offer of double the sum. Jacobson remained loyal to Hoyme and Rasmussen, the latter of whom got his brother Wilhelm to write up a formal purchase agreement with Jacobson. A check for $100.00 was soon in his hands.[17] Competition between the two factions in this case had positive results. Without the need for immediate action, Muskego church would probably have continued to be Jacobson's pig barn. It was now at least the property of the United Lutheran Church, but another competitive situation had to arise for the project to be brought to completion.

In 1904 a third location entered the controversy over the final disposition of the Muskego church. The elderly Reverend H.A. Stub, who had been pastor at Muskego from 1848 to 1855, presented a strong plea in *Lutheraneren*, August 24, 1904, to re-erect the Old Muskego Church on Indian Hill where it had been built and where it would stand alongside the new church. Wilhelm Rasmussen, who had by then left the Muskego parish, was sympathetic but felt that the plea came too late. Rasmus Anderson's previously mentioned article in *Lutheraneren*, October 12, 1904, is an eloquent defense of Stub's position. It reads like the arguments being made today by museum people the world over to preserve total human environments rather than fragments torn from their original sites. "If the old church can be restored on Indian Hill, even though this is off the beaten path, it will be in its rightful place, because it stands on holy ground, and will have a two-fold meaning, when it is sought out as an historic monument."

Anderson and the venerable Stub may not only have been ahead of the times in their concept of preservation but may have recognized that on Indian Hill the church would be outside the major arenas of church politics and therefore on "neutral" as well as "holy" ground. But, however sound the reasoning of the opposition, within less than two months after Anderson's article appeared, the logs of the Muskego church were in St. Paul, as was C.L. Jacobson, the man from the parish who had been hired to supervise the restoration. All money raised for the project had by then already been spent, but the work appears to have been brought to completion in short order.[18]

In *De norske settlementers historie* from 1908, Hjalmar Rued Holand claims credit for having initiated the Muskego church project through a 1897 article in *Skandinaven* in which he supposedly reported on a visit to the church and recommended restoration.[19] The historian E. Clifford Nelson has searched *Skandinaven* in vain for the letter. It is only if Holand was somehow linked with Sebastian Selkirk, an Ibsen enthusiast from Indianapolis who did write such a letter in *Skandinaven*, November 10, 1897, that his story could have some credibility. Even then there is little reason to doubt Anderson's word

Ill. 2. The Kensington runestone with its finder Olof
Ohman and two armed
guards at a public showing
of it about 1929. *Courtesy of
The Runestone Museum*

that Hoyme had discussed the restoration with him already in 1894. Holand's
desire to associate himself with this project, however, is significant. He understood the importance of historic monuments in holding the immigrant group
together and giving it a sense of belonging in the New World. This is precisely
what the Kensington runestone, to which he dedicated much of his life, is
about (Ill. 2).

*A Claim to the Land.
The Kensington
Runestone*

The Kensington runestone, as is well known, was reportedly found by Olof
Ohman in the roots of a tree on his farm in November, 1898.[20] The runic
inscription in translation reads: "8 Swedes and 22 Norwegians on an explo-
ration journey from Vinland westward. We had our camp by 2 skerries one
day's journey north from this stone. We were out fishing one day. After we
came home we found 10 men red with blood and dead. AVM save us from
evil. We have 10 men by the seas to look after our ships, 14 days' journey from
this island. Year 1362."[21]

   The stone, apart from matters of authenticity, has special significance for
Norwegian Americans in several ways. It gives them a national epic (short as it
is), a symbolic right to their land even in the Midwest as descendents of the
first Europeans to have set foot on it, and an icon of almost indestructible
nature that can be returned to as a reminder of their heroic past and their primary position in the New World.[22] It is the most evocative example of Norwegian-American, more properly Scandinavian-American, material culture
to enter immigrant consciousness. None other has been reproduced in granite
many times its original size as a roadside monument.[23] None other has been
the inspiration for a number of plays and pageants that have been performed

in various places over a number of years.[24] None other has been the topic of at least a dozen book-length studies.[25]

One might ask how the Kensington runestone relates to salvaging and preserving material documents from the past. When Hjalmar Holand went to battle for its authenticity in 1908, it had been essentially discarded and was, according to some reports, serving as a stepping stone to the door of the granary on the Ohman farm.[26] It compared, in other words, to the Muskego church serving as a pig house or to the sole of a shoe thrown by the wayside in the Askeladden story. After having received about four months of attention between the time of its discovery late in 1898 and April, 1899, during which it was generally proclaimed a fake, it had been abandoned even by its finder and owner.[27] Holand first uses it as an historic document in his 1908 history of the settlements, the volume in which he also claims credit for having initiated the project to save the Muskego church. Since others, as we have seen, carried that out, Holand became the Askeladden who picked up the abandoned stone. It did not bring him a princess, but it did give him a life mission. Neither did it win for him and his cause half the Norwegian-American kingdom, but it has come close.[28]

Preservation and the Times. The Eighteen Nineties

The record does not say who from the Synod came to Hans J. Jacobson in an attempt to claim the Muskego building for Decorah by outbidding the United Lutheran Church, but it could well have been Haldor Hanson, who in 1900, the year this supposedly occurred, was aggressively collecting Norwegian-American material for the Luther College Museum.[29] Had the emissary been Luther President Laur. Larsen or the Reverend U.V. Koren, Wilhelm Rasmussen would certainly have included the name in his 1904 report of the incident.[30] People of their stature would probably not under any circumstance have gone on this slightly underhanded mission. Hanson was young, comparatively new at the College, and probably unknown in the upper echelon of the United Church.

The correlation in time between the Muskego church project and the development of a Norwegian-American collection in Decorah is almost uncanny. The initial incident in the church effort appears to have been Hoyme's discussion with Anderson in Brooklyn in 1894.[31] In 1895 Hanson was put in charge of the Luther College Museum and in 1899 was named its first curator.[32] His seminal and aggressive activities there in establishing a Norwegian-American collection came to an end when he resigned as curator in 1902, the year the church had been dismantled and stood ready for shipment to St. Paul.

It was the decade from about 1895 to 1905 when the first wave of ethnic awareness swept through the Norwegian-American people, at least as far as their material culture was concerned. One now had for the first time in the immigrant community a substantial adult second generation, people who were adequately American to have little need to hide their ethnic origin. They

Marion John Nelson

were also far enough away from it to be developing curiosity about it, if not an actual feeling of rootlessness and a need to look back. Many by now had also reached an economic level that gave them for the first time an opportunity to reflect on who they were. Cultural activities of any kind beyond the church, school, and newspaper had been limited in the period of settlement. The Atlantic crossing of the *Viking*, a replica of the recently excavated ninth century Gokstad ship, in 1893 and its dramatic arrival at the Columbian Exposition in Chicago on July 12 also contributed to the rise in ethnic awareness among the Norwegian Americans at the time (Ill. 3).[33] The intent of the voyage was to show that Leif Ericson indeed could have discovered America in a ship of his period. The amount of coverage in the immigrant press and of books and pictures distributed indicates the strong impact made by the ship, which was referred to by the national president of the Fair, Thomas Porter, as one of the two attractions that most impressed the public.[34]

Ill. 3. The *Viking*, a full-scale replica of the Gokstad Viking ship sailed across the Atlantic in 1893. It is shown here shortly after being placed under shelter in Lincoln Park, Chicago, in 1921. *Courtesy of J. Harry and Josefa Andersen*

Directly related to the concerns of this article is the fact that the ship was preserved as an historic monument. The leader in this preservation effort was the wealthy Norwegian-American S.T. Gundersen of Chicago. Gundersen began soliciting funds with the hope that the ship could be sent to Washington, D.C., and presented to the Smithsonian Institution without charge.[35] Earlier efforts to raise money among Norwegian Americans for the purchase of the ship had failed.[36] The ship's captain Magnus Andersen together with the captains of other Norwegian ships then in Pensacola, Florida, attempted to have the Norwegian government cover a debt remaining on the building of the ship so that the money raised in Chicago could go toward founding a home in Norway for elderly seamen, a pet project of Captain Andersen.[37] Since the Norwegian parliament turned down the request, the solicited money went toward paying the debt. The donors now, however, made the condition that the ship, which had been sailed to New Orleans, be returned to Chicago.[38] It was presented to the Field Columbian Museum, then apparently under the University of Chicago, on October 13, 1894, and placed on a platform outside the art building in Jackson Park.[39] After being exposed to the weather for twenty-six years, it was in 1921 restored and placed under a shelter in Lincoln Park by the Federation of Norwegian Women's Societies at a cost of $15,000.[40] Here it symbolizes in a more general way than the Kensington runestone the Norwegians' right to a place in America as the first Europeans to set foot on its soil.

Gundersen's preservation effort appears to be the first carried to completion by a Norwegian immigrant group. Since it concerns a replica rather than an original document of immigrant history, however, it has been presented here as an example of the ethnic awakening that occurred in the 1890s rather than the beginning of a preservation movement. The distinction is admittedly academic. As an icon, to be sure, it functions like Muskego church. The Kensington runestone is the perfect example of the ambiguity that can exist between the icon and the document of history.

If Hans Jacobson had let money rather than loyalty to the United Church determine his decision on who should get Muskego church, the Synod would stand as the unchallenged leader of early preservation efforts among the church bodies. As the group nearest the state church of Norway and also the one giving greatest emphasis to the classic tradition in its schools and among the clergy, it was recognized early as the body most likely to become the bastion of the old culture in the New World. When Knute Nelson, then governor of Minnesota, was looking for a place where an Agreement of Transfer dated 1757 from his home farm of Kvilekval near Voss might be preserved, he wrote to Haldor Hanson in Decorah, Iowa, in 1896, "I should like to have this old Deed preserved as long as possible, & I can think of no better place than Luther College—for I apprehend it will be one of the most lasting centers of Norwegian literature & Norwegian education in America."[41]

The early concern of Luther College with preserving a record of Norwegian immigrant history is indeed astounding, not only preceding and excelling other institutions of its own immigrant group in this but putting the group itself at the forefront of all such groups in America. Primary credit for this must go to Laur. Larsen, president of the college, although he chose a protégé to assume direct responsibility for the effort.

In August, 1879, just two years after Larsen first officially acknowledged contributions of objects to the college with the hope that they would become the nucleus of a museum,[42] he was making special concessions to a twenty-three-year-old student, Haldor Hanson, who was having difficulty covering his bills at Luther.[43] In 1888, five years after Hanson graduated from the full six-year program, Larsen attempted to find a position for him on the staff.[44] The Synod was not yet ready to consider an appointment in music, Hanson's major area of interest and expertise, at Luther College so Larsen suggested the possibility of Hanson's teaching mathematics. From 1888 to 1890 he taught mathematics, Latin, and Norwegian in addition to providing the long-established instruction in singing.[45] After Hanson had spent a year of music study in Weimar, Germany, and had taught music for several years in Minneapolis, the Synod finally agreed to a full appointment in that subject for him at Luther with his obligations beginning in January, 1895.[46] Between then and his departure from Luther in 1904, Hanson laid the foundation for Luther's distinguished program in music, primarily in band. [47]

One wonders if music was the only motivation for Larsen's consistent pursuit of Haldor Hanson. On October 12, 1895, the first year of his full appointment, Hanson was put in charge of the Luther College Museum and was also made responsible for the collecting of immigrant newspapers, periodicals, and material relating to Scandinavian music.[48] In 1899, he was named curator of these special collections, the first time this title was used at the college. In December of 1895, two months after he had taken over, the museum was given space in the quarters being vacated by Professor Gisle Bothne in the so-called "chicken coop," a carriage house beside Old Main which had been spared in the fire that gutted the latter in 1889.[49] Already in November, before the new space became available, Hanson was soliciting objects for the opening.[50] The date when the museum was first made officially accessible to the public is not known, but this appears to have been in the spring of 1896. Three years later, donations taken at the door were contributing to the support of the endeavor.[51] The question of concern in this study, however, is just what was being collected and exhibited.

No detailed record of what was in the collection when Hanson took over in October, 1895, has come to light, although David T. Nelson gives a list from an unidentified source in his short history of the museum published as a full issue of *The Palimpsest* in December, 1965. The original collection must have been salvaged in the fire of six years earlier because a small room off a classroom was designated for it when the building reopened in 1890. The newly appointed professor William Sihler was put in charge and described what he found as "a number of boxes of all sorts filled with objects which had been given by persons to whom a museum was a curiosity shop."[52] The collection probably did not include much Norwegian-American material because immigrant history did not emerge as an area of concentration until 1895, when this was recommended at a meeting of the Luther College Alumni Association in Red Wing, Minnesota, on August 16. The Reverend Adolf Bredesen presided and was probably the prime promoter.[53] It was also at this meeting that the alumni agreed to ask the college to put a staff member in charge of the museum who had the time to carry out his obligations, the recommendation which led to Hanson's appointment. By 1900 he was able to refer to the Luther College Museum as a "Norwegian museum," the only one in the country "so far as is known."[54]

While Haldor Hanson was in charge, from October, 1895, to 1902, a detailed record of acquisitions was maintained. The range is very great because the museum covered both natural and cultural history, the latter, to be sure, with concentration on Norway and Norwegian immigration. Responsibility for collecting and maintaining archival and printed materials relating to immigration and Scandinavian music also rested at that time with the museum rather than the library.

From the standpoint of solicitation, emphasis was heavily on immigrant material. No acquisitions policy was stated, but some conception of what it was can be gleaned from a letter written by Hanson to C.K. Preus, later to become president of the college, on November 22, 1895.[55] The immediate purpose was to ask for a historic cane that Preus's father, H.A. Preus, had apparently thought should go to the museum and also to suggest the donation of additional memorabilia from the revered pioneer pastor. But Hanson goes on to say, "Hopefully you also have other objects—historical—Norwegian—related to the College, the Synod, or Norwegians either here or at home—that you would be willing to give up." It is quite clear that Hanson's intent from the beginning of his official involvement was to carry out the recommendation of the Alumni Association that mentions essentially the categories referred to in the letter. The wording of the recommendation suggests that the Alumni Association was thinking primarily of written documents, but Larsen and Hanson seem to have taken for granted that objects too were a part of the historical record.

In an article about Hanson published by *Skandinaven*, July 1, 1927, and reused elsewhere as his obituary two years later, he is referred to as a musician and *bok-kjender* (book expert). His love for the printed word is revealed by the exceptional collection of Norwegian-American publications he assembled, including the unusual, such as school catalogues, student publications, and publishers' book lists, as well as the usual newspapers, periodicals, and books. But Hanson must also have had an unusual sense of the importance of material culture in documenting the everyday life of a people. As Hanson modestly stated in a report of May 15, 1900, "The Museum has made a special effort to gather a collection of Norwegian materials, older and newer, examples of Norwegian fine and domestic arts. Much of this was brought to America by immigrants, and it is important to rescue as much of this as possible before it is too late."[56]

Hanson's acquisitions record, which runs from October 13, 1895, to the end of 1901, reveals that he brought together hundreds of items which document not only the domestic and fine arts of the Norwegians but almost every aspect of their everyday lives. Objects brought from Norway dominate, but things produced by the immigrants in America are also far from lacking. If museum activity in Decorah had ceased with Hanson's resignation as curator in 1902, the Norwegian-American people would still have possessed a remarkably comprehensive collection of their early material culture.

The concentration within the immigrant collection at the end of 1901 was on household materials, especially those going out of use and therefore in danger of disappearing.[57] There were over fifteen ale-drinking vessels, six with eighteenth or early nineteenth-century dates. Three were bowls with two animal-head handles (*kjenger*), and one was a well-carved drinking horn dated 1758. Seven were from Voss and Hallingdal, two from Numedal, and one from Hardanger. Containers for food or other household goods vie with drinking vessels in prominence. Fifteen are mentioned specifically, among which are three *ambar* (covered containers generally used for carrying or serving *rømmegrøt,* sour cream porridge), six pails, a butter tub, and a butter mold. The remainder are *tiner* or *esker,* boxes for a variety of uses. Candlesticks are also well represented. Pots and pans, bottles, a pitcher, and a rolling pin fill out the household collection. The limited amount of lefse-making equipment and irons for traditional pastries suggests that these were still too much in use for relegation to a museum, a fact that is borne out by their prevalence in immigrant homes to this day.

Trunks were apparently also still too common to be considered in need of rescuing "before it is too late." Almost every immigrant brought one, and many two or three, but only one had been accessioned by the museum at the turn of the century. As late as 1928, according to a report on June 7th of that year in the *Mount Horeb Mail,* Isak Dahle was excluding trunks (and spinning wheels) from the objects he would consider purchasing for Little Norway, his private museum in Wisconsin. A little later, they were getting rare and were accessioned in great numbers at Decorah. Now they are being made and decorated by immigrants as furniture symbolic of their origins. The only other piece of furniture at the Luther College museum in 1901 was a *kubbestol* (log chair) made in Wisconsin in the 1850s. It was undoubtedly considered a passing type already but, like the trunk, was ultimately revived as a symbol of ethnicity.

In textiles, the total lack of handwoven coverlets, objects which later came to the museum in large quantities, suggests that they too may still have been in use and not considered endangered. This is supported by references even now to such pieces having been on Grandma's couch or having served as Grandpa's favorite napping blanket. A visitor to the museum as late as 1990 when seeing the early coverlets on display said that he had one in the trunk of his car that he used for lying on when working under the car. To be sure, here was a fine handwoven coverlet somewhat the worse for wear.[58]

Most of the textiles in the collection around 1900 related to dress. Accessories to women's festive costumes included two Hardanger aprons, two pairs of woven garters, a breast plate, and four pairs of embroidered gloves and mittens. These represented Telemark, Hallingdal, and Valdres. One full bridal dress said to be 150 years old is listed. Non-textile accessories to female dress included a substantial amount of traditional jewelry, several family collections of some size in addition to individual pieces. Among the latter are 7 *søljer* (brooches), 3 buckles or clasps, 2 rings, and one bridal chain. Although Carol Colburn elsewhere in this volume has documented that the traditional brooch has continued to be worn by Norwegian-American women without break from immigration to the present day, some women already by 1900 must have felt that their peasant jewelry belonged in a museum as documents of an earlier life.

Men's accessories were as well represented as women's. While there are only 4 pipes, probably of the very long traditional type, there are 12 snuff and tobacco boxes, many described as having unusual age and character. The convenient commercial containers in which these products were sold in America soon made the fine old handmade boxes quaint relics from the past, as were signet rings and seals, of which there are 4. Even the knives in sheaths, traditionally carried by almost every man, were also a vanishing phenomenon. Three were accessioned into the collection. Of the 5 canes, also objects on their way out as elements of proper male dress, 3 were mementoes of early pastors. Retaining the cane as a remembrance of a man seems to have been common.

The shoes collected before the end of 1901 are a good indication of what was happening to this major item of dress. There are no leather examples, but there are wooden shoes of Norwegian, Norwegian-American, and Dutch origin. In the tool collection there is a complete set for making wooden shoes as well as separate wooden shoe chisels, but equipment for leather shoe making is missing. The leather shoe had taken over and the wooden shoe was disappearing.

When Hanson defines the immigrant collection at the museum in 1900 simply as "older and newer examples of Norwegian fine and domestic arts," he is probably doing so because these are what were expected in a museum collection. The concept of presenting the lives of average people through the things with which they worked was not well established outside Scandinavia, the area where it originated, when Hanson was doing his collecting during the last years of the nineteenth century. His description appears to be something of a cover-up. He was in actuality bringing together a remarkably comprehensive assemblage of material relating to a passing technology and way of life. The artistic quality of what was collected does not seem to have been a major concern.

The relationship of Hanson's collecting to that in the Scandinavian folk museums becomes especially evident when one looks at the tools and implements. Those for making wooden shoes have already been mentioned. Other sets include bookbinding equipment from 1860. There are carpenter's tools covering about the full range for making furniture, including a plane dated 1784. The tools for log building include the marker used for creating a tight fit between logs (*meddrag*) referred to in the article by Reidar Bakken. It represents a refinement in traditional Scandinavian log building that was soon abandoned by the immigrants. A spinning wheel and many loom accessories are found although there is no actual loom.

Among farming equipment is both a yoke and a shoe for oxen, but little horse equipment. The latter is represented only by a traditional set of hames from Valdres, parts of the harness that were totally different from those used here. Two corn planters, undoubtedly of the hand type, were accessioned, probably because the horse-drawn planter was taking their place. Both a frame for millstones and a separate set of the stones themselves were in the collection. Other miscellaneous farming equipment included wood stanchions, sheep shears, cow and sheep bells (one dated 1764), and a branding iron from Voss. The most remarkable purely functional object in the collection was Lars Reque's *kubberulle* (log-wheeled wagon) from the 1840s, the only one with wheels that are actual slices of a log known to have survived from the immigrant period (Ill. 4). It was accessioned in 1898 with the note "meget værdifuldt minde fra nybyggerlivet" (very valuable memento from life in the settlements). This kind of editorial comment is extremely rare in the record, indicating that Hanson got more excited about documents of socioeconomic life than about most examples of fine and domestic arts.

The collection of fine arts brought together by Hanson is well-rounded but small compared to what might be called the immigrant ethnological collection. Hanson himself contributed a group of pen and ink drawings by Herbjørn Gausta. This established immigrant artist, probably at Hanson's persuasion, donated his large and important painting of immigrant life called *The Bargain* in 1898. Ten other paintings by Gausta and two by the younger immigrant artist Alex Grinager are said by David T. Nelson to have been in the

collection before Hanson took over.[59] Hanson also accessioned a painting by Nils Hagerup, a west-coast artist of Norwegian origin, two pastels by the Norwegian Nils Bergslien; a very early painting from the Fet church in Norway; and plaster busts of Ibsen, Bjørnsen, and Ole Bull. Even objects related to the art of music, Hanson's major interest, were limited but representative. There was a Hardanger violin from 1817 and a psalmodikon, the one-stringed instrument used to lead singing in early immigrant churches and schools. Two other instruments were mementoes of music life at Luther College.

Before considering what determined the nature of the collection and how it was brought together, a word must be said about photographs and mementoes. The latter are not named as a category in Hanson's report of 1900, perhaps because they are more related to popular concepts of collecting than to an academic museum. He may have wanted to break the association of the museum with a curio shop.

While one might expect the mementoes to be largely of cherished Norwegian things, they are more often immigrant-related.[60] The Norwegian-American church is especially commemorated through such objects, suggesting indeed the concept of relics, physical evidence of a spiritual heritage. Hanson himself, we recall, solicited mementoes of the early church father H.A. Preus. Muskego and Koshkonong in Wisconsin, where the organized church had its conception and birth, were especially well represented. Mementoes from them include a piece of the oak tree at Koshkonong under which the first service there was held, an ornament from the old pulpit at Koshkonong, a small collection of miscellaneous items from the same area, the previously mentioned hardware and fragments of wood from the door of the Muskego

Marion John Nelson

church, and a doorknob given by C.L. Clauson himself from what he calls the first Norwegian-American parsonage, apparently his own house, at Muskego.

Related fragments from other sites of religious significance include the weather vane from the old Spring Prairie church, pieces of the Renville church (destroyed by a cyclone), and another chunk from a tree under which an early service was held. The Synod pastors were represented not only by a collection of their signatures, but also, as has been seen, by such things as pipes and canes. One of the latter was used by the Reverend H.G. Stub when he climbed what is often considered Norway's highest mountain, Galdhøpiggen, a Norwegian-American staff of Moses. The respect for a cane as *pars pro toto* of a man is beautifully illustrated in a story told by O.M. Norlie. "The cane which Eielsen [the leading figure in a pietistic strain in the church] used and which comforted him on his long pilgrimages he gave to his friend, Reverend Ole E. Hofstad; Hofstad gave it to his favorite deacon, Mathias J. Aus, Canton, South Dakota; Aus gave it to O.M. Norlie, reared on the Dakota prairies as his neighbor; Norlie gave it to the Luther College Museum, the greatest depository of Norwegian pioneer articles in America."[61]

Mementoes are often laughed at as historical documents in our pragmatic age, but they are a category of material culture that is loaded with information about a group's values, aspirations, and psychological needs. That the majority of mementoes in the Decorah collection around 1900 are from the early immigrant period reflects a desire in the people to establish its own history apart from that of either Norway or America. The material also suggests that at the folk level the early period of settlement was passing from history into mythology, a set of beliefs that rises above history and becomes the base on which a further culture builds. When that happens, mementoes relating to those beliefs become not only fragments of an essentially lost past but concrete evidence of their truth. Hardware saved from the Muskego door as a memento of the first Norwegian-American church becomes in itself evidence that Muskego was the first church. During the same period the Kensington runestone came to light and would soon acquire its irrevocable place in immigrant culture.

Hanson did not mention the mementoes in his report but he proudly made reference to another category of objects in the collection that represented something more than themselves, namely photographs. The building of a photographic collection began the first month of Hanson's tenure at the museum, October, 1895. He systematically set out to get a pictorial record of those things that could not easily be incorporated into a museum collection, people and architecture. By May 15, 1900, he had photographs of 180 buildings and 124 individuals of significance in Norwegian-American history. This was in addition to 30 photographs of groups at Luther College. Unfortunately, neither the vernacular architecture of the average immigrant nor these immigrants themselves were included in this record, rather surprisingly considering the nature of the collection of objects. Actual examples of vernacular architecture began to be collected in 1913, but photographs of it and of everyday life were not a part of collecting policy until the 1960s. The record was being made by photographers like Andrew Dahl of rural Madison, Wisconsin, even before Hanson's time, but neither Hanson nor other history museum curators were then collecting the full range of photographs being taken.

The immigrant collection at Luther College in 1901 did not give the coherent impression it does in this presentation because there is no evidence of its being displayed apart from other material until Knut Gjerset became curator in 1922. There were also less appropriate objects in the collection than have been mentioned here, such as the foot of an immigrant from Fergus Falls, Minnesota, that had been frozen and amputated.[62]

The remarkably comprehensive collection of immigrant material brought together by Hanson between late 1895 and early 1902 poses several questions. How was it assembled? How was its character determined? And, how did it relate to other museum collections at the time?

Although public requests for historical materials were occasionally made in Hanson's time, much of the collection resulted from personal solicitation. We have seen an example of this in Hanson's letter to C.K. Preus asking for his father's cane. In the same letter he makes reference to having "the boys" work for the museum, each in his own area, during the Christmas holidays.[63] In a letter to President Laur. Larsen, August 4, 1899, from Willmar, Minnesota, Hanson says he is traveling around working for the museum.[64] That he went from place to place soliciting materials is supported by the fact that donations from one locality often appear together in the acquisitions book. Friends and colleagues also worked on solicitation for him, and their names are occasionally listed with the acquisition. The Reverend Adolf Bredesen, for example, solicited the *kubberulle* and much more.[65] Kr. Magelssen and C. Sperati are among other names that appear as solicitors in Hanson's time.

The only written indication that has come to light regarding what Hanson was looking for in immigrant material culture is his previously mentioned request to Preus for "objects—historical—Norwegian—related to the College, the Synod, Norwegians here or at home . . . " and his after-the-fact description of what he had tried to collect: "Norwegian materials, older and newer, examples of fine and decorative art . . . before it is too late."[66] Concentration was definitely on those things that were losing functional significance and therefore in danger of disappearing from the record of immigrant life.

The great question is what led to the collection of so much material relating to the everyday life and work of the immigrant when this emphasis was not standard in museum collections at the time. One might expect to find the answer in the personal interests and dispositions of the leading figures, Hanson, Larsen, and others at the top; but one must also consider to what extent they could determine the direction the collection took. As the people in charge of or actually doing the soliciting and accessioning, they certainly had some control. Of importance as well, however, was the folk nature of the population among which the collecting was being done. The prominence of the folk in Norwegian society has already been mentioned. It was even more prominent in immigrant society before a social hierarchy within it had developed.

The families of students would have been the major contacts for Hanson when he solicited for the museum. The students themselves were being considered as solicitors in 1895.[67] Early writings about Luther College often mention that the students were mostly farm boys. Although there were some funds for purchases, most of the objects were donations, a situation which gives donors themselves a role in shaping the collection.[68] When they sent things in as a response to a general appeal, the selection was almost completely theirs. Rejection in these circumstances would have been difficult. The accessioning of the amputated foot may reflect this situation rather than the curator's judgment.

What the farmers had most of were simple everyday things; and they may, as practical people, actually have considered these their most important possessions even before museum curators began recognizing their significance. Workers have high regard for the tools and implements of their labor. The fact that these may have seen better days does not necessarily diminish this regard. It is the Askeladden mentality that we again meet here. The hoards of old objects on the farms in Norway have the ordinary and the exceptional lumped together without distinction. When the common people themselves do collecting, it is often of old tools and implements. Such private assemblages can be found on small farms and on the walls of restaurants and taverns throughout America. The great machines from the early days of industrialized farming, such as steam engines and threshing separators, are often kept in village sheds by a core of local enthusiasts and brought out annually for ritual performances that are usually a tremendous success with the local public. When the condition of these objects is such that they cannot carry out their ritual duties, they are pulled to some high spot near the road where all who pass must pay homage. If Hanson did not solicit grindstones and corn planters, he might still have been given them.

The Norwegian-American Museum had acquired its folk character already in the 1890s in part because members of a small elite immigrant group, like their peers in Scandinavia, became aware of the significance of the common man in their history but also because the overwhelming majority in the group among which the collection was assembled were just emerging from folk status. A museum recording the group's history would of necessity be a folk museum.

A natural place to turn in seeking sources for the democratic nature of collecting at the Norwegian-American Museum is Scandinavia, the area credited with originating the folk museum. During Hanson's time, direct connections are hard to document, although circumstantial evidence suggests that some may have existed. Haldor Hanson came to America at age nine and is not known to have revisited Norway before he began to work with the museum.[69] To what degree Larsen followed museum developments in Scandinavia or to what extent he as president guided Hanson in his work at the museum remains a question.

Information on Larsen's interest in or involvement with the museum is conspicuously sparse. He must have been supportive because he publicly acknowledged the original contributions, expressed the desire that they would continue, assigned a space for the collection and a person to be in charge in 1890, cultivated Hanson, in whom he must have recognized special museum potential, and in 1902 gave top priority to a library-museum building, an issue involved in the conflict with the faculty and the church council that led to his resignation.[70] In spite of all this, his daughter Karen in her extensive and excellent biography of Larsen mentions the word museum only twice and in purely incidental ways. Haldor Hanson, with whom Larsen appears to have been close as both a student and a staff member, is not mentioned once.

Eilert Sundt, the remarkable theologian and sociologist who laid the theoretical foundation for the development of the folk museum in Scandinavia, was about to leave teaching as an assistant at the university in Christiania (now Oslo) when Laur. Larsen matriculated there in 1850.[71] Sundt had already won national attention for his studies of tramps and gypsies in Norway and his work in improving their circumstances.[72] He had several years earlier completed the theological program at the university which Larsen was just entering. Sundt continued for the next twenty-five years to publish studies of the life and culture of the poor in Norway, including their building customs and crafts as well as their social practices.[73] As an historian, theologian, and someone who is said to have retained unshaken "confidence in the basic soundness of the Norwegian rural population," Larsen could not have avoided being aware of Sundt's work.[74]

By 1895 there must also have been among Norwegian intellectuals in Decorah some awareness of the Swede Artur Hazelius, who had since the early 1870s been collecting folk materials in Sweden and Norway for the Nordic Museum in Stockholm.[75] The museum had opened on a small scale to the public already in 1873, but the collecting of Norwegian material did not get seriously under way until the following year.[76] Hazelius' activity got wide publicity when the outdoor branch of the museum, Skansen, now generally recognized as the first public open-air museum, was opened in 1891.[77]

As early as the summer of 1882 in Norway, however, visitors to the royal estate on Bygdøy outside Oslo could on Sundays and holidays enter a large farmhouse moved in from Telemark with all its original furnishings.[78] Larsen was in Oslo that very summer and could well have taken the opportunity to see this new attraction in the city.[79] The building had been a gift of the farmer-owner Ole Hove to King Oscar II of Sweden and Norway, who covered the cost of moving it and making it available to the public.[80] During the next five years, four more buildings, including the Gol stave church, were added to the complex on Bygdøy and visiting hours were increased.[81] Reference to these developments could also well have appeared in the immigrant press, a matter still to be investigated.

The preservation of the Muskego church and the first phase of collecting immigrant ethnic materials in Decorah could have been inspired in part by the work of Hazelius and King Oscar II but were probably not influenced by either Anders Sandvig, the founder of Maihaugen in Lillehammer, or Hans Aall, the leading figure behind the founding of the Norwegian Folk Museum. Their activity only slightly precedes that in Decorah and would not have been generally known. The Folk Museum was established on December 19, 1894, but it did not open to the public until thirteen years later.[82] Anders Sandvig began collecting about 1887, but he did not have adequate storage space for extensive collections until he moved into a new house in 1894.[83] This is also the year he bought his first early farm building as the beginning of an open-air museum.[84] Ten years would pass, however, before Maihaugen opened with ten historic structures on the site where it would remain.[85] The development period for both these institutions coincides very closely with that of the early immigrant preservation and collecting efforts but does not precede them sufficiently to be considered a model at this point. The situation changes later.

In the precise nature of the folk materials being collected—the typical rather than the exceptional—Hanson was also abreast of his Norwegian colleagues. Hans Aall said in 1920 that this approach first occurred to him in the summer of 1894. "It couldn't be right," he thought, "to seek out and preserve only that which is considered beautiful and pass up all that otherwise played a part in early life."[86] Hazelius also came to this realization after having begun his collecting, although considerably earlier than Aall did.[87] Sandvig's original interest appears also to have been in the individual special object, but by 1902 he was firmly committed to showing material coming from the full range of society and representing work as well as celebration.[88] By the spring of 1896, according to his acquisitions record, Hanson was collecting tools and other very ordinary everyday things, and his comment on the special significance of the log-wheeled wagon was made in 1898. He, Larsen, and his Scandinavian counterparts were building on a common attitude toward history based in an academic tradition that included the work of Eilert Sundt, and they were also dealing with a common society that historical circumstance had given a predominant folk character. This, more than direct cross influence, may account for the parallels in Norwegian and Norwegian-American developments in collecting and preservation at the turn of the century.

The American Context of Preservation Among the Immigrants

The American context of the Norwegian-American activities must also be considered. These were once thought to be well in advance of other comparable collecting and preservation efforts in this country, but that assumption has had to be slightly altered since Simon Bronner of Pennsylvania State University published *Folklife Studies from the Gilded Age* in 1987. Bronner brings to light a previously neglected wave of interest in folk and ethnic material culture among folklorists during the 1890s, mainly in connection with the Chicago World's Fair of 1893. The extravagant display of technological progress at the Fair brought about a corresponding interest in both what Americans were building on and what they were losing. The book reveals that there were parallels in America for what went on in Decorah, just as there were in Scandinavia, but precise documentation of mutual awareness is also lacking here.

Folklorists in the English-speaking world up to the late nineteenth century had been primarily concerned with the beliefs and oral traditions of the peoples they studied. There now came to be an increasing interest in other aspects of primitive societies, primarily their material culture. This resulted in part from increasing contact between the English-language folklorists and those of Germany and Scandinavia, where the concept of folklore had always been broader, as reflected in their terms for it. In Germany these were "volksleben" and "volkskunde," while in Sweden it was simply "folkliv," a word that gradually entered English as "folklife" and by the 1960s was replacing the word "folklore" in several major institutions.[89]

The folklorists of the Gilded Age, however, tended to limit their concern with material culture largely to objects relating to beliefs and customs rather than "subsistence and technology."[90] Arts, crafts, and everyday household items were theoretically considered a part of folklore by such late nineteenth-century scholars as Fletcher S. Bassett of the Chicago Folklore Society[91] and W.J. Hoffman of Pennsylvania,[92] but little was done with this idea in practice. A growing interest in immigrant ethnic cultures among the Victorian folklorists, however, did relate directly to what was going on in Decorah. Among the extensive folklore exhibits in the Anthropology building at the Chicago World's Fair, for which Stewart Culin of Pennsylvania was responsible, was one devoted to Chinese-American workers.[93] The 1880s and 1890s also saw the beginning of serious studies relating to the Pennsylvania Germans, a people who had since the eighteenth century been recognized for their cultural distinctiveness but had not been given much scholarly attention.[94]

Haldor Hanson would probably not have been aware of developments leading to the folklore exhibits at the Fair in 1893, but he could well have seen the exhibits themselves. He knew Chicago from his year of music study there in the mid 1880s, and in 1893 he was teaching music in Minneapolis from which there was easy access by train to Chicago. The folklore exhibit seems to have been prominent enough to have caught the attention of any interested visitor. Culin says that it "afforded the greatest opportunity to the student and collector of folklore that has ever been presented upon this continent."[95]

While Bronner's work reveals that the collecting activities in Decorah were not without an American context, it also makes clear that they did in one way anticipate developments in this country. That was in the attention given subsistence and technology. In this they have their closest American parallel in the slightly later collecting of the remarkable Pennsylvanian Henry Chapman Mercer, who in 1897 shifted his interests from archaeology to folk technology.[96] Bronner presents him last among his Victorians, probably because he entered folklife studies late but probably also because he leads more directly than the others into the twentieth century.

Certain parallels between Hanson and Mercer are almost uncanny although there are also extreme differences, not least in their ultimate impact. They were born on the same day, June 24, 1856, and died four months apart, Hanson in December of 1929 and Mercer in March of 1930.[97] They shared a lifelong attachment to one group, Mercer the Pennsylvania Germans of Bucks county, where he was born and where he died, and Hanson the Norwegian Americans of the Midwest. Both were Renaissance types: Mercer a lawyer, archaeologist, historian, curator, and potter; Hanson a musician, archivist, curator, and publisher. There the basic personal similarities cease. Mercer approached being a mad genius of tremendous energy and creative powers, while Hanson was a highly gifted and hardworking man, too sensitive to claim his place in the world. There was also a difference in their origins and personal circumstances. Mercer came from a family that had been long established in this country culturally, professionally, and financially. His education was through private tutoring, boarding schools, and Harvard University. Hanson was of rural immigrant background and was educated largely in a small public school and at Luther College.

What most relates Mercer and Hanson in the context of this study is that both developed a passion for collecting in the late 1890s, Hanson for the Luther College Museum and Mercer originally for himself but ultimately for the Bucks County Historical Society. Both were innovative in giving tools and implements a place in their collecting, Hanson simply as a part of a larger whole and Mercer as a major area of concentration.

Mercer's description of how he began collecting what he called "tools," but which included all kinds of practical implements and utensils, indicates how innovative the concept seemed in 1897 even to this well-informed man. He had gone to a junk dealer to find a pair of tongs for an old-fashioned fireplace. "When I came to hunt out the tongs from the midst of a disordered pile of old wagons, gum-tree salt boxes, flaxbreakers, straw beehives, tin dinner-horns, rope-machines, and spinning wheels, things I had heard of but never collectively saw before, it occurred to me that the history of Pennsylvania was here profusely illustrated from a new point of view." He goes on to tell of the wild buying spree that followed. This led to the vast and now irreplaceable collections in the Mercer Museum, previously the Bucks County Historical Museum. He credits the fact that so much material had been saved to those folk collectors considered earlier, "these unthanked and non-mercenary hoarders," and to the abundant supply of wood in America that made outbuildings for storage possible.[98] Hanson had begun collecting precisely the kind of objects Mercer enumerates two years before the Pennsylvanian made his discovery.

The similarity between Hanson and Mercer, as between Hanson and the Scandinavians Hazelius and Sandvig, would ultimately have been greater if Hanson had got his building and stayed with the effort in which he had made such a remarkable beginning. He did not have the toughness or the personal wealth to carry it through on his own as did Mercer, nor did he have the same degree of support from his group enjoyed by his Scandinavian counterparts. He also lacked the persuasiveness of Hazelius and Sandvig.

Continuing the Legacy of the Nineties: New Impetus from the Norse-American Centennial

The character which the collection in Decorah acquired under Hanson between 1895 and 1902 remains to this day. Twenty years passed during which the museum had no strong leader. In 1911, after responsibility for it had been passed among several faculty members, President C.K. Preus himself became the chief administrator and retained that position until his death in 1921. Objects added to the collection during his presidency and curatorship continued to represent the full range of immigrant life. Three deserve special mention.

The year before Preus assumed curatorship of the collection, he obtained for it a carved Norwegian-American altar being stored in a St. Paul warehouse.[99] The carver, Lars Christenson of Benson, Minnesota, an immigrant from Sogndal, Sogn, Norway, was still working on the lower section in 1904 when he brought it for exhibition to the Minnesota State Fair. Since the people of Benson, where he had hoped it could be installed in a church he helped found, showed little interest in it, he did not go to the effort and expense of getting it back home after the Fair. How Preus discovered it in 1910, the year of the artist's death, is not known. The altar was, to be sure, an exceptional rather than an everyday object, but its character seemed so primitive that its significance was not understood by the average immigrant of his time. In his long obituary published in the Benson newspaper, no mention is made of the altar.

Preus's recognition of the Christenson altar's significance indicates that his philosophy was completely in line with that of his predecessors and followers in steering the course of the institution. He acted in the Askeladden tradition.

This acquisition in 1910 also made the Luther College Museum a pioneer among American institutions in the collecting of folk art. The first wave of American interest in it did not begin until later in the decade and then primarily among artists and private collectors.[100] When the first national survey of American folk art, called *The Index of American Design,* was made in the 1930s as a Works Progress Administration (WPA) project, the Christenson altar was included. It was referred to by Erwin O. Christensen, the director of the project, as "probably the largest and most ambitious single piece of religious folk carving" in America.[101]

The second acquisition from the Preus years that should be mentioned is a model of Anders Sandvig's open air museum in Lillehammer made for the Norwegian Centennial Exhibition of 1914 in Oslo (Ill. 5).[102] It was obtained and presented to the Luther College Museum by Professor M.K. Bleken, one of the faculty members who had earlier shared in the administrative responsibility for the collection. The model is the first concrete indication of a connection between the museum effort in Decorah and museum activities in Norway. The acquisition of it probably relates to the fact that C.K. Preus in 1913 had formally accepted for the museum its first early immigrant building, the Egge-Koren log house, the third of the three acquisitions from his era to deserve mention (Ill. 6).[103]

The first building in the Luther College Museum's open-air division was in part a memento because it had served for several months as the parsonage of the Reverend U.V. Koren, the first pastor called from Norway to a parish west of the Mississippi.[104] Yet, when President Preus expressed his thanks for it to the donor Paul Egge, with whose parents Koren and his wife Elisabeth had

Ill. 5. Model of the Maihaugen museum, Lillehammer, Norway, purchased by M. K. Bleken for the Luther College museum, 1914. It is evidence of early connections between museum developments in Norway and what was taking place in Decorah. *Courtesy of Vesterheim*

Ill. 6. The Egge-Koren log
house, moved to Luther
College for preservation in
1913, flanked on the left by
the Haugan house and the
Kaasa drying house and on
the right by the Washington
Prairie parochial school-
house, all moved to this site
around 1930. *Courtesy of
Vesterheim*

lived, he referred to it as a document of early immigrant life rather than a memorial to a specific person. "It is true," he said, "that many of these old log houses have been used for firewood and have served a good purpose as such but, it is also good that some can remain with their oak beams, hard and gnarled as they are, so they can tell descendants of their parents' and grand-parents' hard and gnarly days in the struggle and sacrifice of settlement. They also tell how lay and learned men faithfully shared sorrows and joys, one on the other, to establish God's church among our people."[105]

If one can assume that the Egge-Koren house was conceived as a first step in founding an open-air division of the Luther College Museum, which the subsequent acquisition of the Maihaugen model suggests, the house represents the first application of the open-air museum concept in America.[106] By the time additional buildings were added in 1929,[107] however, Henry Ford had already for three years been working on the idea of an outdoor village at Dearborn, Michigan, and in 1927 had moved an old general store to the site.[108] This was not his first effort at historic preservation. In 1919 he had moved and restored his birthplace and had in 1924 done the same with the Wayside Inn from Massachusetts, but these were not thought of as constitut-ing a unified open-air complex. That idea came to him in 1926, thirteen years after the Koren-Egge house became part of the museum in Decorah. Although pinpointing the beginning of the open-air museum in America is difficult, Don Yoder of the University of Pennsylvania recognizes the work in Decorah as the pioneering effort in founding an open-air museum in the United States.[109]

The person who would again bring strong leadership to the museum in

Marion John Nelson

Decorah was Knut Gjerset, who after his appointment at Luther College in 1902 had gained international recognition for his histories of Norway and Iceland. Although he did not assume responsibility for the museum until 1922, Gjerset descends rather directly from Haldor Hanson, with whom he had much in common. Their early contacts were close, and they shared a comprehensive and democratic approach to building the museum collection. Both men were of rural Norwegian stock and came as children with their parents to farms in small rural communities of the Upper Midwest.[110] There they stayed until they left for immigrant educational institutions in preparation for professional careers. Gjerset was in his second year at Willmar Academy when Hanson, who by that time had graduated from Luther College and had also studied music in Chicago, came to teach there from 1885 to 1887. They shared these years as teacher and pupil at this small and intimate institution.

Gjerset, like Hanson, is said to have been recruited for his position at Luther College by Laur. Larsen, although his appointment did not begin until the fall of the year Larsen stepped down as president in 1902.[111] Hanson and Gjerset together submitted their resignations in 1904 because of a policy statement for the college prepared by President Preus which stressed theological preparation over liberal education. Gjerset, however, retracted his resignation when the faculty adopted a revised statement prepared by him.[112] Hanson left for Chicago and never returned. Eighteen years passed before Gjerset took over his older colleague's position as museum curator.

Gjerset immediately recognized that a museum of the Norwegians in America must of necessity be a folk museum. In a letter to Ole Rølvaag of September 5, 1924, he says, "Consider the artifacts which must be found in a museum if it is to be a Norwegian museum. There will be old chests, artifacts of iron made in the father's own smithy, materials which the mother has woven, etc."[113] He looked on such objects also as "a valuable supplement to the historical material about Norwegian settlers in America to be found" in libraries and archives. He already recognized the uniqueness of what had been done at Decorah in collecting objects that can document the lives of the common people. "As far as we know," he says, "the Norwegian group is the only one that has seriously undertaken the task of creating a historical museum with collections which will illustrate their life and culture and the general conditions surrounding them from the time when their fathers and mothers first set foot on American soil."[114] His words establish that he recognized two things, the significance of the common people in history and of material culture in documenting their lives. His position is much like that of the younger Norwegian-American historian Theodore Blegen, whom Don Yoder recognizes as the key figure in establishing a democratic approach to the presentation of American history.[115]

Gjerset was the first to articulate what the museum had been doing, and he seemed happy to build on that. One shift in emphasis that had occurred slowly since the inception of the immigrant collection was from Norwegian material brought with the immigrants to material more representative of their life and culture in America. Movement in this direction was seen already during Hanson's curatorship in the kinds of mementoes and photographs that were collected. Two of the three major acquisitions during the C.K. Preus years were also distinctly immigrant, the Christenson altar and the Egge-Koren house. In the brochure *Luther College Museum* that Gjerset wrote in 1923, the year after he assumed responsibility for it, he says, "Of the various exhibits the pioneer collection is not only the most valuable but in many ways the most interesting" (Ill. 7).[116] When the museum received a gift of five truckloads of Norwegian objects weighing 8,800 pounds from the museums of Norway in connection with the 1925 centennial of organized immigration to America, Gjerset is reported to have considered "even this magnificent gift" as "of somewhat subsidiary importance, as the chief aim of the museum was to gather together articles illustrating the life of Norwegian pioneer settlers in America."[117]

With his orientation toward immigrant material, Gjerset was probably happy to accept responsibility for the major exhibition to be held in St. Paul in recognition of the Norse-American Centennial, an activity that occupied much of his time in 1925.[118] His intent was "to visualize to the present generation the contributions of the Norse pioneers and descendants" (Ill. 8).[119] The exhibitions, of which he was the overall coordinator, were held in the Women's Building on the Minnesota State Fairgrounds, the site chosen as the center for the national recognition of the occasion. Just eleven years earlier, the newly founded Nordmanns-Forbundet in Norway had taken the lead in working with Norwegian-American organizations on a comparable immigration exhibit held in Christiania in connection with the centennial of Norway's constitution. It had systematically dealt with all the major aspects of immigrant life, primarily through models, photographs, and texts.[120] The fact that it was held in Norway, where immigrant artifacts would have had to be sent, undoubtedly accounts for its character.[121]

Judging from photographs, the purely historical exhibition in 1925 was very similar to the exhibition of 1914. This formal presentation of immigrant history, however, was supplemented by a room with a rather miscellaneous collection of tools and implements drawn largely from the material assembled by Haldor Hanson over twenty-five years earlier (Ill. 4). The Household Arts exhibit, on the other hand, which had been assigned to the Women's Auxiliary before Gjerset was made general coordinator, was a massive display of objects from immigrant homes unlike anything previously assembled (Ill. 9).[122] Although not directly the product of Gjerset's efforts, this exhibit was a dramatic demonstration of his belief in the significance of material things from the everyday environment of average people as documents of history. Such material, he felt, "in the hands of the writers of history and students of American culture and social life would be most valuable."[123]

Marion John Nelson

Ill. 7 (top). Selections from
the collection of immigrant
pioneer household objects
and furnishings in the
Luther College museum as
installed in the "chicken
coop" by Knut Gjerset
about 1923. *Courtesy of
Vesterheim*
Ill. 8 (bottom). Knut Gjerset
(right) and the Reverend
Bernhard E. Bergesen (left)
inspecting utilitarian pioneer objects for the Norse-
American centennial
exhibition, St. Paul, 1925.
Courtesy of Vesterheim

Gjerset was eulogized for his work on the exhibition by D.G. Ristad in a newspaper review of the entire centennial event. "Of all that went on at the celebration," he wrote, "there was nothing in my opinion that got so near the essence of what it was all about or that was so pregnant with possibilities for the future as the exhibitions in the Women's Building." After recognizing the division heads and other workers, he continues, "But there is none the less one man who above all others deserves the most thanks, that is Dr. Knut Gjerset, curator of the Luther College Museum. It was his broad vision, his intimate understanding, his talent for organization, and, above all, his clearly focused, inexhaustible energy and faith in the possibilities of the exhibition that brought it to such magnificent results."[124]

Only a small part of the objects in the Norse-American Centennial exhibition that had been lent by individuals came to the museum in Decorah. When the exhibition was over on June 9, 1924, the collection at Luther College was not yet officially recognized as the central museum of the Norwegians in America. There was, at the time, still considerable debate as to where such an institution should be.[125] The decision came in the fall of that year when the Norwegian-American Historical Association was being formed and when Luther College, at the recommendation of the organizing group, changed the name of the Luther College Museum to the Norwegian-American Historical Museum.[126] The first action representing its central position occurred in the spring of 1926 when the recently incorporated historical association asked that custody of the massive gift of objects presented by museums in Norway to the Norwegian-American people through the association be assumed by the newly renamed Decorah institution. This was accepted on June 5, 1926, by the

Marion John Nelson

Luther College Board of Regents, which remained for another thirty-eight years the governing body of the museum.[127]

Beyond giving clearer definition to the goals of the museum, Gjerset's major contribution to it was in considerably enlarging its collections, giving organization to the way they were displayed, and in 1932–1933 bringing them together from their four locations at the College to a central building in downtown Decorah. This was the Arlington House, which had been constructed in 1877 as a hotel and had served from 1890 as the Lutheran Publishing House (Ill. 10).[128] It continues to be the main building of the museum just as Gjerset's philosophy of the institution continues to be its theoretical base.

That the two earliest major collecting and preservation efforts of the Norwegian Americans were institutional—the preservation of the Muskego building by the United Church and the founding of the Norwegian-American Museum by Luther College, an institution of the Synod—reveals the broad recognition of such efforts in the immigrant group. Hoyme was the driving force behind the Muskego project, but he was acting as president of his church

Ill. 10. The former Arlington House hotel and Lutheran Publishing House built in 1877 in Decorah, Iowa, and obtained through the efforts of Knut Gjerset for the Norwegian-American Historical Museum collection in 1931. The building is shown here after the restoration and renovation of the early 1970s. *Courtesy of Vesterheim*

body. Larsen was this force in founding the museum but was acting as president of the college and therefore as a representative of another church body. Hanson and Gjerset, in spite of their personal dedication to the museum, were carrying out obligations officially assigned to them as professors at the college. In Hanson's time these also reflected rather directly the interests of the Synod. It was to U.V. Koren, Synod president, rather than to college president Laur. Larsen, that Hanson submitted his resignation in 1901.[129]

A Norwegian-American preservation effort in Duluth, Minnesota, between 1927 and 1930 began as institutional, like the others considered, but was carried out through the gift of an individual. In 1926 Captain Gerhard Folgerø of Bergen, Norway, like Captain Andersen in 1893, had a ship of Viking type built, which he called the *Leif Erikson*. He sailed it from his hometown to Boston, Massachusetts, between May 23 and August 12. It was only 42 feet long, little more than half the size of the originals and of Captain Andersen's *Viking*, allowing the voyage to be made with a crew of only four men. After spending the winter on the east coast, the vessel sailed through the Great Lakes to Duluth, where it arrived on June 23, 1927.[130]

The *Leif Erikson* was built in Korgen, Nordland, which may account for Nordlandslaget scheduling its annual meeting in Duluth to coincide with the ship's arrival. Already at the society's banquet the very day the ship came, Congressman William Carss recommended that the people of Duluth buy it, place it in Lakeshore Park, and rename the area Erikson Park.[131] Four days later Attorney John Jenswold recommended at a meeting of the city commissioners that the city should put up $2,500, half the amount needed to buy the ship, and the community would raise the rest.[132] The arrangement proved to be unnecessary because the philanthropist J.B. Enger, who had already given Duluth the land for its Enger Park Municipal Golf Course, purchased the ship and presented it to the city. He stipulated that it be placed in Lakeshore Park as Congressman Carss proposed, but two years passed before this was accomplished.[133]

Private Collecting and Preservation of Norwegian Antiquities. The Example of Old Stock Americans

Generally in the history of collecting and preservation, individual efforts have preceded the institutional, the one often leading to the other. Artur Hazelius and Anders Sandvig began as private collectors and even operated their own museums before beginning the process of institutionalizing them.[134] Several private collections of historic rural buildings existed in Christiania before the Norwegian Folk Museum was organized in 1894.[135] Mercer did most of his collecting of folk materials as a private venture before he turned them over to the Bucks County Historical Museum,[136] and Henry Ford established his innovative museums at Dearborn, Michigan, privately long before they were brought together under a museum corporation.[137] Preservation efforts often follow the same pattern. A family feels that its fine home should remain intact as a memorial to ancestors and an educational attraction for the area. Family

members attempt for a while to maintain it but must generally soon approach the community or a historical society about taking it over. The early role of institutions in the collecting and preservation efforts of the Norwegian Americans is exceptional.

Institutional activities in democratic societies should reflect the broad interests of the people in general. That this was true of the institutional preservation efforts of the Norwegian Americans is evident from related private endeavors among them. Few sizeable ones, however, got underway until after the Muskego project had been completed and the museum in Decorah was well established. These private efforts in the immigrant community, like those in Scandinavia and among Americans in the East, tended to feed into institutions. Since an institutional collection with an emphasis on Norwegian-American material came into being early at Luther College, it became the major recipient of later private endeavors.

Old stock Americans appear to have shown an interest in Norwegian folk and medieval material before the immigrants did. When this interest developed among the latter out of pride or a desire for identity, they were in a sense linking into a movement that was already underway for different reasons.

The first modern building based on a stave church either here or in Norway was constructed in 1880 as St. Mark's Episcopal Church at Islip, New York, by William K. Vanderbilt (Ill. 11).[138] The designer was none other than the prominent American architect Richard Morris Hunt. The Fortun Church in Sogn, which four years later was moved to Fantoft outside Bergen, is said to have been one of the models. The Norwegian building at the Columbian Exposition of 1893 in Chicago, also modeled on a stave church, was bought by

Ill. 11. St. Mark's Episcopal church, Islip, New York, designed by Richard Morris Hunt and built in 1880 as what appears to be the first modern structure inspired by Norwegian stave church architecture. This view from the mid-1890s shows the original Hunt building in the background with an 1893 addition between it and the original porch in the foreground. The church is evidence that interest in the antiquities of Norway existed among old-stock Americans before revealing itself in the immigrant group. *Courtesy of St. Mark's Episcopal church*

the wealthy Cornelius Billings of that city, presumably not a Norwegian American, for his estate on Lake Geneva, Wisconsin, that was later purchased by the Wrigley family of chewing gum fame.[139] The purchase by Isak Dahle, dealt with elsewhere, came later (Ill. 12).

According to the late granddaughter of Ole Bull, Sylvia Bull Curtis, the Norwegian violinist's American wife took great interest in Norwegian folk art as early as the 1860s and 1870s. Many of the pieces collected by Sara Thorp Bull came to Massachusetts when she returned to her family after Ole Bull's death in 1880.[140] An important Nativity tapestry from seventeenth-century Gudbrandsdalen, an early trunk with exceptional wrought iron, and an elegant Norwegian rococo chair from her collection were given to Vesterheim by Sylvia Curtis in the 1980s. This was apparently not the only collection of its kind in Massachusetts. The *Wisconsin State Journal* of Madison reported on June 28, 1928, that the founder of Little Norway in Mount Horeb "Isak Dahle has received word that there is an excellent collection of Norwegian antiques in Ipswich, Mass., and he will go there in a few days and attempt to purchase

Marion John Nelson

some of them." The nineteenth-century American collector Henry Armitt Brown of Philadelphia had, apparently on a tour of Scandinavia in 1870, purchased Norwegian folk material, including a Wise and Foolish Virgins tapestry from seventeenth-century Gudbrandsdalen that was given to Vesterheim in 1987 by Brown's granddaughter.[141]

The collecting of Norwegian antiquity continued among Americans in Philadelphia. After the turn of the century, Isabel Spackman and her husband of that city assembled among other things on world tours a substantial collection of Norwegian artifacts that passed with her death in the 1940s to the Delaware Museum of Art in Wilmington. Early in 1992, twenty-five objects from that collection were sold by the museum through the auction house Pook and Pook, Inc. of Downingtown, Pennsylvania.[142] Much of the Norwegian material which appears regularly at Christie's, Sotheby's, and other major auction houses in the East must be of similar origin.

Even in the Midwest, collecting of folk material brought to the area by immigrants appears to have begun among non-Norwegians. In 1911 the collection of John H. Terens (presumably not Scandinavian) of Mishicot, Wisconsin, was sold in a bankruptcy case. In the great miscellany of objects from natural and cultural history were the following Norwegian items: a carved set of hames, a carved tankard, an "ancient" mountaineer's club, and a case with a Norwegian beaded belt and thirty-nine pieces of traditional jewelry and other ornaments of dress.[143] It is only for the contents of this case that the specific origin is known. They were purchased by Terens from a Hanmerstad (probably a misspelling of Hammerstad) family of Gibson, Wisconsin, about 1880.[144]

The earliest Norwegian American known to have been concerned privately with the collection and preservation of Norwegian antiquity in America on a somewhat large scale is Jens Johnson of Minneapolis. He emigrated from Innvik in Nordfjord, Norway, in 1877 and served as a land agent and later an immigration and passenger agent for the Northern Pacific Railroad for nearly forty years before his death in 1929.[145] It is the role he played in the western expansion of Norwegian settlement and his contribution to Norwegian singing societies that received most attention in his obituary and other publicity about him, but there is also evidence of his having been an early and avid collector. In August, 1896, Johnson donated a wooden candlestick from Innvik church, another early copper candlestick, a traditional brooch with spangles, a brass buckle, an old English watch (immigrant watches were often English), a Norwegian document from 1643, and several coins to the Luther College Museum.[146] Donations apparently continued during the period in which records are incomplete, between 1902 and 1922, because Gjerset in his 1923 museum brochure says, "A pair of brass candlesticks dating from 1400, a carpenter's broad axe, probably from about 1500, and many other articles, equally rare and valuable, have been given to the collection by Mr. Jens Johnson of Minneapolis, Minn., one of the most active patrons of our museum."[147]

Johnson's positions as land, immigrant, and passenger agent for a major western railway gave him the opportunity to obtain objects from newcomers needing cash. Some cultivation of him on the part of the Luther College Museum is not surprising. On September 12, 1922, less than a year before he made his kind remarks about Johnson in the brochure, Gjerset had prepared the following certification on which he had also secured the signatures of the presidents of the church and the college: "This is to certify that Mr. Jens Johnson, of Minneapolis, has been authorized to collect objects of interest and value for the Luther College Museum. Mr. Johnson renders this service without any compensation, and we bespeak for him a courteous reception wherever he may present the needs of our museum with a view to increasing the collection and making it as complete and valuable as possible." At this point Johnson's health was already failing, and the acquisitions record lists only five objects—an inlaid picture frame, an early plane, a whale oil lamp, an iron snowshoe for a horse, and a chest—as having come to the museum through Johnson's efforts, all during 1923 and 1924.

In the early 1970s, the Reverend Warren Sorteberg of Our Savior's church in Minneapolis approached the museum in Decorah about a woman who had a collection she felt should go to Vesterheim. It proved to be the elderly daughter of Jens Johnson, Ruth (Mrs. W.E.) Herber, who said her father had resisted giving his personal collection to the museum in Decorah because he felt Luther College had pressured him too much to do so. This makes the very formal letter of certification as a solicitor presented to him when he was seventy-five years old and in failing health appear possibly as an attempt to flatter the venerable old gentleman into donating his own collection. No comparable letter to any of the many others who solicited material for the collection has come to light. Although the daughter admitted that material had gone out of the collection since her father's death almost half a century earlier, she still had sixty-six objects, many of great significance, to present to Vesterheim.

Peter D. Peterson of Eau Claire, Wisconsin, was a slightly younger contemporary of Jens Johnson who, unlike the latter, gained his reputation as a collector rather than for accomplishments in his profession, that of saloon-keeper. His occupation is, in fact, never mentioned in the fairly extensive published information about him. In the city directories of Eau Claire in the early 1900s, when he already had his city address at 411 Putnam Street and when his name appears on a separate list of saloonkeepers, his occupation in the main listing is given as farmer.[148] He apparently did not consider saloonkeeping an adequately respectable profession for listing in the directory at the time.

Peterson is described as looking completely respectable, but certainly not like a farmer. Eyvind Ager of Eau Claire, now in his 90s, remembers him as "a fine looking man, always well dressed . . . wearing a white shirt, starched collar, and a black bow tie."[149] At another time he concludes, "I am inclined to believe he ran a very orderly place."[150]

The last observation was probably correct, because Peterson was a good friend of the very orderly temperance advocate Waldemar Ager, Eyvind's father. Peterson is said to have visited him often, and Ager was not only a pallbearer at Peterson's funeral but wrote a kind obituary in his newspaper *Reform* where he refers to the departed saloonkeeper as "a kind and congenial man who had many friends."[151] Peterson's family has given a somewhat different picture of his character. Nieces report that when they visited Mrs. Peterson, "Uncle Pete . . . kept to himself in his room and at times was quite grumpy."[152] A granddaughter refers to him as "a shrewd collector" who "invested everything in his collections much to Grandma's dismay, for there were things she would have liked."[153] He let her family trunk, which she is said to have wanted, go to Decorah with the sale of his collection.[154]

It was probably dedication to the Norwegian heritage that paved the way between the saloonkeeper Peterson and the temperance advocate Ager. Ager wrote in his obituary of Peterson, who was born in Namdalen, North Norway, in 1859, and came to America at age twenty-four, that he "had deep feeling for Norway, kept up with Norwegian literature and everything related to his countrymen over there."

Ager's statement is of significance in trying to determine the motivation for Peterson's collecting. The material is so extensive and diverse, including armor, firearms, china, glass, stamps, and coins, that it might seem more the product of an obsession with ownership than of any specific interest. Norwegian material, however, appears to have had special appeal (Ill. 13). He is said to have begun picking up things already when at sea as a boy of sixteen (echoes of Askeladden),[155] but a relative of his wife from Norway who visited him in 1926 got the impression that it was after visiting Norway in 1908 that his serious collecting began. When in Skjåk, Gudbrandsdalen, the area from which his wife Kari Harsem (Harsheim) came, he had "bought up all he could get hands on of antique carved pieces, etc."[156] While obtaining much material in the immigrant community, Peterson, according to Ager, also continued to buy abroad: "He went back to Norway several times and each time took the opportunity to enlarge his great collections."[157] Pieces from Harsheim remained prominent.

Just as Johnson is thought to have utilized his position as immigrant agent to obtain objects for his collection, Peterson is known to have utilized his as saloonkeeper for the purpose. In the 1970s an elderly visitor to Vesterheim, on seeing some primitive woodcarvings from the Peterson collection, remembered them from an Eau Claire bar where they had been given to the owner for drinks. The bar was undoubtedly Peterson's famous saloon.

Profession and hobby were indeed very closely linked for Peterson. Eyvind

Ager recalls that the gun collection, which was considered one of the largest in the country, was also exhibited in the saloon. In the window, according to Ager, was a sign that read "Museum Buffet."[158] Peterson's enterprise therefore belongs to a large category of establishments in which the serving of food and drink has been combined with collecting and exhibiting historic and aesthetic materials. In private clubs, such as the eighteenth-century Norske Selskab in Oslo or the much later Union League clubs in America, this combination is standard. Another commercial example comparable to Peterson's, especially appropriate for mention here, was the Buckhorn in Hayward, Wisconsin. Although owned by the Swiss old-time musician and student of folk music Otto Rindlisbacher, the collection which gave the place character included many Norwegian musical instruments. They too have come to Vesterheim through the generosity of his daughter Lois Albrecht. Less ambitious examples of bars and restaurants in which the owners display their collections are ubiquitous throughout the Midwest and elsewhere.

The popular appeal of places that combine the display of collections with the serving of food and drink has led to some museums in recent years solving their problems of audience and even support by incorporating a major restaurant into their complex. If Vesterheim should move in the same direction by expanding its Dayton House restaurant, the Peterson collection could ultimately find itself back in circumstances related to those under which it came into being.

While completely private in origin, the Peterson collection was already moving toward institutionalization around 1920 when the owner lent the material that could not be accommodated in his saloon and residence to the Eau Claire Public Library for display on the second floor.[159] It was his hope that the city would buy it for $10,000, $3,000 less than an appraisal obtained by the library, as the basis for a public museum.[160] Since the idea did not receive adequate support, Knut Gjerset, who had for some years shown interest in it but felt it should remain in Eau Claire, entered the picture. He negotiated with Peterson in 1930, just three years before the collector's death, to buy the collection—with the exception of the coins, stamps, and "several valuable and prized pieces that he [Peterson] gave to members of his family and other relatives"—for $6,125.[161] No itemized list of the material has come to light, but David T. Nelson's estimate of "more than 1,000 items" is not an exaggeration. The miscellaneous nature of the Peterson material blurred the focus of the museum in Decorah but added to its core collection some important objects from Harsheim, numerous other Norwegian items, and the exceptional woodcarvings (apparently Norwegian-American) already mentioned.

The private collector in the early twentieth century with the best understanding of material culture as documentation of Norwegian and immigrant life was Martha Brye (1864–1945) of Coon Valley and later La Crosse, Wisconsin.[162] She knew this life intimately, having grown up on the farm of her parents Lars K. Brye from Hol in Hallingdal and Anna Maria Unseth from Biri, both from prominent families with deep rural roots. Such traditional activities as spinning, dyeing, weaving—abandoned in many immigrant homes—continued on the Brye farm during Martha's childhood. The family was kept in constant contact with Norway by often housing newly arrived immigrants, sleeping as many as twenty people at a time.

After Martha's mother died in 1890, she had to assist her father, who was steeped in early traditions from Hallingdal. She gleaned much from him and from her immigrant surroundings, making lists of Norwegian proverbs heard in daily conversation and of the quaint occupational nicknames given men and occasionally even their wives. Shortly after 1900 she learned how to take, develop, and print photographs, and in 1913 she wrote an article, "The Brye Relatives," with her father for the December issue of *Hallingen.*

Martha's education included a teaching certificate from the Ward School in North La Crosse and graduation in 1898 from a two-year program in nursing offered by the Tabitha Hospital in Chicago. This was followed by a long career as a physical therapist in La Crosse, primarily at the Gundersen Clinic. But of more importance in the context of this article, she had a natural sense for history, documenting in writing or photographs much of what she experienced. Her collecting of objects was more a part of this documentation process than a desire to possess.

Collecting objects relating to her heritage is thought to have begun early in Brye's life, but special impetus was given it when she spent six months in Norway in 1921. There she visited museums and churches, keeping careful record of what she observed. She not only visited but entered into the kind of life she had known only through her father's stories, living for a period on a *seter* in the mountains, tending the goats and making cheese and the cream porridge *fløtegrøt*. To quote her niece Laura Aune, "She returned home with enthusiasm, having seen the richness and beauty of things weathered with age. She felt it more important than ever to continue preserving historic objects."

Both Brye and Peterson appear to have been first shocked into a full realization of the richness in the material culture of their ancestors when they visited Norway, Brye for the first time and Peterson after twenty years in America. Both also felt a desire not only to enter that heritage by surrounding themselves with the remnants of it but to share it by making those remnants available to others. Martha Brye could not put her material on permanent public exhibition in La Crosse as Peterson did his in the Eau Claire Public Library because there was no appropriate place for it. Brye's collection, however, was put on temporary display in La Crosse as indicated by the following newspaper announcement: "An exhibit of great interest to the many Norwegians of La Crosse and to others as well was shown last week in the social rooms of Our Saviors Church. It is the property of Miss Martha Brye of 909 Vine Street, who inherited a nucleus of the collection from pioneer grandparents and has added to it throughout her lifetime. There are several ale bowls beautifully painted, a salmodikon, spoons hand carved from wood and ramshorns, linen home woven and lace made in a pattern so old that for many years the method was a lost one until revived some years later, a china soup tureen and platter 200 years old. Many exquisitely woven tapestries are in Miss Brye's collection and mittens knitted in elaborate designs with different colored yarns. Several Early Americana are included, a brass bed warmer, a call bell used in the first public school in Coon Valley and a hand hammered brass kettle. This is not one tenth of the whole display which one should see to really appreciate."[163]

The precise date of the above exhibition has not been determined but Brye's address indicates that it was after she had joined her sister late in life, perhaps between her retirement in 1934 and her death in 1945. It probably just preceded her donating much of her collection to the museum in Decorah, an institution she had followed with interest since her nephew, later to become the Reverend Leif Evens, attended Luther College around 1915. No date has come to light for this donation either, nor a complete list of it, but it was still possible in 1964 when cataloguing of the collection in Decorah got underway to identify seventy-five objects as having come from Martha Brye. They are so representative of the full range of objects ordinarily brought from Norway for setting up a household on the prairie that many of these are being used as the core of a display titled "Typical Contents of an Immigrant Trunk" (Ill. 14).

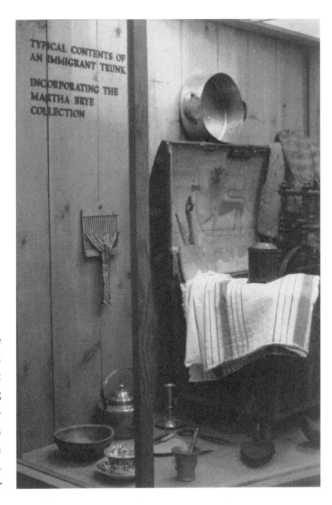

Ill. 14. A portion of the "Typical Contents of an Immigrant Trunk" exhibit at Vesterheim, consisting primarily of material collected by Martha Brye, La Crosse, Wisconsin, between about 1900 and 1940. *Photograph by author*

While many early private collections came to Vesterheim, one led to the founding of another Norwegian-American museum regularly open to the public during the summer while remaining in private hands. It was the assemblage of artifacts brought together on an immigrant farm near Mt. Horeb, Wisconsin, by a third-generation immigrant, Isak Dahle, whose ancestry was primarily from Nissedalen, Telemark. The official name of the museum is Nissedahle, coined from the place and family names; but it is popularly known as Little Norway. This outdoor complex originated in 1927, supposedly as a retreat for the bachelor owner, his friends and family; but it has always been considered an immigrant memorial and has always to some degree served a broader public. Since 1937 it has been officially available to visitors on a regular basis. The collection is in magnitude and comprehensiveness second only to that at Vesterheim.[164]

Isak Dahle was the Askeladden type, a collector from childhood.[165] He spent his early years in Mt. Horeb, where his parents and later his brother Otto operated a dry-goods store, but he went off to school at an early age and

Little Norway.
A Private Museum
for the Public

as a young man settled in Chicago where he became a successful insurance agent who invested his money well.[166] This, and the fact that he was a bachelor,[167] made adequate funds available for the Nissedahle project until the crash of the stock market in 1929 and the depression that followed. In a letter dated October 7, 1933, Dahle writes, "Like all other men who were rich in the gay 1928 and 29's I am now broke."[168] The project had by then won the enthusiastic support of many family members and friends, the people for whom it was originally intended and who had from the beginning carried out much of the actual work.[169] They were also to carry it on, not only after the funds on which it was being built had been wiped out but after the guiding spirit, Isak Dahle himself, had passed away in 1937 at the young age of fifty-four.[170] Dahle's mother Anne lived on and remained "its motivating inspirational force," as Isak had given her credit for being from the beginning, for another fourteen years.[171]

Three fundamental circumstances lay behind the founding of Little Norway: Dahle's collecting interests, his love of the countryside he had known as a boy,[172] and the inspiration of his mother. The initial incident that led to the project, however, was travel in Europe with his mother during the fall of 1925 and early winter of 1926 which included a trip to Norway. There he discovered the richness of his ancestral heritage and saw how the Norwegians were preserving that heritage in their museums.[173]

The pattern of rediscovery through a trip to Norway that has been seen in the collecting histories of Peterson and Brye repeated itself in Dahle. About a year after the trip, early in 1927, Isak Dahle and his brother Otto bought the site that was to become Little Norway, a farm they are thought to have known from wandering as boys through the countryside around Mt. Horeb.[174] It had been purchased about 1865 by Østen Olson Hougan (later to make Austin the family name) of Tinn, Telemark, who constructed a farmstead of log buildings which had never been replaced.[175] After his death in 1905, his widow, with help from the family, continued to farm the land until her death in 1920. The youngest daughter, Lena, took over until her death in June, 1926. The original furnishings of the farm were sold at auction in October of that year, just three months before the availability of the farm was drawn to Isak Dahle's attention. The original appearance of the farm is now known through six photographs from the winter of 1927 (Ill. 15).[176]

What resulted over the remaining eleven years of Dahle's life was the materialization of an immigrant's conception of his own ethnicity, a conception that corresponds to that of most Norwegian Americans, especially those who rediscover their cultural heritage after once having been Americanized. This accounts for Little Norway's immediate and ongoing appeal to the public and its significance as an immigrant document. It has, of course, the additional significance of being a large, comprehensive, and fine collection of Norwegian and Norwegian-American artifacts.

Ill.15. The Østen Olson Hougan farm as it appeared in the early months of 1927 when it was purchased by Isak Dahle as the site of Little Norway. *Courtesy of Little Norway*

Ethnicity is to the individual an undifferentiated concept, an entity in which the past is telescoped into a single present, that which we are or conceive ourselves to be. It is the culmination of what we have been, think we have been, or wish we had been. It is the personal mythology on which we construct our lives, shared to varying degrees with a group. Little Norway is a direct and honest expression of such ethnicity as it formulated itself in a third-generation immigrant from Norway and has formulated itself in general among Norwegian Americans.

What is disturbing to scholars but perfectly acceptable to the public in Little Norway is the complete fusion of the Norwegian and the American in a way that never happened historically but can easily happen in the mind. Dahle honestly admitted that what he was and what he presented was as much a product of mind and imagination as it was reality. The "legends of Nissedal," the area of Telemark from which three of his grandparents came,[177] began, he says, with "mere germs of facts . . . Handed down through the generations, the few known actualities have been interwoven with fantastic imagination and unique superstition until they have become word pictures far beyond the reach of present-day comprehension." Of the museum he said, "While the spirit of old Norway will always be the guiding hand in the development of Nissedahle . . . the effort as a whole will be dedicated to the traditional legends of the Norseland."[178] The constant reference to "spirit" and "legend" is the key to an understanding of Nissedahle.

It is an article of faith with many Norsemen who emigrated that they are more Norwegian than their lives and surroundings reveal. They must therefore use material culture props to prove that they are what they conceive themselves to be. The farm that Isak Dahle took over must have been one of the rare total environments from the early immigrant period that remained in 1926. If it could have been kept as it was in the natural setting out of which it had grown, it would put both the composite farmsteads of Old World Wisconsin and the rather heavily restored Jacobson farm at Vesterheim to shame as documents of early immigrant life; but it would then not have become the equally significant document of how Norwegian Americans of the third and later generations perceive their past, and it would probably not have been able to support itself. While Dahle had the good judgment to begin with a completely authentic immigrant farm, his goal was to make it "a truly Norwegian outdoor museum . . . the living, breathing picture-book of Norway."[179]

In line with the above goal, the buildings were furnished as much as possible with material either from Norway or constructed in the Norwegian tradition. Many things were imported, enough so that the Norwegian law of 1928 prohibiting the export of material from before the middle of the nineteenth century was looked on as a substantial block to the project.[180] Material that had come with the family, however, had been incorporated from the beginning and continued to be added.[181] Material obtained through advertisements in newspapers, donations from families who wanted their Norwegian things preserved, and purchases from individuals and antique dealers filled out the furnishings.[182] Whatever could not be obtained in original examples was made by local immigrant craftsmen.[183]

With material coming from many sources, objects of American origin but representative of immigrant life also found a place among the furnishings at Nissedahle, to the consternation of visitors who wanted it to be a true "Little Norway." Thea Dahle, Isak's sister, who with her husband Asher Hobson, professor of economics at the University of Wisconsin, operated and/or owned the complex essentially from 1931 until their own deaths in 1986 and 1991 respectively, found it necessary to defend the American material at Nissedahle. "One criticism we often hear," she said in a speech to the P.E.O. women's club of Madison, "is 'I wish they would take out those things which are not strictly Norwegian'—let me say here we do not claim to be strictly Norwegian—we simply want the things the Norse pioneers used at that time in this country." At another point in the speech as well she emphasized the immigrant aspect of the museum, referring to it as "a memorial to these early Norwegian pioneers of America" in contrast to her brother's description of it as a "replica of Norway's haunted hills and homes."[184] The ambiguity, well founded in immigrant psychology, gives Little Norway its authenticity as a Norwegian-American monument.

While the interiors of the buildings on the Austin farm were made essentially Norwegian by Dahle, with built-in beds and trestle tables not typical of immigrant furniture, the exteriors, while heavily restored, retained originally much of the character of pioneer buildings (Ill. 16). The decorative boards on

Ill. 16. The Østen Olson
Hougan farm after recon-
struction as Little Norway
but shortly before the addition of the Norway building
in 1935. *Courtesy of
Little Norway*

the ridges and ends of the roofs that alter this on some of them are of more recent origin. The major early change, curiously enough, was the addition of massive exterior chimneys, a characteristic not found in either Norwegian or Norwegian-American houses but associated with the romantic conception of the Lincoln log cabin.[185] The earliest new construction, the springhouse of 1927, was the first to break abruptly with the farm's immigrant character by being given a central turret of three receding structures suggestive of those on Norwegian stave churches.[186]

It was indeed another building modeled on a stave church, the Norway Building from the Chicago World's Fair of 1893, that finally tipped the scale in favor of the Norwegian rather than the immigrant even in Nissedahle's exterior appearance (Ill. 12).

After the Fair, the Norway Building was re-erected on Cornelius Billings' estate at Lake Geneva, Wisconsin, which was later purchased by William Wrigley. Dahle had been aware of it for some time but did not take steps to obtain it until after the Chicago World's Fair, A Century of Progress, of 1932–

1933, when he saw a newspaper picture of the Fortun (Fantoft) Church outside Bergen that again brought the building on the Wrigley estate to mind.[187] William Wrigley had died and the property was in probate with a son, Philip, assuming responsibility. Dahle must have moved fast. Already in his letter of October 9, 1933, to the contractor W.E. Stone he says that the "building has been given to me for removal to Little Norway." Negotiations continued, however, until 1935 when he officially got not only the structure without charge but $700 for dismantling it and removing it from the property.[188]

Reconstruction of the building at Nissedahle was near completion already by the late fall of 1935.[189] Having been designed by the Norwegian architect Albert Waldemar Hansteen and built in Trondheim for dismantling and re-erecting, the building lent itself well to the move.[190] Progress even so was not as rapid as Dahle had hoped because the exterior needed more repair than anticipated.[191] With this 25 x 60 foot building now towering over the little farm, Nissedahle acquired more the character of a rural community in Norway than a humble immigrant farm. Being an exhibition building, the new structure also made Nissedahle clearly a museum.

Some ambiguity had always existed in the relation of Nissedahle to the public. It is often stated that the complex was conceived as a private retreat; and yet it was given considerable early publicity as a "Norse memorial."[192] A public announcement of a Tweiten family reunion to be held at Nissedahle appeared in a newspaper from about 1927. Mrs. Dahle, to be sure, is listed as hostess, and she had family connections with the Tweitens. An article in *Mount Horeb Mail* on June 6, 1929, little more than two years after the farm was purchased, says that "there have been as many as 350 cars at Nissedahle on one Sunday." The damaging effect of this influx, however, led to the following announcement in the same article, " 'Nissedahle,' or 'Little Norway' as it is popularly called at Mt. Horeb, will be closed to the general public after June 15." This implies that it had been essentially open to that point. The article goes on to say that it would remain available with special permission on weekdays, and this opportunity must have been generously utilized. The *Capitol Times* of Madison reported on June 26, 1936, that 30,000 people had visited Little Norway since 1928.[193] Most of these had come as members of clubs and organizations that paid thirty cents per person for group visits. When the museum officially opened in 1937, the family and staff already had considerable experience in dealing with the public and in running the museum as a business, although it is said not to have become self-supporting until 1960.[194]

Isak Dahle had intended that his hobby would be completely institutionalized upon his death, which occurred in 1937, the year it officially opened to the public. Both in the invitation to visit which he sent with an album about Nissedahle to Crown Prince Olav and Crown Princess Märtha, apparently in 1933, and in a letter to Philip Wrigley on July 1, 1935, he mentions the Norwegian-American Historical Association, the University of Wisconsin, St.

Olaf College, and Luther College as possible recipients of his estate. In the 1935 letter the American-Scandinavian Foundation was added to the list. His actual will, however, gave the estate in trust to his mother for her lifetime with the stipulation that Nissedahle should be offered to the Wisconsin State Historical Society or sold within the family.[195] The change was probably made because of the increasing interest his sister Thea and her husband Asher Hobson were showing in the complex. The offer to the State Historical Society was made but turned down because the operation was not self-supporting. The Hobsons purchased Nissedahle in 1947 after having assumed major responsibility for its operation at the death of the founder ten years earlier.[196] His mother was to remain with them for an additional four years.

While Nissedahle was never completely private, neither has it ever taken the character of a completely public institution. The owner lives on the grounds, which resemble a private park over which the residence looks. A visitor has the feeling of being admitted into a private realm, a family's realization of who they feel they are and where they came from as Norwegian Americans. This realization finds resonance in many from their ethnic group and arouses wonderment in many from without.

Jens Johnson, P.D. Peterson, Martha Brye, and Isak Dahle are major representatives of a phenomenon that also existed on a much smaller scale as grass-roots activity in the immigrant community. It will be covered only in a schematic way here. Usually the concern is with keeping together and preserving the family mementoes, but sometimes it goes beyond, as it did for those mentioned above, to include similar material that can be obtained from neighbors, at auctions, or in secondhand and antique shops. Keeping the old things in the family or the community is generally the rationale for the collecting, but why this should be done or what should ultimately become of the material is seldom clearly defined. There is in the phenomenon that clinging to the past, to the physical vestiges of one's ethnicity, which gives psychological satisfaction but can be hard to justify in practical terms. It is a manifestation of that Askeladden mentality in which the ultimate importance of the deed is understood only by the doer. To others, like Askeladden's brothers, it may seem folly.

Isak Dahle, working as an individual, became involved with the preservation of buildings as well as smaller artifacts; and in this he too had counterparts on a smaller scale among Norwegian Americans. Grass-roots historic preservation parallels collecting but is done not only by individuals or families but by local groups as well. Both types are here being considered together under the general discussion of individual rather than institutional efforts because of their small scale and highly localized character.

Grass-roots historic preservation generally takes the form of retaining one or more old buildings on the farm even if their function has been assumed by

Grass Roots Preservation. Architecture

new structures. These gradually become respected and are given the little repair necessary to prevent their total decay. In some cases they serve new functions, such as areas for storage, woodworking, or play; but in others they just stand or become the place where other old things are kept. The preservation of buildings in such cases relates closely to the preservation of objects. Characteristic designations for these little historic units are "Grandpa's granary," "the old house," or "Marit's *stue.*" Group efforts at a grass-roots level are generally undertaken within church organizations or by local historical organizations and often consist of moving an early building to the church grounds, the fairgrounds, or a city park.

The earliest known effort by a small group to preserve a building relating to the Norwegian Americans was the move of the Tank cottage in Green Bay, Wisconsin, to that city's Union Park, now Tank Park, in 1907–1908.[197] Although Nils Otto Tank was completely Norwegian and has his place in immigrant history through organizing the Norwegian Moravian colony that ultimately became Ephraim, Wisconsin, the preservation and restoration project appears to have been carried out by Americans. The South Side Improvement Association, a group of businessmen in a section of Fort Howard that had recently been annexed to Green Bay, saved the historic structure from demolition by the move in an effort to upgrade the area. Writings on the history of the region by Deborah Beaumont Martin probably account for the historic awareness that led to this remarkably early preservation effort. The group associated with the initial restoration of the house and its first presentation to the public was the Tank Cottage Committee, organized by Mrs. Arthur Courtney Neville some time after the move.

Of greater interest to these groups than the Norwegian Nils Otto Tank, who lived in the house from 1850 until his death in 1864, was that it had been built by French settlers as one of the earliest of its type in Wisconsin and that Mrs. Caroline Tank, who continued to live in the house until her death in 1891, was a Dutch heiress from Pennsylvania who had made a strong cultural as well as economic impact on the region. Thus, by fortunate chance, Norwegian Americans have had one of their earliest historic landmarks preserved for them. That they recognized what had been done is revealed by Hjalmar Holand's reference to the move in his *De norske settlementers historie* of 1908.[198] He believed that the house had been purchased by the city, probably because it was placed in a city park, but the work had actually been that of local groups.

One of the earliest known efforts to preserve a dwelling by a completely Norwegian local group was moving the so-called "Little Iowa Cabin" in Winneshiek county, Iowa, to the grounds of the parsonage at Glenwood Lutheran church in 1926. A group within the congregation, organized the previous year as the Little Iowa Pioneer Association, carried out the project and three years later donated the building with its contents to the Norwegian-

American Historical Museum in Decorah, where it now stands as the Haugan House (Ill. 6).[199]

The pastor at Glenwood, the Reverend Olaf Brevik, was probably the motivating force behind the group because he is listed as president of the association and also as the first person on the committee assigned to work with the building. The inspiration behind both the organization and the specific project may well have been the founding of the Norwegian-American Historical Association in Northfield, Minnesota, and the reestablishment of the museum at Luther College as the Norwegian-American Historical Museum. All this happened in 1925–1926, and Kristian Prestgard, editor of *Decorah-Posten,* in his speech at the dedication of the "cabin" is reported to have "envisioned the time when such pioneer societies will be organized in all the Norwegian communities in America and when the historical and archaeological work now represented by the Norwegian-American Historical Association and the Norwegian Historical Museum will get the united support of all the local pioneer societies and museums."[200] His words not only suggest the link which may originally have existed between the larger institutional developments and this local effort but an acceptance of centralization and cooperation in what was being done. One must recall in this connection that Little Norway was also founded at the time and that both the association in Northfield and the museum in Decorah were mentioned by Dahle as possible recipients of his creation.

A project related to the above was carried out at Highland Prairie church near Bratsburg, Minnesota, sometime around 1930 by the woodcarver and folk builder Tarkjel Landsverk, who had previously owned the house involved.[201] It was well furnished with early household objects and continues to be well maintained on the site to which it was originally moved.

Moving an early local building to the church grounds became a common practice among Norwegian Americans, appearing to progress northward from Decorah. In 1934 at Union Prairie church, west of Lanesboro, Minnesota, such a project was undertaken at the initiative of the pastor, P.J. Nestande.[202] The building was more than furnished, becoming a virtual museum with what a journalist described as hundreds of objects from early pioneer days in the parish.[203] Vandalism and theft became a problem, leading to the sale of the small objects at public auction some time after 1955. Though locked, the house is maintained by the congregation as a roadside monument on U.S. 14 between Preston and Lanesboro and was given special attention in 1990 when the church celebrated its 125th anniversary.[204]

These three examples from a rather limited geographic area are typical of the many from the period that must exist elsewhere in the country, although a survey among the 7,000 members of the Vesterheim museum in 1990 brought to light more preservation efforts from after than before World War II.

Completely private or family efforts at the grass-roots level to preserve historic buildings appear to precede those of groups and generally do not involve a move. In a history of Houston county, Minnesota, from 1919, Guri Erickson (Mrs. Erick Ellestad) of Blackhammer is said to be "much interested in early history, and has preserved the log buildings erected in the 50s by her foster parents."[205] It was also in Houston county that a blacksmith shop, which initially served also as a residence, built about 1855 by Mikkel Sinnes from Vrådal, Telemark, was preserved on the Anton Skree farm with its original blacksmithing and shoemaking equipment. The preservation was very conscious, at least on the part of Anton Skree, who was on the farm through the entire first half of the twentieth century. His son Darrell was instrumental in having the building with its contents transferred to Vesterheim in 1972, another example of a private effort feeding an institution.[206]

The original 1870s house built by Anders O. Wickney in rural Northwood, North Dakota, was also carefully maintained by the family after it went out of use with the construction of a new house in 1916.[207] The early house was given to Vesterheim in 1982 by the builder's granddaughter Ruth Wickney and was moved intact, needing only thorough refurbishing to be preserved as it originally was.

Many of the early houses preserved as mementoes on immigrant farms are still *in situ,* and only a thorough combing of the countryside could bring them all to light. An example is the Lars Rudi cabin, near Sacred Heart, Renville county, Minnesota, built by its namesake from Opdal in Numedal, Norway, in 1868.[208] It was bought by a neighbor, Ole Enestvedt, in 1912, just one year before Rudi died in it, and it stood empty after 1914. In 1922 Enestvedt took measures to preserve it as a memorial to early pioneers in the area, among whom Rudi had been the major religious and educational leader. The house was furnished with material from the early period of settlement and is still maintained by the descendants of Ole Enestvedt, serving the purpose he established for it. In 1986 it was accepted for listing on the National Register of Historic Places.

A number of similar preservation efforts dating from before World War II that had by 1950 become generally known or were even operated as small private museums are described by Tora Bøhn. Her article from 1956 reports on a year of sponsored research done in 1949–1950. The three sites given most attention after Nissedahle are Albert Skare's "The Hidden Farm," MacFarland, Wisconsin, the collection of which is now in a local public museum; the Torsgaard farm near Westby, Wisconsin, the collection of which has been sold at auction; and the Heg farm buildings in Muskego near Milwaukee, Wisconsin, now in a memorial park maintained by the community.[209]

Early churches too were often preserved at the local or grassroots level. The motivation was not only respect for a local icon but a desire to retain a symbol of some early element in Norwegian-American Lutheranism that was losing

its identity through mergers. A striking example of the latter is the continued use on an alternate seasonal basis of both churches at East Koshkonong, Cambridge, Wisconsin, although the theological differences that accounted for them were resolved in 1917 and the two groups themselves became a single congregation in 1961.[210]

The clinging to symbols of lost identities may explain the preservation of a number of churches built by followers of the early nineteenth-century lay preacher Hans Nielsen Hauge. The earliest of those remaining and probably the first to be consciously preserved is a Hauge church in Perry township near Daleyville, Wisconsin (Ill. 17). It was built in 1852 and used until 1878 when a larger building was constructed several miles away.[211] Here the congregation through the merger of church bodies in 1917 lost the Hauge Synod to which it belonged but retained the Hauge name. Little is known about the old church from 1878 until the mid-1920s, but nothing was changed and reference was made at that time to annual gatherings having been held there "under the auspices of the Ladies Missionary society of the Hauges Lutheran church," the congregation that had moved to the new building.[212]

Widespread attention was drawn to the old Hauge church in Perry when an all-day 75th anniversary celebration was held there on August 21, 1927. Professor Julius E. Olson of the University of Wisconsin was the afternoon speaker, and the *Mount Horeb Mail*, probably exaggerating, reported a crowd of about two thousand people.[213]

The magnitude of the anniversary celebration undoubtedly resulted from negotiations which had taken place in the spring of 1926 between professors Gjerset, Eittrem, and Jacobson at Luther College and Reverend Joseph M.

Ill. 17. The Hauge log church from 1852 at Daleyville, Wisconsin, as it appears after having been given a protective coat of clapboard siding in 1927. *Photograph by author*

Green of Chicago, a brother-in-law of Isak Dahle who a year later would begin work on Little Norway, regarding a move of the church to the Norwegian-American Historical Museum in Decorah. Consent from the departed congregation to which it still belonged had been obtained, and the move was scheduled for June.[214] A counter-movement stalled the plan, and a subscription for funds to put siding over the logs, refurbish the building, and construct a surrounding fence had yielded $830 in cash plus much donated time and material before the end of the centennial year. The work by then had also been completed and $327.31 was invested as a fund to support the further maintenance of the church in its original location.[215] H.A. Stub's recommendation for Old Muskego was carried out at Perry, leaving the first Norwegian-American church built west of Madison preserved on its site. It is now being maintained by the Perry Hauge Log Church Restoration Association.[216]

What occurred at Perry was essentially repeated near Kenyon, Minnesota, but almost twenty years later and without the threat of having the building moved. The Hauge congregation there was founded about 1860 but did not begin construction of a church until 1871 and did not consider it complete until 1889.[217] In 1903 this congregation too built a larger church several miles away, but, like the congregation at Perry, it continued to maintain the old building, even allowing further burials in the cemetery. It also suffered a loss of identity with the demise of the Hauge Synod in the merger of 1917. In preparing for the centennial of the congregation in the late 1950s, a local group refurbished the old building and made improvements on the grounds. Since then the church, which is now maintained by the cemetery society of the Hauge congregation that built it, has been used about once a year for a memorial service in Norwegian. The situation at Kenyon, in turn, has a parallel in a Hauge church north of Decorah, Iowa, indicating that the preservation efforts referred to are examples of a common pattern.

Not only old churches associated with passing theological directions, however, were preserved as mementoes of earlier times. Valley Grove, in rural Nerstrand, Minnesota, belonged from the beginning to the Norwegian Synod, which remained a strong element in the merged church, but the congregation retained its first building constructed between 1862 and 1868 facing its larger new church of 1894.[218] As one of the first churches in the early parish titled The Norwegian Evangelical Church of Goodhue county, the old building must already in the 1890s have been considered a historic landmark. It has continued to be maintained without major alterations, serving a variety of needs for the congregation.

Even the new Valley Grove church has stood empty since 1973, when most of the remaining members transferred to the church at Nerstrand; but before the congregation was dissolved, the two churches were made the property of The Society for the Preservation of the Valley Grove Church and The Valley

Grove-Grace Cemetery Association. The buildings were also at that time nominated to the National Register of Historic Places. They continue to have the mysterious appeal of twin churches felt also at East Koshkonong, an appeal associated by Norwegians with the so-called sister churches of medieval origin at Gran in Hadeland, Norway.

*Grass Roots
Preservation.
Objects*

The elevation of certain smaller objects or groups of objects with some age to the status of family treasures for preservation began shortly after the immigrants arrived. Seven or eight examples come to Vesterheim annually, many having been brought to this country or made here in the 1860s and 1870s. The transfer to the museum now is generally due to lack of heirs, difficulty in equitable division among heirs, or concern that the children will not respect the objects. When there has been a century or more of preservation, selling often seems improper. A standard comment when people give something is "We couldn't think of selling it." Much also goes to local historical societies or other museums or is indeed passed on to another generation. The amount of the latter is difficult to estimate, but the number of inquiries that come to Vesterheim about the conservation of such materials is considerable. To the above must be added those things that even after several generations of preservation lost their ethnic significance to the owners or were sold for other reasons.

A number of fine early objects of ethnic character, of course, never had much emotional significance to the owners and were disposed of to collectors as soon as they no longer served a practical purpose or when their cash value began to exceed their practical or emotional value. An early example was the sale about 1880 of traditional Norwegian jewelry and other objects by the Hammerstad family of Gibson, Wisconsin, to John H. Terens. Great numbers of Norwegian immigrant objects were sold around 1930 by the dealers Mr. and Mrs. Edwin B. Trimpey of Baraboo, Wisconsin, of which nineteen trunks are known from photographs at the State Historical Society of Wisconsin.[219] The amount that can still be accounted for in the Norwegian-American community, however, is great.

Two specific examples of objects that have functioned as ethnic cult symbols in Norwegian-American families will stand for the hundreds that exist. In 1918 Mons and Christe Guttormson posed in front of their log house in Folsom, Wisconsin, for a photograph in which the only prop is the spinning wheel they brought from Luster, Sogn, when they emigrated in 1872 (Ill. 18a). Fifty-two years after that picture was taken, their great-great-grandchildren, Mark and Eric Casida, in Berkeley, California, were photographed behind the same wheel (Ill. 18b). Several years later, Eric at age thirteen made a computer artwork representation of it for a family notecard that included the following verse by seventeen-year-old Mark:

Ill. 18a (top left). Mons and Christe Guttormson of Folsom, Wisconsin, pictured in front of their old house in 1918 with the spinning wheel they had brought from Luster, Sogn, Norway, as immigrants in 1872. *Courtesy of Mark Casida*

Ill. 18b (top right). The Guttormsons' great-great-grand-children Mark (left) and Eric (right) Casida with the wheel seen in Ill. 18a. *Courtesy of Karl Casida family*

Ill. 18c (bottom). The family wheel represented in computer graphics by Eric Casida at age 13 in 1973 for a notecard containing a family epic poem by his seventeen-year-old brother Mark. *Courtesy of Eric Casida*

Marion John Nelson

Ill. 19. Thorbjørg Olas-
datter Aga Jaastad about
1915 in Rushford, Minne-
sota, donning the festive
costume she brought from
Aga, Hardanger, Norway,
as an immigrant in 1869.
Such occasions had become
family ritual. *Courtesy of
Margaret T. Jaastad*

"Time passes:
A generation goes,
Another comes.
The two are united
By a thread
Strong and flexible
Spun on a wheel
Spun on a symbol."

The object retained its significance as an ethnic symbol not only through several generations but through major revolutions in technology.[220]

Thorbjørg Olasdatter Aga, who married Endre Jaastad in 1869, brought her complete festive costume with her when she immigrated to Rushford, Minnesota, later in that same year. Although she did not wear it regularly, she would on occasion don it for the children and grandchildren.[221] One such occasion about 1915 was recorded on a family snapshot (Ill. 19). In it the proud traditional stance of the seventy-year-old woman with an admiring young girl looking on has all the ritual characteristics of clan perpetuation found in Adolph Tidemand's several paintings from the 1860s of grandmother showing her bridal crown to admiring grandchildren. The dress passed on to a daughter and also went to California where it too remains as a symbol of family ethnicity after a second migration.

Conclusion   In spite of Tora Bøhn's impressive list of privately preserved heirlooms, which included several major urban collections in addition to the four farm collections already mentioned, she concluded after interviews with people who told about how little they had kept of the large amount brought and of the hundreds of Norwegian objects sold by such dealers as Trimpey that "at this time, Norwegian immigrant objects with any artistic or cultural interest have to a large extent gone astray or been destroyed."[222] It was probably in comparison with what still existed around 1950 in the rural districts of Norway that Bøhn drew her conclusion. The amount of immigrant material that exists in Norwegian-American families, in museums, and among collectors proves her wrong, at least in an American immigrant context.

Since other immigrant ethnic groups, with the possible exception of the Pennsylvania Dutch, have given less scholarly attention to the role of ethnic materials in their lives than the Norwegian Americans, reliable comparisons are difficult to make. Representatives of these other groups, however, are consistently surprised at the amount of material they find in Decorah or in private Norwegian-American collections compared to what is known from their own people.

The early interest of institutions in preserving the material record of the Norwegian Americans and the extensive private collecting and preservation

Marion John Nelson

activity among them at all levels of society indicate that even in this country Norwegians distinguish themselves by an Askeladden mentality as relates to old and seemingly useless things. They put them in their satchels as they go their merry way, saying, "We have such things to do. We have such things to carry." Those things from the past have indeed served them well as a body of material to which most Norwegian Americans relate because it goes back to the point of their common origin. Language, music, and customs change, but most old things remain the same, standing as tangible and direct links with an earlier culture and life that continues to give cohesiveness and identity to the group.

NOTES

1. P. Chr. Asbjørnsen and Moltke Moe, "Prinsessa som ingen kunde målbinda," in *Norsk folkedikting. Eventyr I* (Oslo, 1936), 126–129.

2. "Jeg har nu vanket i 7 Mands levetid. Den 8de mig fornyet har, forlænges skal hans liv. JJ.S.M. 1517," Acc.801. Cat. 14.A.46. Luther College Collection, Vesterheim. The date, presumably an estimate on the part of the painter who did the refurbishing and added the inscription, is probably too early.

3. Tonte Hegard, *Romantikk og fortidsvern. Historien om de første friluftsmuseene i Norge* (Oslo, 1984), 195–199.

4. Anders Sandvig, *I praksis og på samlerferd* (Oslo, 1969), 71–189.

5. Both were in Minneapolis, where the author was made aware of the sale.

6. The information is from Norma Vanderpan, Brookings, South Dakota.

7. The legal establishment of the Norwegian-American Historical Association did not occur until 1926, but this resulted from planning that got well underway at meetings in Decorah, Iowa, and Northfield, Minnesota, in 1925, after the Norse-American Centennial celebration of June 6–9 that year. Odd S. Lovoll and Kenneth O. Bjork, *The Norwegian-American Historical Association 1925–1975* (Northfield, Minnesota, 1975), 15–17.

8. An authoritative account of the origin of the Norwegian Lutheran Church in America is found in E. Clifford Nelson and Eugene Fevold, *The Lutheran Church among Norwegian-Americans, I* (Minneapolis, Minnesota, 1960).

9. Gerhard Rasmussen, *Lutheraneren*, December 7, 1904. The logs are reported to have been on the Seminary grounds at this time, with C.L. Jacobsen, son of a *klokker* (sexton) in the old church, ready to assemble them. Information on the move of Muskego church is from a compilation of sources prepared by E. Clifford Nelson, summer, 1966, and made available by Paul Daniels, archivist of Luther Northwestern Theological Seminary, St. Paul, Minnesota. This compilation and one prepared the previous year by E.W. Sihler, also at Luther Northwestern archives, are the sources of all information relating to Muskego church. Translations of quotations are also theirs unless otherwise indicated. See also Ill. 4 p. 205.

10. Rasmus Anderson, *Lutheraneren*, October 12, 1904.

11. E. Clifford Nelson discovered a letter from Hoyme to Gerhard Rasmussen in the Rasmussen papers, Norwegian-American Historical Association archives, Northfield, Minnesota, that documents the nature and time of the purchase. The story is also told by Wilhelm Rasmussen in *Lutheraneren*, September 7, 1904. The earliest reference to the church being used as a *grisehus* (pig house) appears to be in a report of a visit to it by Sebastian Selkirk in *Skandinaven*, November 10, 1897.

12. *Beretning for Det trettende aarsmøde for Den forenede norsk lutherske kirke i America* (Minneapolis, Minnesota, 1902), 280.

13. G. Rasmussen, *Lutheraneren*, December 7, 1904.

14. Manuscript for a speech on Muskego church in the Luther Northwestern Theological Seminary archives, 11. Paul Daniels, archivist, has concluded from the appearance of the manuscript that the author may have been Professor Carl M. Weswig. Various dates from around 1940 handwritten on the opening page indicate that the speech was given several times at the annual memorial service held at the church.

15. Manuscript for a speech on Muskego church, 14. I. M. Kalnes is among the few authors to openly challenge this position. In his "Koshkonong built first Norse Church in America," in *The Capital Times* (Madison, Wisconsin), July 1, 1928, he states, "The first church building completed by Norwegian Lutherans in America was a log church in West Koshkonong, completed in December, 1844. . . . Norwegian-American church historians usually designate the log church built in Muskego, Racine county, as the first Norwegian Lutheran church in America, because the congregation there was organized in 1843, the year before the organization of the congregations in West and East Koshkonong, but although building a church was commenced at Muskego before the one at West Koshkonong, it was not completed before the spring following the completion of the West Koshkonong." His facts have not been refuted, but Muskego continues to be considered the first Norwegian Lutheran church in America. See Odd S. Lovoll, *The Promise of America* (Northfield, Minnesota, 1984), 40–41.

16. This translation is the author's. E. Clifford Nelson had mistranslated the first phrase in the last sentence "Isaafald havde den vist ikke nu lagt hvor den ligger" to read "At all events, had they known its location."

17. W. Rasmussen, *Lutheraneren*, September 7, 1904.

18. G. Rasmussen, *Lutheraneren*, December 7, 1904. No reference to a rededication of the church on its new site has been found. Because of the mixed feelings regarding this site, the people responsible for the move may have been reluctant to draw further attention to it at the time.

19. Hjalmar Holand, *De norske settlementers historie* (Ephraim, Wisconsin, 1908), 120.

20. Theodore Blegen, *The Kensington Rune Stone: New Light on an Old Riddle* (St. Paul, 1968), 6. The month of discovery varies in different reports, but Blegen arrived at November after evaluating the sources.

21. The translation is a slightly edited version of that found in William Thalbitzer, *Two Runic Stones From Greenland and Minnesota* (Washington, D.C., 1951), 18.

22. Tom Trow of the University of Minnesota has recently drawn the author's attention to the work of Michael G. Michlovic and Michael W. Hughey, Moorhead State University, Minnesota, who have also dealt with the stone from a sociological rather than an historical

standpoint. Their major concern has been the racial implications in the inscription and its interpretation. See their "Norse Blood and Indian Character: Content, Context, and Transformation of Popular Mythology," in *The Journal of Ethnic Studies,* 10 (Fall, 1982), 79–94.

23. The monument is in Alexandria, Minnesota. It was under discussion in 1928 (see Blegen, *Kensington Rune Stone,* 103) but was not carried out until the 1950s.

24. Michael Brooks lists in the bibliography of Blegen, *Kensington Rune Stone,* 192, *The Runestone Pageant Play* by Bert Merling, a duplicated typescript which he assumed originated in Alexandria, Minnesota, about 1961. It apparently is not the text that was used for a pageant in Alexandria in connection with its centennial because Audrey Bursch of Alexandria in an interview, August 12, 1992, said this text was by Margaret Leuthuer of that city. Both texts are distinct from the play *Viking,* a fantasy about Vikings in Minnesota who could have left the runestone, performed as a musical several summers in the early 1980s north of Park Rapids, Minnesota. Blegen also lists novels and books of cartoons inspired by the stone.

25. Works from before 1968 relating to the Kensington runestone and its background are listed in Michael Brooks' bibliography in Blegen, *Kensington Rune Stone,* 185–205. Much has also been published since.

26. There are contradictions in the reports on its location and use from 1899–1907. See Blegen, *Kensington Rune Stone,* 46.

27. The hiatus of interest in the stone from 1899 to 1908 is dramatically evident in the chronological bibliography in *The Kensington Rune Stone, Preliminary Report to the Minnesota Historical Society by the Museum Committee* (St. Paul, 1910), 61.

28. Holand, *De norske settlementers historie,* 15–21, 120. Holand published a defense of the stone's authenticity in *Skandinaven* (Chicago), January 17, 1908, but this article does not to the same degree use it as historic evidence. The ongoing power of the stone is illustrated by a lengthy article with the headline "Evidence shows Kensington Runestone no Fake" by Rolf M. Nilsestuen, published in the "Opinion" section of the *Star-Tribune* (Minneapolis), July 12, 1991, in which most of the major arguments that have been advanced in support of authenticity are presented uncritically and those that put authenticity in question ignored. The article has the tone of presenting new evidence that solves the historic problem while it merely presents one side of the old debate. The fact that the article is given prominent presentation in a major newspaper indicates that forces are at work here which rise above the vicissitudes of historic investigation.

29. Hanson recorded the donation of the hardware and other parts of the Muskego church door given by Hans J. Jacobson on March 10, 1898.

30. *Lutheraneren,* September 7, 1904.

31. Anderson, *Lutheraneren,* October 12, 1904.

32. David T. Nelson, "Norwegian-American Museum," in *The Palimpsest,* 46:12 (Iowa City, Iowa, 1965), 615, 618.

33. Magnus Andersen, *Vikingfærden 1893* (Kristiania, 1895), gives a detailed account of all aspects of the voyage and its reception.

34. The observation by Porter appears in one of a large number of unidentified clippings about the *Viking* mounted on a board in the collection of Vesterheim. The museum also has two prints for framing commemorating the voyage.

35. Andersen, *Vikingfærden,* 21–23.

36. Andersen, *Vikingfærden*, 6.

37. Andersen, *Vikingfærden*, 26–27.

38. Anderson, *Vikingfærden*, 23–24, 29.

39. Charles S. Winslow, "*Historical Events in Chicago,*" III, 42, 46. This work is in mimeographed form in the Chicago Historical Society. Located by Harry and Josefa Andersen, Chicago, Illinois. Birger Osland, in the manuscript for a speech given in Lincoln Park, July 11, 1952, refers to the University of Chicago as the owner while the ship was at the Field Columbian Museum. Manuscript supplied by Harry and Josefa Andersen.

40. Osland speech, 4.

41. Letter from Knute Nelson, Alexandria, Minnesota, to Haldor Hanson, Decorah, Iowa, November 19, 1896. Luther College archives, 54:1:1–5. Duane Fenstermann assisted in obtaining all materials in Luther College archives.

42. *Kirketidende* (Decorah, Iowa), February 23, 1877.

43. Letters from Haldor Hanson, Grand Mound, Iowa, to Laur. Larsen, Decorah, Iowa, August 13 and 29, 1879. Luther College archives, 96:92:14 and 42.

44. Hanson, Grand Mound, to Larsen, Decorah, May 12, 1888. Luther College archives, 96:147:9. Basic biographical information on Hanson is drawn from Gisle Bothne, *Det norske Luther College* (Decorah, Iowa, 1897), 271; *Symra* (Decorah, Iowa, 1907), 210; and *Festskrift. Den norske Synodes jubilæum 1853–1906* (Decorah, Iowa, 1903), 392.

45. Hanson, Grand Mound, to Larsen, Decorah, July 24, 1888. Luther College archives, 96:148:16. Also Bothne, *Luther College*, 271.

46. David T. Nelson, *Luther College 1861–1961* (Decorah, Iowa, 1961), 148. The reference to Weimar as the place of study in Germany is found only in Nelson.

47. Nelson, *Luther College*, 146, 156. Hanson's appointment was paid in part through student fees and he also, being unmarried, lived with the students. This established a close bond between him and "the boys," as he called them, a bond which made it difficult for him to carry out some of the demands made on him relating to students and contributed to his leaving Luther. Hanson, Decorah, Iowa, to Rev. U.V. Koren, Decorah, Iowa, November 30, 1901. Luther College archives, 96:231:30.

48. Nelson, "Norwegian-American Museum," 613–615.

49. Hanson, Decorah, Iowa, to C.K. Preus, November 22, 1895. Luther College archives, 4:161:35.

50. Hanson to Preus, November 22, 1895.

51. In the accessions book covering 1899, $9.03 is reported as donations from visitors between June 11 and 18.

52. Nelson, "Norwegian-American Museum," 611, 615.

53. Nelson, "Norwegian-American Museum," 613.

54. Nelson, "Norwegian-American Museum," 618.

55. Hanson to Preus, November 22, 1895, Luther College archives, 4:161.

56. Nelson, "Norwegian-American Museum," 619.

57. The presentation of the early collection that follows is based on acquisition records in the Vesterheim archives.

58. The visitor was Morten Tuftedal, Homewood, Illinois, a leader among the veterans of the 99th Battalion in World War II.

59. Nelson, "Norwegian-American Museum," 615.

60. Mementoes from Norway included wood from the Gokstad Viking ship, stone from the Trondheim cathedral, and hardware from the Dalen (Telemark) church door; but these are few compared to those from immigrant sites and personages.

61. O.M. Norlie, *History of the Norwegian People in America* (Minneapolis, 1925), 194–195.

62. The term "less appropriate" may need qualification. The foot has disappeared from the collection, but one could imagine it being exhibited today when historical museums are trying to shock visitors out of the comforts of their own time to the brutal realities of the period being presented. The loss of limbs to frost was indeed a reality on the northern frontier. The man who gave the foot and Hanson who accessioned it may, in being true to their Askeladden heritage, have shown greater wisdom than the curator who, on the basis of common sense, threw it out.

63. Hanson to Preus, November 22, 1895.

64. Hanson to Larsen, August 4, 1899. Luther College archives, 96:216:21.

65. The key role of Adolf Bredesen, Stoughton, Wisconsin, in the Norwegian-American museum has not been given adequate attention. His name appears constantly in early museum records as a donor as well as a solicitor. It was also he who was the leading figure in the Luther Alumni Association meeting at Red Wing, Minnesota, in 1895 when recommendations to the college included appointing a staff member to the museum with time to assume the responsibilities of the position and to make the history of the Norwegians in America a major area of emphasis. Both were carried out by President Larsen, and the museum as we now know it got underway. Bredesen's daughter Inga Norstog, as director of the museum from 1947 to 1960, carried it through the most critical period in its history.

66. Nelson, "Norwegian-American Museum," 619.

67. Hanson to Preus, November 22, 1895.

68. Nelson, "Norwegian-American Museum," 617. The 1,183 purchases that Hanson reported for the period from October 13, 1895, to May 25, 1898, as compared to 3,471 gifts, must have been largely books, archival material, and music, because the accessions book lists few purchases of objects.

69. A visit to Norway might have been expected in the academic year 1891–1892, when Hanson was studying music in Weimar, but no reference to such a visit has been found.

70. Karen Larsen, *Laur. Larsen* (Northfield, Minnesota, 1936), 305.

71. H.O. Christopherson, *Eilert Sundt, En dikter i kjensgjerninger* (Oslo, 1962), 56–66; and Larsen, *Laur. Larsen,* 17.

72. Christopherson, *Eilert Sundt,* 67–82.

73. Christopherson, *Eilert Sundt,* 26–55.

74. Larsen, *Laur. Larsen,* 25.

75. Fredrik Böök, *Artur Hazelius, En levnadsteckning* (Stockholm, 1923).

76. Hegard, *Romantikk,* 193.

77. Böök, *Artur Hazelius,* 347.

78. Hegard, *Romantikk,* 55.

79. Larsen, *Laur. Larsen,* 245.

80. Hegard, *Romantikk,* 55.

81. Hegard, *Romantikk,* 37–56. The buildings were eventually incorporated into the Norwegian Folk Museum that opened to the public in 1907. The only reason for not considering the collection on the royal estate the first public open-air museum is that it was essentially a private venture of the King, although he worked in cooperation with the Society for the Preservation of Norwegian Antiquities and made it available to the public.

82. Hegard, *Romantikk,* 153.

83. Sandvig, *I Praksis,* 46–51, 94.

84. Sandvig, *I Praksis,* 95–101.

85. Sandvig, *I Praksis,* 164–174; and Hegard, *Romantikk,* 109.

86. Hegard, *Romantikk,* 153.

87. Hegard, *Romantikk,* 193.

88. Hegard, *Romantikk,* 193. Sandvig became the first of the leaders in the folk museum movement to take a holistic approach to the presentation of folk society, not putting together individual elements but keeping together entire complexes like the twenty-two-building Bjørnstad farm. "My intention with Maihaugen," he wrote in 1907, "has not been to create a museum with formal exhibitions, neither to collect miscellaneous things from the old days that one comes across accidentally, a house here, a tool there." (Hegard, *Romantikk,* 91.) Bjørnstad is an example of what he did intend to present. In it he is far ahead of Hanson or his immediate successors. The museum in Decorah was not able to realize the preservation of an entire social and economic complex until it took over the Jacobson farmstead in the 1970s.

89. Simon J. Bronner, *Folklife Studies from the Gilded Age* (Ann Arbor, Michigan, 1987), 6; and Don Yoder, *Discovering American Folklife* (Ann Arbor, Michigan, 1990), 25.

90. Bronner, *Gilded Age,* 6.

91. Bronner, *Gilded Age,* 68–71.

92. Bronner, *Gilded Age,* 79.

93. Bronner, *Gilded Age,* 8.

94. Bronner, *Gilded Age,* 75.

95. Bronner, *Gilded Age,* 8.

96. Cleota Reed, *Henry Chapman Mercer and the Moravian Pottery and Tile Works* (Philadelphia, 1987), 17.

97. For sources of information on Hanson see note 45 and obituary in *Minneapolis Tidende,* December 19, 1929. The latter was furnished by Harry and Josefa Anderson. For vital statistics on Mercer see Reed, *Mercer,* xv–xx.

98. Reed, *Mercer,* 17.

99. This acquisition is humbly listed under 1910 in the museum's record book as "Udskaarne Altertavle [carved altarpiece]–Willmar, Minn." The record is not clear, but the altar appears to be one of several items under the heading "Ved prof. C.K. Preus fra Mr. . . . Johnsen." The man for whom the recorder has apparently not known the first name was very likely Jens Johnson of Minneapolis. The remaining information about the altar is from Marion Nelson, "A Pioneer Artist and his Masterpiece," in *Norwegian-American Studies, 22* (1965), 3–17. See also Ill. 18, p. 218.

100. Beatrix T. Rumford, "Uncommon Art of the Common People: A Review of Trends

in the Collecting and Exhibiting of American Folk Art," in *Perspectives on American Folk Art* (New York, 1980), 14.

101. Erwin O. Christensen, *Early American Wood Carving* (Cleveland, Ohio, 1952), 125.

102. Nelson, "Norwegian-American Museum," 623.

103. Nelson, "Norwegian-American Museum," 623.

104. Detailed documentation of this stay is found in Elisabeth Koren, *The Diary of Elisabeth Koren* (Northfield, Minnesota, 1955).

105. O.A. Tingelstad and O.M. Norlie, eds., *Christian Keyser Preus 1852–1921* (Minneapolis, 1922), 381. Reprinted from *Evangelisk Luthersk Kirketidende* (Decorah, Iowa), November 12, 1913, 1269–1271. The aged Elisabeth Koren, who was an honored guest at the dedication, had a less lofty view of the preservation project involving the building in which she as a refined young woman of upper-class origin had experienced her first shock of life among farmers on the frontier. Her comment was simply, "Dere har nok hat meget stræv for det gamle hus." (You must have gone to a lot of trouble with that old house.), 381.

106. There had been other moves of individual residences for preservation before 1913 but without the intent of creating an outdoor historical complex. One which relates to the Norwegian Americans is the house of the Moravian religious leader of Norwegian origin Nils Otto Tank, Green Bay, Wisconsin, which was moved for preservation in 1907.

107. A record book in the Vesterheim archives includes a document dated July 28, 1929, transferring title to the "'Little Iowa' Pionérstue" (now known as the Haugan House) to the Norwegian-American Historical Museum. It was accessioned August 30 of that year, the same month as the parochial school from Washington Prairie and the Tasa drying house. These, together with the Egge-Koren house, represented the full extent of immigrant buildings in the open-air division until the 1970s.

108. James S. Wamsley, *American Ingenuity, Henry Ford Museum and Greenfield Village* (New York, 1985), 17. Additional information on Ford in this paragraph is from the same source.

109. Yoder, *Discovering American Folklife*, 33.

110. Hanson came from Fuse near Bergen to Grand Mound, Iowa, at age nine in 1865 (*Synodes jubilæum*, 392) and Gjerset from Frena in Romsdal to Big Bend, near Benson, Minnesota, at age six in 1871 (David T. Nelson, "Knut Gjerset," in *Norwegian-American Studies, 25* [1972], 27–30). The remaining information in this paragraph is also from these sources.

111. Larsen, *Laur. Larsen*, 294.

112. Nelson, *Luther College*, 180–181.

113. Nelson, "Gjerset," 37.

114. Knut Gjerset, "The Norwegian-American Historical Museum," in *Norwegian-American Studies and Records*, 6 (1931), 152, 160.

115. Yoder, *Discovering American Folklife*, 47. An undated manuscript credited to Knut Gjerset, titled "New Trends in Historical Writing and Research," has come to light in the Luther College archives, 28:4:1, that is a strong statement for a democratic and pluralistic approach to the study of American history. References in it indicate a date of about 1934. The first volume of Blegen's immigrant history had by then already been in print for three years.

116. Gjerset, *Luther College Museum* (Decorah, Iowa, 1923), 15–16.

117. Nelson, "Gjerset," 42.

118. This mammoth exhibition with twenty-two divisions was put together in record time. It was the end of January, 1925, before the Norse-American Centennial Board of Directors invited Gjerset to be responsible for exhibits at the event. The opening was four months and one week away. Unsigned letter to the Board of Directors, January 28, 1925, recommending the appointment of Gjerset, Norwegian-American Historical Association archives.

119. *The Norse-American Centennial, 1825–1925*, 86. Quoted in Lovoll, *A Folk Epic: The Bygdelag in America* (Northfield, Minnesota, 1975), 165.

120. Lovoll, *A Folk Epic,* 97, 115; and models, photos, and other remains at Vesterheim from the exhibition.

121. There was also an exhibition in St. Paul in 1914 which did indeed include objects. It is referred to in a letter from the Reverend B.J. Larsen, Stoughton, Wisconsin, to Gjerset, Decorah, Iowa, January 3, 1922, copied in a record book at Vesterheim, December 28, 1922. On May 17th and several days following, the letter says, there was an exhibition with Professor Andrew Veblen in charge and "Man søgte at samle sammen alle norske oldsager, man kunde faa fat i til Udstillingen." (They tried to bring together all the Norwegian antiquities they could get hold of for the exhibition). Not enough information has come to light about the exhibition to deal with it further at this point.

122. Photographs in the Vesterheim archives best illustrate its size and character.

123. Gjerset, "Norwegian-American Historical Museum," 161.

124. An unidentified clipping in Norwegian signed by D.G. Ristad in the Norse-American Centennial folder in the Norwegian-American Historical Association Archives. Translation by the author.

125. Gjerset's frustration over this situation is well presented by David Nelson in "Gjerset," 40.

126. Gjerset, "Norwegian-American Historical Museum," 155–156.

127. Gjerset, "Norwegian-American Historical Museum," 156.

128. Nelson, "Norwegian-American Museum," 625–634.

129. Original document in Luther College archives, 96:231:30. Although the resignation was for January 1, 1902, Hanson remained with the museum through the year and with the college as a professor of music until 1904.

130. Gerhard Folgerø, "Viking Ship *Leif Erikson*," typescript in the Duluth Public Library identified as "from a leaflet––no imprint." This and other material on the *Leif Erikson* was obtained through Dennis Gimmestad, Minnesota Historical Society.

131. "Norsemen Dock in Duluth after 10,000-Mile Trip," in *Duluth News-Tribune* (?), June 24, 1927. The source is not completely clear on the clipping.

132. *Duluth News-Tribune,* June 28, 1927.

133. *Duluth News-Tribune,* December 25, 1927, April 18, 1929; and "A Viking Skipper's Dream," in *Duluthian* (Duluth, Minnesota), September, 1930, 9.

134. Hegard, *Romantikk,* 93–106, 192–193; Böök, *Hazelius,* 262–331; and Sandvig, *I Praksis,* 71–186.

135. Hegard, *Romantikk,* 32–88.

136. Reed, *Mercer*, 17–19.

137. Wamsley, *American Ingenuity*, 15–25.

138. "A Brief History of St. Mark's Church, Islip, Long Island," four typewritten pages said to be adapted from *Long Island: A Guide to New York's Suffolk and Nassau Counties*, by Raymond, Judith, and Kathryn Spinzia (New York, second edition, 1990). The manuscript was obtained from the church by Harry and Josefa Andersen. Judging from photographs also supplied by the church, additions to the structure in the 1890s made the original stave church portion little more than a dramatic chancel. Fire seriously damaged the church on December 5, 1989, but it has been restored. Its fame rests as much on its Tiffany windows from 1895 as on its unusual architecture. All information on the building is from the one listed source.

139. Ann Wolfmeyer and Mary Burns Gage, *Lake Geneva, Newport of the West 1870–1920* (Lake Geneva, Wisconsin, 1976), 39–42. A news item in the *Lake Geneva Herald*, December 8, 1893, read, "The Norway building at the world's fair has been bought by that sturdy Norsk, C. K. G. Billings, who paid $1,500 for it." This has led to some confusion regarding his ethnicity. Short but detailed biographies in the *Chicago Tribune*, January 19, 1902, 40, and in the *Biographical Dictionary and Portrait Gallery, Prominent Men of the Great West* (n.p., 1892), present Billings as very much old-stock American. He was born in Saratoga Springs, New York, to Albert M. and Augusta Farnsworth Billings and married Blanche McLeish of Chicago's prominent merchant family. There is no indication of contact with the Norwegian community in Chicago. The reporter may have referred to this obviously American purchaser of a Norwegian building modeled on a stave church as "norsk" purely as a joke. His readers in Lake Geneva would have included a good many Norwegians who would have caught the irony.

140. Interview with the late Sylvia Curtis in 1983.

141. Letter in the Vesterheim museum files from Dorothy Burr Thompson, donor of the tapestry and granddaughter of the collector. See also J. M. Hoppin, *Henry Armitt Brown, together with Four Historical Orations* (Philadelphia, 1880), 36.

142. The Pook and Pook Inc. catalogue for the auction of January 24–25, 1992, listing the Spackman collection was made available by William Wangensteen, Minneapolis. Further information was obtained through telephone conversations, September, 1992, with Ron Pook of the auction house and Rowland Elzea, head curator, Delaware Museum of Art.

143. Inventory of Terens' Museum, records of The State Historical Society of Wisconsin Museum, Madison.

144. Letter from Emil Baensch, President, East Wisconsin Trustee Company, to Charles E. Brown, Chief of Museum, Madison, Wisconsin, January 23, 1911. Records of The State Historical Society of Wisconsin Museum. The objects went to the historical society, and the trustee was able to get information on their origin. Both this letter and the inventory were located for me by Carol Larsen, Registrar.

145. Jens Johnson obituaries, *Skandinaven*, August 20, 1929, and *Minneapolis Tidende*, August 22, 1929. Norwegian American Historical Association archives. An article in *Sangerhilsen* (Minneapolis), June, 1914, reports on his active role in the singing societies, but neither it nor the obituaries mention his collecting.

146. Accessions records, Vesterheim archives.

147. See n. 99 for other possible contributions.

148. Eyvind Ager, Chippewa Falls, Wisconsin, supplied these vital statistics in a letter of April 19, 1991.

149. Ager letter, April 19, 1991.

150. Note from Ager referred by Genevieve Hagen, Eau Claire, Wisconsin, February 13, 1991.

151. *Reform* (Eau Claire, Wisconsin), June 25, 1933. Furnished by Eyvind Ager.

152. Letter from Robert E. Solfest, Eau Claire, Wisconsin, March 8, 1991, reporting for several of Peterson's nieces.

153. Letter from Carol Langsjoen, St. Peter, Minnesota, January 22, 1991.

154. Solfest letter, March 8, 1991.

155. Unidentified clipping from about 1930 furnished by Carol Langsjoen.

156. Letter from P. Harsem, Oslo, to family members from the Harsem farm, May, 1960. Furnished by Robert Solfest.

157. *Reform,* June 25, 1933.

158. Ager letter, April 19, 1991.

159. The date of installation in the library has been arrived at through the subheading on an unidentified clipping in English announcing the sale of the collection, which occurred in 1930, saying that it "Has Been Housed for Past 10 Years in Library Here." Furnished by Carol Langsjoen.

160. *Reform,* October 23, 1930.

161. *Reform,* June 25, 1933; an unidentified clipping in English furnished by Carol Langsjoen; and Nelson, "Norwegian-American Historical Museum," 630. The clipping also makes reference to material sold to other museums and individuals. This perhaps accounts for Gjerset's paying almost $4,000 less than Peterson asked for "the entire collection" from Eau Claire. That only a portion of the collection went to Decorah has not been generally known.

162. All genealogical information relating to Martha Brye is drawn from Amalie and Edwin Brye's "The Brye Centennial Reunion, Pioneer Narratives and Family Rosters," a well-researched and historically rich mimeographed work prepared in 1949 and made available by Martha Brye's niece Laura Aune, Rochester, Minnesota. The biographical information is all drawn from an eight-page letter of February 5, 1991, and a three-page letter of February 18, 1991, from Laura Aune. They summarize material from the papers of Martha Brye now with Laura Aune and also her memories of Martha Brye and the environment in which she grew up.

163. Typewritten copy of an unidentified clipping in the Martha Brye papers, furnished by Laura Aune.

164. All material except specifically identified newspaper information on Little Norway has been furnished by Marcelaine Winner, Scott J. Winner, and Brian J. Bigler of that institution and Marleen Rogers, Reference Librarian, Lake Geneva Public Library, Geneva, Wisconsin. The museum has been thought to have originated in 1926, but an article in the

Mount Horeb Mail, June 7, 1928, says that Dahle was first shown the farm with thought of purchase on January 1, 1927, and that the transaction occurred later that year.

165. Thea (Dahle) Hobson, undated manuscript for a speech to the P.E.O. women's club of Madison, Wisconsin.

166. "Little Norway Closed to Public," *Mount Horeb Mail,* June 6, 1929. Brian J. Bigler, interview with Joe Green, Isak Dahle's nephew, February 12, 1991. Marcelaine Winner's notes and memories of her Uncle Isak and Little Norway, 4, give the following information, "Isak lived in Chicago in an apartment on North Michigan Avenue. He was a prominent insurance salesman for Equitable Life Insurance Company. He was a successful investor and available funds were not a problem for him."

167. Hobson, P.E.O speech.

168. Dahle to W.E. Stone, contractor approached for an estimate on the move of the Norway Building.

169. In an invitation to visit Nissedahle sent to Crown Prince Olav and Crown Princess Märtha, apparently in 1933, Dahle included a formal typeset acknowledgment of twenty-nine individuals and couples, both family members and friends, who had helped with the project.

170. Brian J. Bigler, "1987 is the 50-year anniversary for Little Norway," in *Vinland* (Chicago), August 1, 1987.

171. Bigler interview with Joe Green; and Winner, notes and memories. According to the latter, Isak Dahle's will put his estate in trust through his mother's lifetime. Green reported to Bigler that Isak's mother, Anne Dahle, "was the principal overseer to the collecting effort." Isak's credit to his mother is given in the frontispiece to his 1933 invitation to the Norwegian royal couple.

172. Winner, notes and memories. Winner writes that Thea Hobson had memories of Isak and Otto Dahle's enjoyment in hunting and fishing in rural Mount Horeb and of their knowing from youth the actual farm that they later purchased.

173. *Mount Horeb Mail,* February 12, 19, March 5, April 2, 1926; Dahle, invitation; and Hobson, P.E.O. speech. That the museums of Norway were an inspiration is supported by Dahle's saying in his royal invitation that little did the original settlers on the farm know it "would some day become a truly Norwegian outdoor museum in every detail."

174. Winner, notes.

175. Winner, notes. Dahle in his invitation to the royal couple had dated Haugen's settlement "about 1840," but Winner adjusted this to 1856. The obituary of Julie Austin Toland, *Mount Horeb Mail,* October 14, 1926, indicates that the actual date was nearer 1865. Variants in the spelling of the names include Olson, Hougan, and Austen.

176. Winner, notes, and *Mount Horeb Mail,* July 2 and September 23, 1926. According to tradition the farmstead had been vacant six years before Dahle took over, but contemporary newspaper reports indicate that this was nearer to six months. These photographs are included in Brian Bigler and Lynn Madrey's excellent *The Norway Building at the 1893 Chicago World's Fair* (Blue Mounds, Wisconsin, 1992), which appeared after this article had been written.

177. Hobson, P.E.O. speech.

178. Dahle, invitation.

179. Dahle, invitation.

180. While Hobson in her P.E.O. speech interpreted this law as covering material more than 100 years old, Bigler in "1987 is the 50-year anniversary" interprets it as relating to all material made before 1865. That 1928 was the year of its introduction is confirmed in *Mount Horeb Mail,* June 7, 1928, but specific information on its nature is not given.

181. Bigler, interview with Green, and Hobson, P.E.O. speech.

182. Winner, notes. Winner's report on notes from Thea Hobson indicates the wide range of sources for the collection, including the antique dealer James Stavrum of Chicago, who made a scouting trip to Norway for Isak. Solicitations for objects appear in *Mount Horeb Mail,* September 8, 1927, and June 7, 1928.

183. "Isak Dahle Building Norse Farm Memorial," in *Wisconsin State Journal* (Madison), June 28, 1928, makes reference to the built-in beds.

184. Dahle, invitation.

185. The addition of the fireplaces and exterior chimneys occurred with the very first restoration work. An article in *Mount Horeb Mail,* June 7, 1928, states that this work was done "last summer." An article in the same newspaper, July 5, 1928, which identifies all the major craftsmen on the project, includes six excellent photographs which show fireplaces with exterior chimneys on at least three of the buildings although reference is also made to another yet to be built.

186. It has been assumed that the springhouse was built in 1928 (see Winner, notes), but an article in *The Capital Times* (Madison), July 1, 1928, says, "last summer a force of from ten to fifteen men reconstructed several of the log cabins, erected fireplaces and chimneys, built a typical Norse springhouse, drained the marsh, and carried on several other improvements." The *Wisconsin State Journal* article of June 28, 1928, refers to "a locomotive bell" having "been placed for a dinner call" in the steeple of the springhouse, a feature associated with the storehouse in Norway.

187. Winner, notes, reports that a clipping with the photograph is in Isak Dahle's scrapbook from the period of the fair with the note, "This looks just like the Norway Building at Wrigley's. I hope to get it someday."

188. Letter from Cutting, Moore, and Sidley, Chicago, Illinois (apparently attorneys for the Wrigley estate) to Dahle, Chicago, July 3, 1935. This letter and several others relating to the building have been recently brought to light by Bigler.

189. Letter from Dahle, Chicago, to Philip K. Wrigley, Chicago, September 25, 1935.

190. The name of the architect and the place of construction are incised in the body of the building itself. The letter to contractor Stone indicates that the building can be taken down in sections, and photographs at Little Norway of the reconstruction indicate that the building was indeed designed to be dealt with in this way. These photographs have since the writing of this article been made public in Bigler and Madrey's *The Norway Building of the 1893 Chicago World's Fair.*

191. Dahle to Wrigley, September 25, 1935.

192. The words "Norse memorial," suggesting a public monument, are used both in the *Wisconsin State Journal* article of June 28, and the July 1 article in *The Capital Times*, Madison, 1928. The latter, however, also includes the sentence, "The Dahle brothers have adapted this Norse settlement as a hobby, planning it solely for the use of their family and friends."

193. Quoted from Bigler, "1987 is the 50-year."

194. Winner, notes.

195. Winner, notes, reporting on the will.

196. Winner, notes. If Dahle's invitation was extended in 1933, as established by the family, the Hobsons had been superintendents at Nissedahle since their return to Madison in 1931. Isak recognizes their two years of service in this capacity in the acknowledgments that accompanied the invitation.

197. Information on Tank Cottage is from an interview on August 12, 1992, with Dennis Fredrick of the Heritage Hill Foundation, reporting on research done by the Foundation and Heritage Hill Corporation. Some had already appeared in print in "Tank Cottage Revisited," a series of undated newsletters edited by Fredrick.

198. Holand, *De norske settlementers historie,* 235n.

199. The original document of transfer to the museum in 1929 and a handwritten booklet from the same time with a short history of the house and a list of its contents are in the Vesterheim archives. There is also an unidentified clipping in Norwegian reporting on the dedication ceremonies in 1926 when the committee, which according to the handwritten account had been elected by the association to carry out the move and restoration, formally presented the house to the association. There must have been some legal or political reason for the complicated procedure, but what this was is not clear because the committee is identical with the association's Board of Directors.

200. The clipping referred to in the previous note. The article ends with an unidentified verse of extraordinary strength and appropriateness.

> Vi venter paa Hellen en liden Stund
> Og træder saa ind i Stuen.
> Vi kjender vi kommer paa hellig Grund
> Og strygger af Hodet Luen.
> (We pause a moment on the doorstep
> And then walk into the house
> We feel we are treading on sacred ground
> And remove our caps from our heads.)

201. *Highland Prairie Lutheran Church–1934* (Lanesboro, Minnesota, 1934), 92: and Margit Mindrum, *No Change My Heart Shall Fear* (Janesville, Wisconsin, 1975), 38–39.

202. Harold Severson, "Lanesboro Church's Log Cabin Is Reminder of Pioneer Origin," in *Post Bulletin* (Rochester, Minnesota). Date missing from clipping.

203. "Reconstructed Cabin Dedicated to Settlers," name of newspaper missing from clipping, February 18, 1955.

204. "The Pioneer Cabin," a typewritten flyer prepared for the 125th anniversary of the church in 1990 and furnished together with the clippings referred to in notes 202 and 203 by Sara Tollefson, Preston, Minnesota.

205. *History of Houston County* (Winona, Minnesota, 1991), 457.

206. Letter from Jim Skree, Badger Valley, Minnesota, May 13, 1991; and records from Vesterheim archives.

207. All information on this preservation effort has come from Ruth Wickney, Northwood, North Dakota, and is based on carefully kept family records as well as excellent memory.

208. All information on the Rudi cabin is from the application for placement on the National Register made available by Dennis Gimmestad, Minnesota Historical Society.

209. Tora Bøhn, "Norwegian Folk Art in America," in *Norwegian-American Studies and Records,* 19 (1956), 121–122.

210. "East Koshkonong Lutheran Church, 145 Anniversary 1844–1989," a folder prepared in connection with the celebration; and a telephone interview with Pastor H. Stanley Christenson of the congregation, February, 1993.

211. Letter from Stanley Kittleson, Madison, Wisconsin, March 3, 1993, and an enclosed undated history by Harland B. Martinson, "The Old Hauge Log Church," published in *Lutherans of Wisconsin* (Milwaukee) in the summer of 1989.

212. *Mount Horeb Mail,* August 4, 1927.

213. *Mount Horeb Mail,* August 4 and 25, 1927. A celebration at the church reported in *Mount Horeb Mail,* September 12, 1929, had comparable attendance, and the afternoon speaker was Wisconsin Lieutenant Governor H.A. Huber. A fund for the maintenance of the recently restored church had then reached about $500.

214. *Mount Horeb Mail,* March 19 and May 21, 1926.

215. *Mount Horeb Mail,* December 1, 1926.

216. Martinson, "The Old Hauge Log Church."

217. Information on the Old Hauge church at Kenyon is from Harold Severson, *We Give You Kenyon* (Kenyon, Minnesota, 1976), 220–221, and telephone interviews with Jeanne Ellingson and Mildred Lair, Kenyon, March, 1993.

218. All information on Valley Grove Lutheran Church is from a telephone interview with Lillian Wasner, Northfield, Minnesota, March, 1993, and a pre-release copy of a four-page publication by G. M. Bruce, "A Brief History of Valley Grove Lutheran Church" (Northfield, 1993) furnished by Wasner.

219. Bøhn, "Norwegian Folk Art," 125. Information and photocopies supplied by Andrew W. Kraushaar, archivist, The State Historical Society of Wisconsin, Madison. The photographs had come from the estate of Mrs. Trimpey in 1951.

220. Information, photographs, and artwork furnished by Kati Casida, Berkeley, California.

221. Information and photograph furnished by Margaret T. Jaastad, Rushford, Minnesota.

222. Bøhn, "Norwegian Folk Art," 120–136.

Marion John Nelson

Acculturation in Buildings and Farmsteads in Coon Valley, Wisconsin, from 1850 to 1930

by Reidar Bakken
translated by James Skurdall

To a Norwegian, building traditions in northwestern Wisconsin do not appear to have very much in common with building traditions in Norway. This can be said even about such areas of high Norwegian concentration as Coon Valley and Coon Prairie near La Crosse. At first glance the houses seem to be American, and the layout of farmsteads appears to be essentially different from that in the old country. One could get the impression that immigrants in this region adopted American building practices soon after arrival and conclude that a rapid cultural transformation took place in Norwegian-American architecture. This is quite unlike what happened with folk music and the Norwegian language, both of which remained a vital part of everyday life in these districts well into the twentieth century and can still be found there today.

The most visible aspects of this transformation were the point of departure for a study carried out in the Coon Valley region during the spring of 1990. The aim was to determine whether those first impressions of rapid Americanization in building practices would hold up under closer scrutiny or whether one might not discover beneath this apparently rapid transformation a slow acculturation, a more gradual adoption of American customs.

There are very few intensive studies of building traditions in clearly defined areas of Norwegian settlement. Surveys of a more general nature make up the bulk of published material on this subject. Marion J. Nelson of Vesterheim, The Norwegian-American Museum, proposed a more localized study that would build on existing investigations as well as original research. A grant from Norges allmennvitenskapelige forskningsråd (Norway's Council for Humanistic Research) together with the goodwill and cooperation of

Norskedalen Nature and Heritage Center in Coon Valley and The Norwegian Emigrant Museum in Hamar made possible a stay of three months in 1990 to do field work in Coon Valley, Wisconsin, and the surrounding area.

The first phase of this project involved a survey of selected buildings and farms in the valley. The farms chosen were those on which the largest number of old buildings had been preserved. The selection was further limited to those farms that had been established by settlers from Gudbrandsdalen, who comprised the largest group of Norwegians in the area. All well-preserved farms of this group were included in the study. There were twelve in all, with a total of 171 buildings. While measurements were being taken, some of the oldest inhabitants of the area were also being interviewed. As much information as possible was obtained from them on the history of the buildings and any changes that had been made. Photographs of buildings and farms were also taken.[1]

When studying the building traditions of an area, it is important to ask about the origins of the inhabitants. It was already known that settlers from Gudbrandsdalen made up a large portion of the Coon Valley population, a reason this area was chosen. Part of the study, however, went beyond concern with settlers from Gudbrandsdalen to documenting more general patterns of settlement in the region.

In dealing with the population of the Coon Valley area, one cannot consider only the patterns of migration to the region but must take into account the natural environment as well. The valleys and rivers separated by narrow ridges were appealing to Norwegians for several reasons. This was the type of terrain they were accustomed to farming. The prairie seemed forbidding, especially because access to water was a constant concern. This was no problem in the Coon Valley area with its many springs. There was also an abundance of fish and game, a matter of importance on the virtually self-sufficient farms in Norway. However, attachment to the landscape alone cannot fully explain why so many Norwegians settled in this area. Large numbers of Norwegians also settled in areas that would not have reminded them of Norway in the least. There must have been other factors that will not be dealt with here.

The map of the Norwegian settlements in Coon Valley and Coon Prairie, drawn up on the basis of plat books (Ill. 1), shows what the distribution was during the 1890s. There were compact Norwegian populations in the townships of Coon and Christiana, and this concentration continued in the direction of the Mississippi River through the townships of Hamburg and Bergen. Toward the north, south, and east other ethnic groups penetrate the settlements. This map establishes the perimeters of the region with which the Norskedalen Nature and Heritage Center, an institution devoted to preservation, and this article are concerned.

A graph (Ill. 2) compiled on the basis of information about the regional

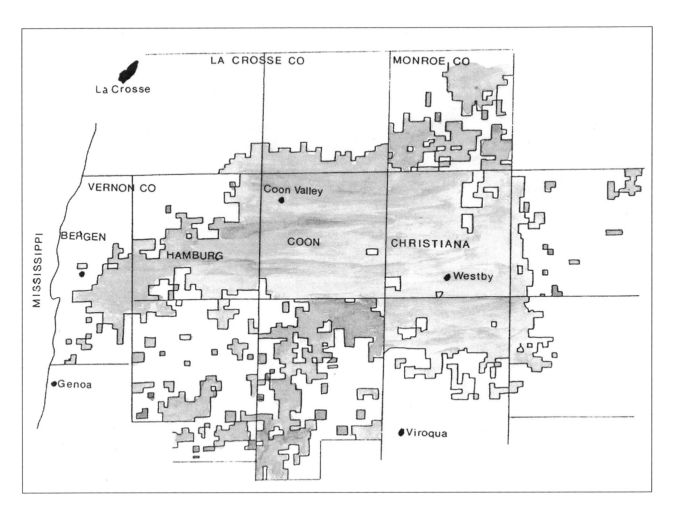

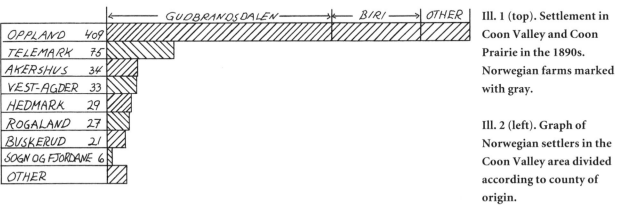

		GUDBRANDSDALEN	BIRI	OTHER
OPPLAND	409			
TELEMARK	75			
AKERSHUS	34			
VEST-AGDER	33			
HEDMARK	29			
ROGALAND	27			
BUSKERUD	21			
SOGN OG FJORDANE	6			
OTHER				

Ill. 1 (top). Settlement in Coon Valley and Coon Prairie in the 1890s. Norwegian farms marked with gray.

Ill. 2 (left). Graph of Norwegian settlers in the Coon Valley area divided according to county of origin.

BIRI	105
ØYER	75
NORTH-FRON	57
GAUSDAL	38
SOUTH-FRON	29
RINGEBU	21
FÅBERG	11
VÅGÅ	6
OTHERS IN GUDBRANDSDALEN	
LAND	34
VARDAL	9
TOTEN	6
OTHERS IN OPPLAND	

Ill. 3. Settlers from Oppland county divided according to township of origin.

origin of 656 of the first Norwegian settlers in Coon Valley and Coon Prairie shows the county of Oppland in the lead, followed by Telemark, Akershus, Hedmark, Rogaland, Buskerud, and Vest-Agder, with nearly an equal number of persons having emigrated from each of the last five. The population is not only predominantly Norwegian, but this graph shows that the majority of Norwegians are also from one region, Oppland, in the central highland of Norway.

Another graph groups the settlers from Oppland according to the township of origin (Ill. 3). This graph reveals that they were primarily from the southern and central parts of Gudbrandsdalen, Norway's central valley, an area that runs essentially from Biri to Land, up through Fåberg, Øyer, Gausdal, and even as far as North Fron in central Gudbrandsdalen. With a focus, then, primarily on southern and central Gudbrandsdalen, it was necessary to look within this region for distinctive traditions that would most likely have been brought with the settlers to the Coon Valley area.

The Dwelling   In 1984 William H. Tischler, a professor at the University of Wisconsin, headed a project for Norskedalen which documented fifty-three log houses in Coon Valley. The project report lists the following types of houses: one-room cabin, modified single-bay house, two-bay house, log house with frame porch (*sval-hus*) and frame house.[2] Of these house types the log house with frame porch is certainly of Norwegian origin. The other types too existed in Norway, including Gudbrandsdalen, though the simplest types were already considered antiquated there at the time of emigration. One can, for example, compare the Struxness house in Coon Valley with the so-called Akershus house

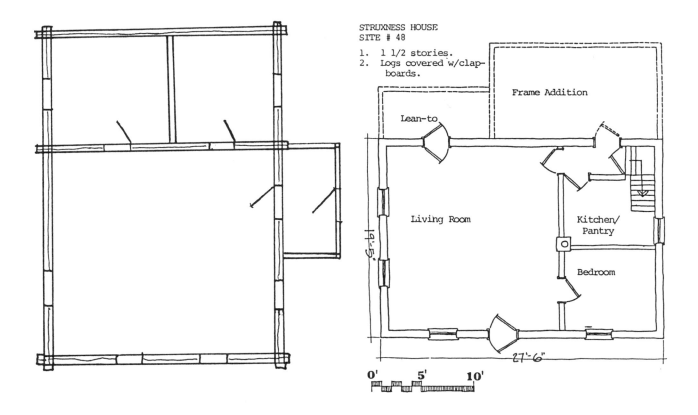

STRUXNESS HOUSE
SITE # 48

1. 1 1/2 stories.
2. Logs covered w/clap-
   boards.

Frame Addition

Lean-to

Living Room

Kitchen/
Pantry

Bedroom

19'-5"

27'-6"

0'   5'   10'

type, the most common floor plan in Gudbrandsdalen up to about 1850 (Ills. 4, 5). Apart from the two extra doors of the Struxness house, which may have been of only secondary importance, the similarities are striking. One can naturally assume that this modified single-bay floor plan had been brought over from Norway. In accordance with typical processes of acculturation, it later underwent modifications under the influence of American building customs.

Tischler's study, which concentrates on the period from 1863 to 1880, also considered the elevation of the houses. Of a total of sixty-three houses, thirty-three had one and a half stories, sixteen were one-floor dwellings, two had two stories and one had two and a half stories. There were no statistics on the remaining twelve houses. The predominance of the one and a half story house is difficult to explain in Norwegian terms.

Only three houses are reported to have had earthen or sod roofs, while fifty had various types of wooden roofs (shingles, shakes, boards, clapboards). One house had an earthen floor, while forty-five had wooden floors. Forty-five houses had one door, six had two doors, and four had three doors. Before

Ill. 4 (left). Akershus house type from East Norway.

Ill. 5 (right). Struxness house in Coon Valley.

1880 the American custom of a front and back door was not adopted to any noticeable extent on the homesteads in Coon Valley. There were eighteen houses with two windows, twelve with three, nine with more than four, and seven had only one window.

Tischler sums up his findings as follows: "The most common early house size on the homesteads was 14' x 16', or if of different dimensions, it enclosed from 200 to 249 square feet of space. Typically, it was one and a half stories in height, had a shingle roof, board floors, one outside door and two windows."[3]

The above statistics reveal much that is surprising to a Norwegian observer expecting continuation of native tradition. To begin with there are the large number of small houses with one and a half stories. These houses have high-pitched rather than the Norwegian low-pitched roofs and proportions that also differ from those of small log houses in Norway. It is clear that they were modeled after the American log cabin. For whatever reason it appears that the majority of settlers immediately adopted the building practices of the area to which they came.

During the period of emigration there was a preponderance of slate roofs in Gudbrandsdalen, although sod roofs were also still common. Tischler does not refer to a single slate roof in Coon Valley and lists only three earthen/sod roofs. The use of slate roofs had to be abandoned because the material was not readily available, a common reason for cultural adjustment in migrant groups. The small number of sod roofs could be attributed simply to the appeal of the American high-pitched roofs which were not suitable for sod covering. Sod roofs may also have been abandoned simply because the climate of the Middle West, with its heavy downpours followed by periods of dry weather, made them impractical. The use of wood as a roofing material was also, like the abandonment of slate, a necessary adaptation to the new environment. The three sod roofs documented in Tischler's study are marginal examples of attempted continuity which proved impractical.

Tischler does not make any mention of how Norwegian building traditions were adapted to American practices. Using his study based on homestead documents one can, however, notice several characteristics of American building that were rapidly taken over: small houses with one and a half stories; high-pitched roofs; and wooden roofs. Using data from his register of houses and from the present research, the following features can be added: whitewashing, interior as well as exterior; deviations from the most standard Norwegian corner joining and other details in log construction; roofs supported by rafters rather than purlins; frame rather than log construction in the upper gable ends; and additions made at a right angle to the original house. All of these characteristics are visible from the outside and make an immigrant house seem quite unfamiliar to a Norwegian observer.

The whitewashing of log houses was as common in Coon Valley as in the rest of the Middle West. This could have been done to draw moisture out of the logs, a characteristic of lime. It is of course also possible that it was done for aesthetic rather than practical reasons. The houses looked better when they were completely white. Whatever the reason, whitewashing is an example of the rapid adoption by Norwegians of an American custom with which they were previously unfamiliar.

Equally rapid adoption of American practices occurred in corner joining and other techniques of log construction. Most corners are dovetailed in ways rarely seen in early Norwegian building. The logs were seldom scribed and slightly hollowed underneath to match the irregular surface of the log below and make room for moss or other insulation as was done in the old country. With the American method, which seems to have originated in Central Europe, the irregular spaces between the logs were filled with pieces of wood, rags, etc., after the wall was completed. Then it was chinked with lime mortar both inside and out. When the whitewash on the logs has worn off, the chinking stands out so clearly that it becomes a significant visual feature of the house. This is precisely the effect people try to achieve today when building new log houses or restoring old ones, an effect that a Norwegian is not used to at all.

The reasons for rapid Americanization in log construction as in other aspects of the house may simply have been a matter of adapting to new circumstances. The settlers had easiest access to deciduous trees, oak in particular, and the gnarly logs would have been more difficult to join tightly than those of the coniferous trees in the old country. Yet this still does not explain the preference for the American type of dovetail joining. Again, whatever the reason, the adoption of American customs was rapid and highly visible.

Raftered roofs and frame-constructed gable ends are typical of the old houses in the area. Roofs supported by ridgepoles and/or purlins are exceptions. In Norway too one can find frame construction in the gable, and roofs with rafters also occur. What strikes one is the high frequency of roofs with frame-constructed gables and roofs with rafters in Norwegian-American log houses. It shows that the tradition of the American log cabin continued essentially unbroken even though the immigrants came from an area with different and varied traditions. This is also shown in the practice of placing an addition perpendicular to the house, not common in Norway but widespread in the American Midwest.

What impression does one get on a closer inspection of the less conspicuous features of the houses? One must turn to the floor plans to investigate more closely the slow process of acculturation that the present research reveals. The house on the Bakke farm at Viroqua has a floor plan that is both interesting and typical. It can be seen as two smaller houses that have been joined together (Ill. 6). The left side of the house when viewed from the front is built of logs, the right side is of frame construction. The part of the house built of logs has a large parlor and a rather narrow entry hall. The location of

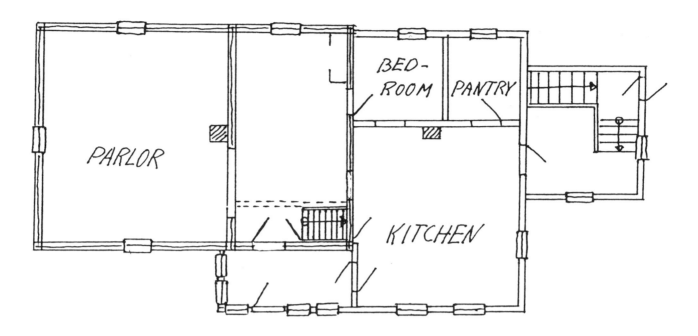

the outside door in this hall makes it possible to classify the log part of the building as a Norwegian three-room house. This floor plan originated during the Middle Ages, and in certain regions of Norway, western Norway in particular, it was by far the most common type of dwelling right up to the beginning of this century. Owner Lawrence Bakke's grandfather, Knud Olson, who presumably built the house, emigrated from Ringebu in central Gudbrandsdalen. Three-room cottages were also common in Ringebu, although around 1800 the main entrance would have led directly into the main room. This type of house had been the dominant type in eastern Norway from about 1600. The pastor and sociologist Eilert Sundt in his treatise of 1862 on rural building traditions gave it the name Akershus house because of its frequent occurrence in the county of Akershus.[4]

The right side of the Bakke house, the part which is of frame construction (excluding the entry hall that has been added on), also has a large room, in this case the kitchen, as well as two smaller rooms, but here the entrance leads into the main room. This part of the house too fits Eilert Sundt's description of an Akershus house. The fact that the two sides of the house have been joined perpendicular to each other has already been referred to as a common practice in the American Middle West. In Norway, the addition would have been end to end. Thus, the exterior of the house is American in appearance, while the two interior floor plans are in accordance with Norwegian tradition. It is tempting in this connection to call attention to the prevalence of other aspects of Norwegian folk culture inside this house, the Ringebu dialect, Norwegian food, and the entire spectrum of Norwegian traditions that had remained so vital in this region. Lawrence Bakke relates, for example, that his

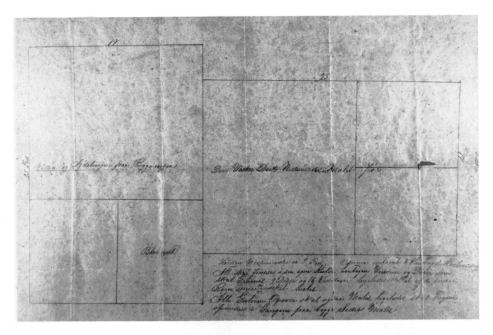

great-grandparents had had a contract stipulating that they would have a place on the farm. It also guaranteed them a small plot of land for growing potatoes and the like, plus beef, pork, wood and some cash. This was, in other words, a retirement contract modeled after the Norwegian *kårkontrakt*, a type of document frequently found on other farms in the Coon Valley area as well. What is found here is a contrast between the American exterior form of the buildings and a Norwegian organization of space and way of life inside and around them.

A comparable example is the house on the Terry Rudie farm in Coon Valley. The house was built in 1895 by Ivar Nesset and Ole Sund, both of whom came from Gudbrandsdalen. Ivar Nesset's original sketch of the floor plan with handwritten instructions to the painter has been preserved, and it clearly shows that the house actually comprises two three-room dwellings joined perpendicular to each other (Ill. 7). Seen from the outside, the house seems to be entirely American in style, with respect to both the decorative trim and the perpendicular juxtapositioning of the two halves (Ill. 8).

Ill. 7. The carpenter's drawing for the Terry Rudie house in Coon Valley.

Ill. 8. Facade of the Terry Rudie house.

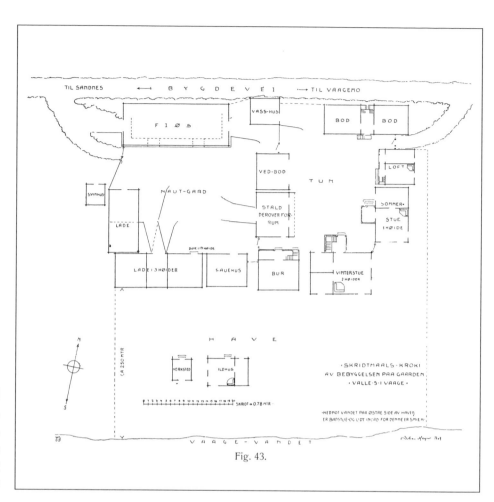

Ill. 9. The double farmyard
on Søre Valde in Vågå.
*Courtesy Johan Meyer,
Fortids Kunst i Norges
Bygder: Gudbrandsdalen III
(Oslo, 1977)*

Fig. 43.

The Farmyard   The arrangement of the farm buildings on farmsteads in Norway varies according to the different regions in which they are found. They can be laid out in either open or closed rectangles, in rows, or in clusters. Today there is a preponderance of farms of the open-rectangle variety in eastern Norway. The fact that they often have an oblong shape may reflect an older double farm-yard arrangement. Such double farmyards have existed for a long time, being mentioned, in fact, in documents preserved from the Middle Ages. In this system the main house and other domestic buildings had their own courtyard, and the buildings for the animals a separate yard. The double farmyard was once very common throughout eastern Norway, and is also found on the Swedish side of the border.

Today the double farmyard is found mainly in Gudbrandsdalen, and it was well known there during the period of emigration.[5] Buildings were numerous and relatively small. Using Johan Meyer's 1909 survey of Søre Valde in Vågå as an example, one can see that the farm consisted of two rectangles, with the horse barn, storehouse, woodshed, and wellhouse forming a dividing line

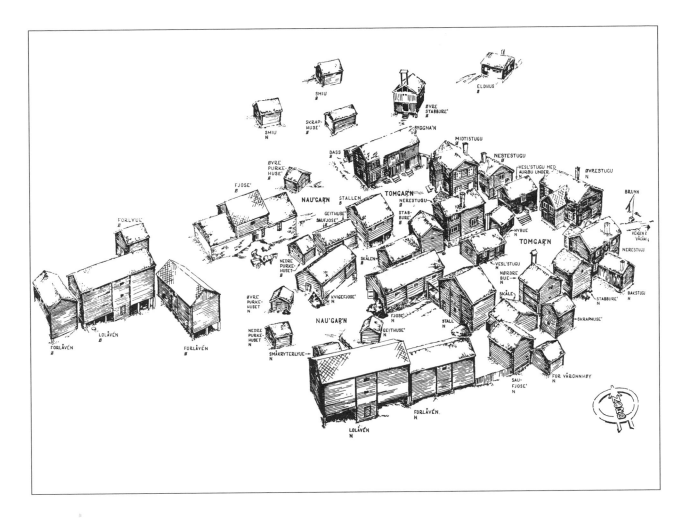

between the area around the dwellings and the barnyard (Ill. 9). With the dividing of farms comprised of several clusters of buildings, the double farmyard arrangement could become very complicated, as exemplified by the layout at Kvarberg, Vågå, around 1900 (Ill. 10). There were actually two smaller farms at Kvarberg, each with its own buildings, and each with a courtyard and a barnyard. The fact that the horsebarn was situated between the courtyard and the barnyard on both says something about the special importance of horses in early agrarian society.

How then were the early farms in Wisconsin laid out? In connection with the planning of a Norwegian farm at Old World Wisconsin, an outdoor museum of the State Historical Society, extensive fieldwork was carried out in an attempt to find an answer to this question. The plan was to reconstruct a farm at the museum that would be authentic and representative of a pioneer Norwegian farm in Wisconsin.[6] One of the original researchers on the project, Bjarne Breilid, presented the following conclusions in 1974: "The layout varies greatly, but there are a couple of noticeable trends: The house is nearly

Ill. 10. The farmstead at Kvarberg in Vågå where two farms with double farmyards are combined. *Courtesy Arne Bing, Norske gardstun (Oslo, 1968)*

always placed at a higher level than the other buildings on the farm, and there seems to be a tendency to place the buildings so that they form a triangle, an L-shape, or a shape approaching a crude half-circle. The rectangular pattern also occurs, but the triangle is more frequent, even when several buildings have been added so that an enclosed area could easily have been achieved.

"Thus we look in vain for a definite, regular pattern such as on a great many German farmsteads . . . We get the feeling as we study the different farmsteads that the thing uppermost in the mind of the builder was the practical aspects of the farm layout in relation to its particular topography."[7] Mark H. Knipping and Richard J. Fapso, who did additional research for Old World Wisconsin, in a report published in 1978 also confirmed that the layout of the different farmsteads varied considerably: "If any generalization can be made regarding Norwegian farm layouts, it is that there are no consistent patterns."[8]

These conclusions represent the current status of research with respect to the arrangement of buildings on Norwegian farms in Wisconsin. They point toward some kind of sudden transformation and suggest that traditions of the Norwegian farm layout were not brought across the Atlantic by Norwegian immigrants. The studies carried out for Old World Wisconsin, however, covered large geographical areas, including those with settlers from various regions of Norway. In a small district such as Coon Valley the situation is quite different. This study will attempt to test the validity of conclusions drawn from previous research by focusing on a local area in which the majority of farmers had emigrated from the same district in Norway.

The double farmyard was a cultural concept among the inhabitants of Gudbrandsdalen who emigrated to Coon Valley. Because it was no longer prevalent in other districts, it had come to be regarded as typical for Gudbrandsdalen. Of the twelve farms selected for this survey, six proved to have layouts strongly suggesting a double farmyard.

The Harvey Lunde farm (Ill. 11) in Washington township is a typical example. It was established in 1854 by Hans Hansen Dahlen from North Fron in central Gudbrandsdalen and passed down to the present owner through his mother's line. A granary situated in the middle of the farmyard separates the courtyard around the house from the barnyard and machine shed. A garage also helps to indicate this dividing line. The house is still standing on its original site, sheltered by two spruce trees, and the barn was rebuilt on the old foundation after a fire. Numbers were reported to have been visible on the logs of the granary indicating that it had been moved, but they cannot be seen today. Such a move would have occurred before 1887 since a photograph taken that year shows it standing on the same spot as today. The courtyard near the house is not as clearly delineated as the barnyard, and it includes a spring house, outhouse, and woodshed. A brooder house was situated for a time near the woodshed, but buildings such as these did not have foundations and were often moved.

It was while surveying the Lunde farm that the possibility of double farmyards having been used by Coon Valley farmers from Gudbrandsdalen first began to be considered. This farm includes the buildings which are pivotal to the double farmyard arrangement, the house, the granary, and the barn. During the course of the field work attention was focused on this configuration, which came to be referred to as the "granary in the middle" arrangement.

According to Tischler the granary and the horse barn were among the first buildings to be put up on a pioneer farm. Since Hans Hansen owned seven horses in 1880, he must have had a barn for them.[9] There are no documents indicating where it might have been situated, but all of the horse barns listed in this study were attached to the barn. It has already been noted that in Gudbrandsdalen the horse barn was often located on the dividing line between the two yards. Without wanting to attach any particular importance to the fact, the garage, the modern-day horse barn, is situated on this same spot on the Lunde farm and on several other farms. Research has also shown that the house, granary, and barn are, as a rule, among the oldest buildings on farms today. Since any barns exclusively for horses that once existed have been torn down, the rest of this study will focus on the former three buildings.

The farm now owned by Sue Erlandson (Ill. 12) was established by Johannes Skjonsberg from Øyer in south Gudbrandsdalen in 1861, the year he emigrated. Egil Haugen, who took over the farm in 1931 and owned it for thirty-nine years, was able to provide detailed information about various farm buildings.

The house and the granary are old, while the existing barn was built in 1919–1920 on a new site. The new location of the barn put it in line with the house and the granary, the latter being situated between the other two buildings. This made the division of the farmyard even more visible than it had been up to then. But the farm had the features of a "granary in the middle" farmyard even before the construction of the new barn.

On farms in Coon Valley the tobacco shed, in most cases constructed after the general configuration of buildings had been established, usually stands apart from the farmstead proper. The other buildings on the Erlandson farm date from the 1930s or later and are therefore not relevant to this investigation.

Today there are no indications that the Terry Rudie farm (Ill. 13) once had a double farmyard. It was built by John Rudi, who emigrated from South Fron in central Gudbrandsdalen in 1866. The distance between the house and the barn is considerable, and the house is shielded from the sun and the rest of the farm by a belt of spruce trees.

Informants were able to tell me where the old house had been located before 1895, and where the barn had stood up to 1893. The old plan shows that prior to this time the granary had been situated about halfway between the barn and the house. In this location it had divided the farm into a courtyard and a barnyard.

The same layout as in the Rudie farm is discernible in the old plans of the

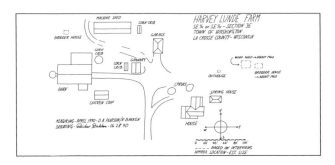

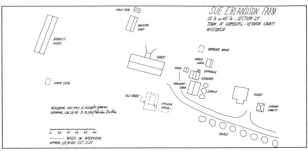

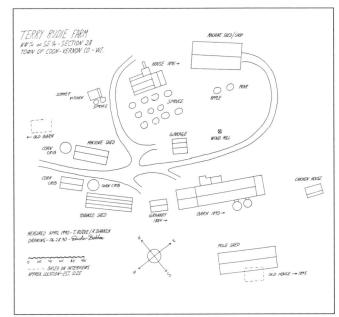

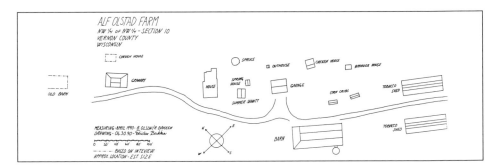

Ill. 11 (top left). Harvey Lunde farmstead.

Ill 12 (top right). Sue Erlandson farmstead.

Ill. 13 (center). Terry Rudie farmstead.

Ill. 14 (bottom). Alf Olstad farmstead.

Reidar Bakken

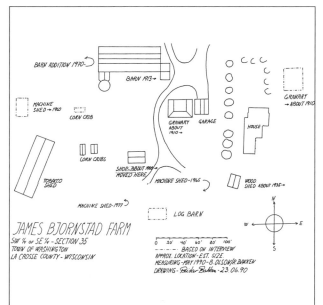

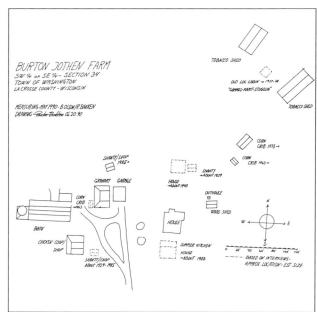

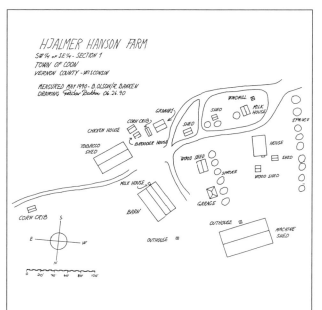

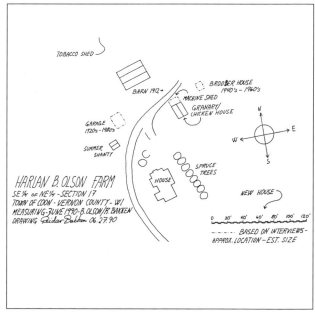

Ill. 15 (top left). James Bjornstad farmstead.

Ill. 16 (top right). Burton Jothen farmstead.

Ill. 17 (bottom left). Hjalmer Hansen farmstead.

Ill. 18 (bottom right). Harlan B. Olson farmstead.

farm Alf Olstad owned (Ill. 14) before he died in 1990. Today there are hardly any indications of a divided farmyard, even though the garage is situated in the middle. Noting where the old barn used to stand, it becomes apparent, however, that the granary was once situated between the house and the barn. When Alf Olstad's uncle, Ole Olstad, built a new barn on a new site in 1913–1914, this arrangement ceased to exist.

The James Bjornstad farm (Ill. 15) has a clearly discernible divided farmyard layout today, with the granary and the garage situated in the middle. According to the owner, however, the granary was moved from another site around 1910. A new barn was built in 1913 to replace the old log barn. This means that this divided farmyard dates back only to 1913, which suggests that early in this century there was still a tendency to follow traditional patterns in the layout of farm buildings. The family came from Skabu in central Gudbrandsdalen.

The layout of the Burton Jothen farm (Ill. 16) is reminiscent of the arrangement on the Lunde farm. It has two distinct parts separated by the granary and the garage. As they are closer to the barn than on the Lunde farm, the barnyard is reduced in size. The barn was built in 1906, and the location of the old barn is not known. The house is sheltered by a spruce tree and a pine. The house on the south section of the farm was moved to Norskedalen in 1983. Although there used to be several houses on the farm, their locations still clearly suggested a double farmyard. The tobacco sheds as usual are located beyond the confines of the farmyard, and a log cabin known as "Old Marit's Cabin" once stood out in the same area. It was torn down in 1927–1928.

Many of the small buildings on the Hjalmer Hanson farm (Ill. 17) have been moved there from other locations. The buildings as a whole comprise two separate farmyards, with the woodshed and the garage situated between them. A row of spruce trees planted as a windbreak accentuates the division. The garage was built in 1930, and before its construction the divided yard was not as discernible as it is now. This farm is also atypical to the extent that the granary does not help mark the boundary between the two yards. The large number of buildings on the Hanson farm, however, as on all the farms discussed, makes it typical of the farms in Gudbrandsdalen with double farmyards. The family came from South Fron in central Gudbrandsdalen.

Finally there is the Harlan B. Olson farm, a farm which has a different layout, but one which may have originated in Norway nonetheless (Ill. 18). It is a small farm, established by settlers from Tretten in southern Gudbrandsdalen. One can see that the buildings are arranged to form a rectangular farmyard. This was a pattern found on smaller farms in Gudbrandsdalen and presumably brought over from the old country. It is, however, a pattern that was also used among other ethnic groups in Wisconsin.

Although the data is limited, it includes all well-preserved farms established in the Coon Valley area by settlers from Gudbrandsdalen. Six of the farms referred to—half of the farms included in this study—show or have shown indications of a double farmyard. There is also one farm with a rectangular pattern. The farmyards of the other five farms treated in this survey cannot be classified as types originating in Norway.

These findings come as a surprise when compared with conclusions drawn from previous studies. One would not have expected the influence of Norwegian traditions on the layout of these farms to be so easily identifiable. Before arriving at any firm conclusions, however, one must first consider the historical development of the various types of double farmyards in the area.

The type was already clearly established on the Lunde, Jothen, and Erlandson farms toward the end of the last century. It is not possible to say whether this development could be traced back to the beginnings of these farms, but it seems likely. The double farmyard was introduced about 1910 on the Bjornstad farm, when the granary was moved, and sometime around 1930 on the Hanson farm, when the garage was built. The Hanson farm has the atypical feature of having a granary that is not situated in the middle, as it is on all of the other farms with this layout. If the Hanson farm is omitted, one can on the basis of existing evidence date the establishment of double farmyards in Coon Valley to a period from the 1880s to around 1910. If the Hanson farm is included, the period is extended to about 1930. The evidence suggests but cannot document earlier use.

During the same period there was also a development away from the double farmyard on the Rudie and Olstad farms. The house on the Rudie farm was moved in the 1890s. Construction of the barn on its present site in 1913–1914 changed the layout on the Olstad farm. It seems likely that the double farmyard had existed on both of these farms from the time they were first established.

For interpretation one would like to have more data. The most important buildings connected with the double farmyard, the house, the barn, and the granary, have been preserved on only a few farms. The selection of examples was therefore limited. If the data seems insufficient for drawing any solid conclusions, it nonetheless illustrates cultural processes that took place in Norwegian communities in America. On the basis of farmyard patterns the farms can be divided into five groups for the period from about 1880 to 1930: 1. Farms that were established with double farmyards and retained them. 2. Farms that established double farmyards at a later date. 3. Farms that were established with double farmyards but did not retain them. 4. One farm with a rectangular farmyard. 5. Farms with other types of layouts.

As far as the first four groups are concerned, one can see a specific development of a cultural concept that was prevalent in the region from which the settlers or their parents had emigrated. Not only was the double farmyard something the people knew from direct experience, it was also described in the literature of the day. It thus became, particularly during the first decade of this century, a clearly defined concept with special local status. Several cultural processes can be detected in the developments on the different farms: traditions, traditionalism, acculturation, and revival.

Tradition explains the fact that some settlers from Gudbrandsdalen established double farmyards in Coon Valley when they first arrived. They were carrying on a practice brought with them from the old country. If one accepts the view that the one rectangular farmyard was also based on Norwegian practice, it too falls into the category of tradition.

Traditionalism implies a more conscious attitude with respect to keeping certain cultural concepts alive. The number of double farmyards documented in this study, and the fact that some of them were established after other types had become prevalent, suggests that conscious retention may have been at work. The status the double farmyard had achieved as a result of the attention given it in research and literature may have influenced the preservation of it.

Adaptation or acculturation occur in the farms on which there was a development away from the double farmyards that had originally existed.

The fact that at least two farms with double farmyards were established in Coon Valley during the early part of this century might be viewed as a revival of Norwegian tradition, but no documentation of this exists. The word revival implies the reestablishment of a tradition that has been broken. It has an important place in music and the decorative arts but cannot be expected to any degree in something as rooted in function as the arrangement of farm buildings.

Norwegian traditions in the organization of the farmstead were not preserved in Wisconsin as a whole. This means that the farms in this study with neither a rectangular nor a double farmyard are the most typical. They represent a transformation that took place without intermediate stages.

Conclusions The field work carried out in Coon Valley confirms the impression that Norwegian immigrants were rapidly influenced by American building practices. Yet it also documents continuation of some building traditions from Norway. There are in particular similarities between the floor plans of houses in Coon Valley and those of the Norwegian three-room house and Akershus house. While the exteriors of the houses are American, the interiors have retained more of Norway. The houses of Norwegian Americans are not as completely American as they appear to be at first glance, and we are left with the impression that the rapid transformation was only a partial and perhaps superficial one.

Earlier studies of farmsteads in Wisconsin have not documented very many typically Norwegian features. By focusing on farms in the Coon Valley area this study identified several examples of the Gudbrandsdalen double farmyard. Some of these appear to be as old as the farm itself, while others were established between 1880 and 1930. The fact that the double farmyard was not only a tradition brought over from Norway, but one that was also introduced on farms that may originally not have had it shows that it was deeply rooted in this immigrant community.

The double farmyard was once widespread in Norway and gradually became limited primarily to Gudbrandsdalen. Even there it is now disappearing, especially in the south and central parts, where it is the victim of industrialized agriculture. The area of its ongoing use in Norway may soon be limited to parts of northern Gudbrandsdalen as it seems always in Wisconsin to have been limited to Coon Valley.

Informants:

Bakke, Lawrence, b. 1907, Viroqua.
Bjornstad, James, b. 1928, Coon Valley.
Hage, Olga, b. 1914, Westby.
Hanson, Hjalmer, b. 1907, Coon Valley.
Hanson, Verna, b. 1926, Coon Valley.
Haugen, Alva, b. 1915, Coon Valley.
Haugen, Egil, b. 1906, Coon Valley.
Jothen, Burton, b. 1915, Coon Valley.
Jothen, Lillian, b. 1921, Coon Valley.
Lunde, Harvey, b. 1936, Coon Valley.
Olstad, Alf, b. 1911, Coon Valley.
Rudie, Edvin, Coon Valley.
Rudie, Lawrence, Coon Valley.

Notes

1. Hjalmar R. Holand, *Coon Prairie* (Minneapolis, 1928). English translation (Decorah, Iowa, 1977).

2. William H. Tischler, *Early Buildings, Farmsteads and Landscapes in the Coon Valley Norwegian Settlement of Wisconsin* (Madison, 1988), 35.

3. Tischler, *Early Buildings*, 31.

4. Eilert Sundt, *Om bygnings-skikken på landet i Norge* (Oslo, 1862, reprinted 1976), 77.

5. Hilmar Stigum and Kristofer Vistad, *Vår gamle bondekultur* (Oslo, 1971), 69.

6. Bjarne Breilid, *Report on Norwegian Research and a Proposal for a Norwegian Farm Complex at Old World Wisconsin* (Stens, Wisconsin, 1974), 7.

7. Breilid, *Report on Norwegian Research*, 8.

8. Mark H. Knipping and Richard J. Fapso, *The Anders Ellingsen Kvaale Farm, Early Norwegian Commercial Agriculture, circa 1865* (Stens, Wisconsin, 1978), 27.

9. Wisconsin Agricultural Census, La Crosse County, Town of Washington, 1880.

"Good Building Stone and a 'Lay of the Land' that Makes for 'Hominess' ": Norwegian-American Settlement Patterns and Architecture in Bosque County, Texas

by Kenneth A. Breisch

T HE N O R W E G I A N settlement which was established on the American frontier in Bosque county, Texas, during the latter half of the nineteenth century represents a rare surviving example of a rural Scandinavian-American community.[1] Its architecture, therefore, lends itself well to a study of immigrant material culture. Because of the self-sufficient nature of their social and economic ties, moreover, the immigrants who settled after 1853 within a 150 square mile triangle of land between Clifton, Meridian, and Cranfills Gap remained relatively isolated from surrounding Anglo-American and German-American communities for more than five decades—and even to this day the communities they established retain a strong self-identity. This colony, which by 1890 was composed of some 1,300 Norwegians, thus maintained much of its traditional Norwegian culture well into the twentieth century.

An exceptionally significant component of the Bosque county Norwegian heritage is a group of several dozen farmsteads that were established during the early years of settlement between about 1854 and 1885. In spite of facing a harsh, unfamiliar climate and topography—one, for instance, with very little timber for building—the Norwegian pioneers who settled in this region of central Texas continued to maintain a traditional sense of community, while at the same time adapting new architectural forms and building technologies from their Anglo-American neighbors to the east. The forms of settlement and building that resulted from this meeting of cultures precisely define the way early Norwegian settlers in this area accommodated themselves to existing circumstances.

Although a handful of Norwegians had arrived in Texas before him, the "father" of Norwegian immigration in Texas was Johan Reinert Reiersen, who seems to have begun to develop definite plans for an organized settlement in the United States during the early 1840s. In 1843 Reiersen suggested in a letter to Christian Grøgaard, a sheriff in Lillesand, that "if one desires to leave his fatherland and found a new society in a foreign country, then who lays the first foundation becomes important. The elements should be kept as pure as possible so that the settlement in its initial organization does not contain the germs of its dissolution. This purification is the surest guarantee of future prosperity and happiness, and accordingly should not be ignored. I therefore wish that the society be constituted of men who, in the first place, have some means—several hundred dollars each to spare for a beginning—and who, in the next place, are known as moral, orderly, industrious, and friendly people. They should be limited at first to a fixed number—50 or 100 such men or families.

"The whole society would buy land in one location, and as large an area as possible. I have thought that each one should have no less than 160 acres, which for a hundred families would comprise around 16,000 acres. The whole society would pay *pro rata* for the most necessary expenses, as for example a saw, with either man or horsepower to cut lumber for houses, a gristmill, etc., and would see to it that they have in their midst various professional men. Everyone able to bear arms should have his rifle and be obliged, whenever necessity commanded, to take his place in the field. Transportation for the whole expedition would be provided at common expense according to a proportionate ratio, and each one who joins the society should be obliged to contribute his equal share for the expenses incurred by the society in searching for or discovering a suitable place."[2]

In 1844, after having traveled through the Midwest and Texas to investigate potential sites for his colony, Reiersen expanded his notions in his widely read travel guide, *Veiviser for norske emigranter til de forenede nordamerikanske stater og Texas* (*Pathfinder for Norwegian Emigrants to the United States of America and Texas*). Here he suggested that Texas, in spite of its warm southern climate, might, in fact, offer advantages over Illinois and Wisconsin, areas in which earlier Norwegian immigrants had settled. "The argument that we Norwegians require a very cold winter for our physical well-being, even though we endure the extreme heat of an oppressive summer without falling sick," wrote Reiersen, "seems to be illogical and to run counter to common sense." Texas had the obvious advantage of enjoying much milder winters, and he was unconvinced that the summer heat was any worse than in the North. According to Reiersen, the healthfulness of a region was dependent not so much on how far north or south it was, but on its elevation, its distance from rivers, the density of its forests and prairies, and, as well, on "whether the settlers themselves take or neglect the necessary hygienic precautions and so avert or invite sickness."[3]

This defense of Texas as a potential area of settlement was no doubt encouraged by observations Reiersen had made during his short visit there early in 1844. While visiting Austin he had met with the president of the Republic of Texas, General Sam Houston, "who expressed great interest in having Norwegian immigrants choose Texas as their new fatherland."[4] At this meeting Houston also assured Reiersen that the Republic would do everything it could for these immigrants; he believed that the recent Mexican and Comanche Indian hostilities had both come to an end and were not likely to cause problems in the future. Consequently it would be an opportune time for a new colony. In his *Veiviser,* Reiersen himself mentions as an example of new settlement in the Republic a "German Company" that was bringing immigrants to a large tract of land it had acquired on the Colorado River west of Austin. This was undoubtedly a reference to the Fischer-Miller Land Grant that had been made by the Republic to Henry Francis Fischer, Burchard Miller, and Joseph Baker on June 7, 1842, and renewed in September of the following year, less than eight months before Reiersen himself visited Austin. Although actual colonization of this tract would not begin for some time, the stated intention of the contract was to allow one thousand German, Dutch, Swiss, Danish, Swedish, and Norwegian immigrants to settle between the Colorado and Llano rivers.[5]

The example of this type of organized colonization seems to have influenced Reiersen's own thinking, for he went on to note in his *Veiviser* that in addition to having settled in the North, earlier Norwegian immigrants had also made an error in their pattern of settlement, which had been to scatter their farms widely over a large area of land. This, Reiersen thought, inevitably led to a dissipation of their political power. As a result, the local government and schools would be so dominated by Anglo-American settlers that the foreign-born would be forced to assimilate into this culture, thereby losing "their own language and character."[6] If, on the other hand, Norwegian immigrants were to buy up just half of the land in any one township, they could control both the elections and the schools. In doing this, moreover, these settlers could claim the best land, allowing less desirable tracts in between these claims to be used as common woodland and pasture until a time when they might be purchased by the settlers to accommodate growing families.

"One need not worry about the unoccupied land being bought up by the Americans," Reiersen argued, for "they are not inclined to push in among a foreign population so large that it controls local elections. This pattern of settlement would yield important advantages for both the present and the future. The scheme would also allow the settlers to set up the school system and manage their affairs as they think best."[7]

In May, 1845, Reiersen took an initial step toward realizing this concept when he, his father Ole, and five other Norwegians set sail for New Orleans. Here Ole purchased a $500 Headright Certificate from the Texas Consul,

Kenneth A. Breisch

Ill. 1. Johan Reinert
Reiersen Cabin, c. 1845,
near Brownsboro,
Henderson county, Texas.
*Courtesy of the University
of Texas, Institute of Texan
Cultures at San Antonio,
Texas*

which entitled him to 1,476 acres in the Republic. In July, Ole claimed land on the western edge of what was then Nacogdoches county, about 75 miles southeast of present-day Dallas. At the time this was largely unsettled territory on the edge of the East Texas "Piney Woods."[8]

According to Johan Reiersen, who preempted additional land adjacent to his father's homestead, their new property was composed of high, rolling country that abounded in oak, ash, hickory, and walnut trees, interspersed with prairie. Wild game in this region was plentiful, and the soil was excellent for growing a variety of crops such as corn, wheat, rye, barley, oats, cotton, tobacco, and sugar. According to Elise Wærenskjold, an early settler and propagandist for Texas, the Reiersens were soon joined by "a few American families and an old Norwegian bachelor, Knud Olsen, who had come from the Northern states. . . . This was the meager beginning of a Norwegian settlement in Texas."[9]

Although Johan Reiersen apparently intended to name this colony New Normandy, it eventually became known as Brownsboro. Here, at the top of a hill overlooking a valley that ran through their property, the Reiersens erected a small house. This structure, according to Johan Reiersen, consisted of "two log rooms 16 feet square, with a 10-foot hallway between them and porches on both sides." According to Wærenskjold this building, which seems from the description to bear a close resemblance to a traditional Southern American "dogtrot" cabin, was built by an American.[10] Near the house, which has been heavily altered and covered with wooden siding, is a smaller two-room structure, which has been identified as the Reiersen smokehouse or kitchen (Ill. 1). Though of somewhat cruder workmanship, aspects of this building's

construction seem to fall within the general patterns of traditional Norwegian
log building. These patterns are most clearly reflected in the Reiersen cabin's
tightly spaced, planked logs and the interior log partition, which is square-
notched into the outer wall, a combination of features typically not found in
neighboring Anglo-American log buildings of the same period.[11]

By the end of 1846 the population of Reiersen's small Norwegian colony
had grown to about fifty, but the full-scale settlement that he had envisioned
never materialized, as many prospective colonists bypassed Texas for the
north. To make matters worse, many of this first wave of pioneers, observed
Wærenskjold, had "settled, contrary to Reiersen's advice, in very unhealthful
places. Thus eight families crowded into two small rooms which an American
had built in the bottom lands, completely surrounded by grainfields. The
American, who knew how unhealthful it was, wouldn't live there himself but
was glad to rent his undesirable place to the Norwegians. Three families also
built themselves a cabin in the bottom lands. . . . All went fairly well until the
warm season arrived; then almost everyone became ill. With the exception of
J. R. Reiersen's family, whose house lay on a high and healthful ground. Consequently many were discontented, and some died."[12]

Perhaps at least in part because of this experience, Johan Reiersen, Wærenskjold and her new husband, and several other of these early colonists
established a second colony in 1848 that they called Four Mile Prairie
(*Firemils-sletten*), about thirty-six miles northwest of Brownsboro. The following year—though no new immigrants arrived from Norway—witnessed a
slow migration of settlers from Normandy to Four Mile Prairie. Knud Olson
Hastvedt, for instance, wrote that in 1849 he and Torge Tvedt went to Four

Kenneth A. Breisch

Mile Prairie to build a house for Wilhelm and Elise Wærenskjold, who had been married the previous September.[13] A surviving photograph of this structure reveals what appears to be two large rooms with end chimneys, set to either side of a wide breezeway (Ill. 2). Reflections of the "dogtrot" house are found even in this Norwegian-built house. It was apparently of wood-frame rather than log construction, with vertical board and batten siding across the front facade and horizontal clapboard siding on the side gables. According to Wærenskjold, either type of sheathing required interior paneling "to be any good," and was the best type of construction for those who could "afford to buy lumber right away." Those who had "little or nothing to start out with," on the other hand, "had best build a log house, since [they] can improve that as [they] go along."[14]

According to Hastvedt, "it was not long" after working on the Wæren-skjold house before Torge Tvedt bought a half-section of land from them. "There was better prairie around here and more open land, so we liked it better."[15] The Hastvedt family soon followed, as did others. An analysis of United States Census abstracts indicates that there were 105 native-born Norwegians living in Texas in 1850. Of these, fifty-six were living in Van Zandt county at Four Mile Prairie. In spite of Hastvedt's claims, many of the new settlers still remained dissatisfied with the land they found in this area. They also found it difficult to cope with the extremely hot and humid climate and the continuing outbreaks of malaria and other diseases common to the region. As a result, by 1852 plans were being formulated to move to higher and drier lands still farther to the west.[16]

By most accounts, the Norwegian who initiated this movement was Ole Canuteson. In 1850, he and his wife Ellen and their children—along with Cleng Peerson—had moved from LaSalle county, Illinois, to Dallas county, where they joined Johannes and Kari Nordboe, who had homesteaded there in 1841. Peerson, who was now almost seventy years old, had apparently visited both Normandy and Four Mile Prairie in 1848 and then returned to Illinois, where he convinced the Canutesons—who had themselves just arrived from Norway—to accompany him on a second trip to Texas. After again visiting with Johan Reiersen in 1850, Peerson moved in with the Nordboes on their Dallas county farm, while the Canutesons claimed a homestead nearby. Shortly after his arrival, however, Ole Canuteson began to investigate other land southwest of Dallas in the Bosque River Valley, west of the village of Waco. In the summer of 1853, he claimed three hundred and twenty acres in an area that was to become part of Bosque county in 1854.[17]

This same year, the Canutesons were joined by a second group of Norwegians from Four Mile Prairie, who were apparently led by Peerson. According to Axel Arneson, who arrived in Bosque county in 1873, all of these settlers had been impressed by the quality of the land which they found there, as well as the "abundance of wood and water . . . good building stone and a 'lay of the land' that makes for "hominess.'" Equally as important perhaps, the valleys, "one beyond the other, each separated by a range of hills—mountains they called them," formed "an ensemble that strongly reminded them of the home valleys from which they came."[18] Within three years of this expedition, Norwegians from East Texas had preempted ten homesteads in the southwestern section of the county and by 1860 there appear to have been just over one hundred Norwegians in the area, living on fifteen separate farmsteads—only slightly fewer than the number of immigrants then residing at Four Mile Prairie and Brownsboro. Ten years later, the population in Bosque county had grown to over 350 and the number of homesteads tripled to about forty-five.[19]

Although they were separated by as much as fourteen miles, the pattern of settlement determined by the earliest pioneers clearly established the parameters of the future colony. Topography and siting, in fact, appear to have played a significant role in the development of the settlement as a whole. Farms were often established on the slope of a valley wall, or near the top of a small hill, with a view towards other farmsteads or the parish church. Several of the first pioneers, such as Ole Canuteson or Berger Rogstad, for example, chose extremely distinctive locations for their homes at the tops of what were to become known as Normandy Hill and Rogstad Mountain. These sites served in turn as focal points for the development of several small rural communities, which usually consisted of one to two dozen closely grouped farmsteads, a small school, and occasionally a church. As in Norway, the organization of these rural districts, or *bygder,* was determined by the topography, with natural barriers such as creeks and valley ridges forming their boundaries.[20]

An excellent example of this type of settlement pattern can be observed in the Upper Meridian Creek Valley, just below Rogstad Mountain, where Berger Rogstad and his wife had settled about 1855 (Ill. 3). In 1863 and 1864 they were joined by the Swenson, Olson, Reiersen, and Skeinland families, who each preempted 160-acre tracts along the southern slope of the valley midway between the crest of Rogstad and Jenson mountains and the Meridian Creek bed. Over the next three decades others followed, first, like the two Knudsons and the Ilsengs, claiming land in similar locations, then filling in areas left between the farmsteads of the original settlers, and finally, preempting less desirable sites above and below the first claims. While recalling the colonization strategy outlined by Johan Reiersen in his *Veiviser,* as well as his admonition not to settle in bottom lands—a warning which proved all too prescient in East Texas—the settlement pattern in the Upper Meridian Creek area also strongly recalls traditional Norwegian agrarian practice where it was common for farmers to plant grain on the side of hills or mountains so that they could take advantage of the slope as they walked uphill to cut it by hand.[21]

In the Upper Meridian Creek Settlement, or Upper Settlement as it came to be known, many of the earlier homesteads were also clustered midway up the

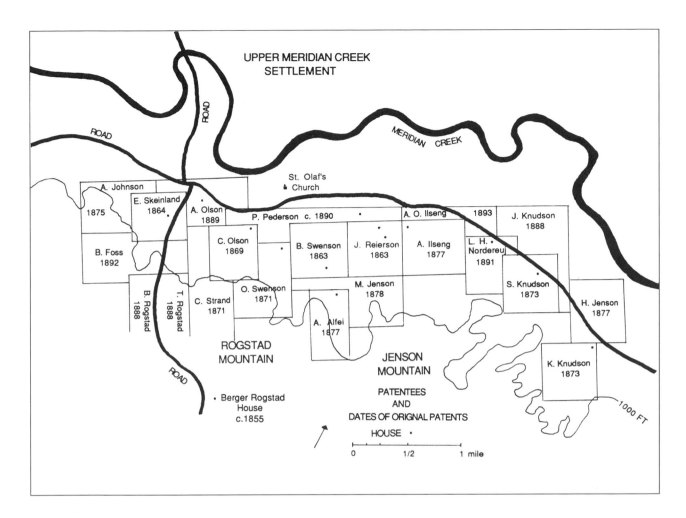

UPPER MERIDIAN CREEK
SETTLEMENT

ROAD

ROAD

MERIDIAN CREEK

A. Johnson
1875

E. Skeinland
1864

A. Olson
1889

St. Olaf's
Church

P. Pederson c. 1890

A. O. Ilseng 1893

J. Knudson
1888

B. Foss
1892

C. Olson
1869

B. Swenson
1863

J. Reierson
1863

A. Ilseng
1877

L. H.
Nordereu
1891

B. Rogstad
1888

T. Rogstad
1888

C. Strand
1871

O. Swenson
1871

M. Jenson
1878

A. Alfei
1877

S. Knudson
1873

H. Jenson
1877

ROAD

ROGSTAD
MOUNTAIN

JENSON
MOUNTAIN

K. Knudson
1873

1000 FT

Berger Rogstad
House
c.1855

PATENTEES
AND
DATES OF ORIGNAL PATENTS

HOUSE •

0   1/2   1 mile

slope of the valley, giving them not only a majestic view of the rolling landscape to the north and the west, but also, after it was built in the late 1880s, of
St. Olaf's church, which was prominently situated on the rise of a low hill not
far from Meridian Creek near the middle of the district (Ills. 3, 4a). As in Norway, the church stood alone as the symbolic center of the community or
parish.

Because the relatively mild winters of central Texas required fewer indoor
activities than in Norway, the Bosque county Norwegian farmsteads themselves tended to be much less complex than those which the immigrants had
left behind. Most Norwegian-Texan farms, in fact, appear to have been composed of little more than the main house and a small group of log or stone
outbuildings. These ancillary structures included such building types as bank
barns, vegetable cellars, corn cribs, springhouses, detached, or "summer,"
kitchens, and storage or work sheds. High stone fences of exceptional size and
quality surround many of these farms and enclose additional pens and
pastures.

Ill. 3. Nineteenth-Century
Norwegian Settlement in
the Upper Meridian Creek
Valley, Bosque county,
Texas. *Courtesy of Kenneth
Breisch, The Texas
Historical Commission*

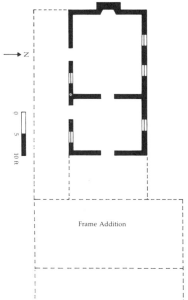

Ill. 4a (above). Bersvend and Kari Swenson House, c. 1865, Bosque county, Texas. *Courtesy of Kenneth Breisch, The Texas Historical Commission*

Ill. 4b (right). Plan of the Bersvend and Kari Swenson House, c. 1865, Bosque county, Texas. *Courtesy of Kenneth Breisch, The Texas Historical Commission*

N

0 5 10 ft

Frame Addition

Kenneth A. Breisch

The largest ensembles of these structures—such as that found on the Karl and Sedsel Questad farm, with its impressive complex of stone buildings and fences, built it is said by other Norwegian immigrants in exchange for passage from their homeland—not only convey the impression of prosperity, but transplant to Texas soil the character of the traditional Norwegian farm (Ills. 5, 6, 7, 8). As in Norway, the topography of the site clearly determined the location of the farmstead and the seemingly informal arrangement of its buildings. The placement of the stone fences, the house, and several of its nearest outbuildings—a "blacksmith shop" and combination kitchen/spring-house—demarcate a rectangular yard, similar in form to the type of tradi-tional Norwegian *tun* common to the Questads' native province of Hedmark.[22]

At the Questad place as well as on a number of other farmsteads, such as the Ringness farm, imposing work and storage buildings, which now are often referred to as "blacksmith shops" in recognition of their owners' skill at what appears to have been a highly respected craft, dominate the farmyard, often competing with the main house itself for prominence (Ills. 8, 9). In the hot Texas climate it seems likely that much of the actual smithing would have been performed outdoors. There is, in fact, little evidence of large scale forges in any of these buildings, so it seems likely that they functioned more as multi-purpose storehouses and workshops. Rectangular in plan, with a gable entry and attic, or loft (there is also evidence that the Ringness building once had a gable-end porch), these buildings bear some resemblance to the wooden *loft*, or storage buildings, that similarly dominated the *tun* of the traditional Nor-wegian farm (Ill. 10).[23] Though constructed of randomly laid limestone

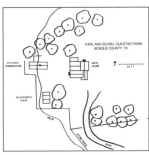

Ill. 5. Karl and Sedsel Questad Farm, c. 1855–1870. Bosque county, Texas. *Courtesy of David Moore, The Texas Historical Commission*

Ill. 6. Site Plan, Karl and Sedsel Questad Farm, c. 1855–1870, Bosque county, Texas. *Courtesy of Kenneth Breisch, The Texas Historical Commission*

Kenneth A. Breisch

Ill. 7 (opposite page, top). Springhouse and Kitchen, Karl and Sedsel Questad Farm, c. 1855–1870. Bosque county, Texas. *Courtesy of David Moore, The Texas Historical Commission*

Ill. 8 (opposite page, bottom). Blacksmith Shop, Karl and Sedsel Questad Farm, c. 1855, Bosque county, Texas. *Courtesy of David Moore, The Texas Historical Commission*

Ill. 9. Blacksmith Shop, c. 1860–1870, Jens and Kari Ringness Farm, Bosque county, Texas. *Courtesy of Kenneth Breisch, The Texas Historical Commission*

blocks, the impressive quality of their finish, careful proportioning, and monumentality, like the size and decoration of the homeland *loft,* clearly were intended to reflect the wealth and prosperity of the farm and the stature of its owner within the community.

Although the Norwegian *loft* was not typically used for smithing, the Bosque county "blacksmith shops," like the *loft,* seem to have been used both as storehouses and, when the situation required, as shelter for guests or newly arrived immigrants. The "blacksmith shop" on the Questad farm, for example, is said to have been the first permanent structure erected by Karl and his family, who preempted their farmstead in 1854. A later account by Johanna Rogstad, a granddaughter of Berger and Anne Rogstad, suggests that her grandparents "lived in the blacksmith shop on the Questad place" for a short period after their arrival in Bosque county the same year.[24] It may very well be that the Questads, too, used this building as an early home, although they are also said to have erected a log building as their first shelter. Local legend also identifies several of these structures as places of refuge and defense during infrequent Indian raids.

According to tradition, and as many of them had done earlier in the Piney Woods of East Texas, a number of the earliest Norwegian pioneers in Bosque county, such as the Questad and Ringness families, are supposed to have lived in small log houses, or stone and wood dugouts, when they first arrived. The oldest identified examples of Norwegian log building in Bosque county, however, date to the late 1860s or early 1870s.[25] Like the Adolf and Christine Godager cabin, these are all small, single-pen buildings with end gables and central doorways (Ill. 11). Characteristically the workmanship of the Bosque

Ill. 10 (opposite page). *Stabbur* in Numedal. Photograph by
Darrell Henning. *Courtesy of the Photographer*
Ill. 11 (top). Adolf and Christine Godager Cabin, c. 1874,
Bosque county, Texas. *Courtesy of David Moore, The Texas
Historical Commission*
Ill. 12 (bottom). Andreas and Olia Alfei House,
c. 1870–1880, Bosque county, Texas. *Courtesy of Kenneth
Breisch, The Texas Historical Commission*

county cabins, where the lack of adequate timber supply made fine log construction all but impossible, contrasts markedly with that of their Norwegian and even East Texas counterparts. In particular the irregularity of the logs normally seems to have required heavy stone and clay chinking of the inevitable gaps left between them.

As was not uncommon in European folk cultures, the raising of these cabins was often a cooperative venture. This process was described by Carl (Charlie) Knudson, the son of Knud and Gunhild Knudson. Charlie was born at Four Mile Prairie in 1867, six years before Knud and his father Salve preempted land in the Upper Settlement of Bosque county. According to Charlie, "Salve and Knud settled on adjoining farms of 160 acres each, where they [sic] was sufficient land which would not have to be cleared of trees before the first crop could be planted. For a short time, until their log house could be built, they camped under an oak tree in a little lean-to made of lumber which they brought with them. . . .

"As soon as they could the two pioneers set about building houses for themselves. They cut and trimmed the logs themselves in the plentiful timber in the hills and dragged them to the sites. Then the neighbors came from all around to raise the one-room houses. Two men sat on opposite sides of the walls and received the logs as they were handed up to them, notched them with axes and set them in place. The chinks between the logs were plugged with clay and rocks."[26]

In contrast to good building timber, limestone was abundant and it very soon became the preferred building material, with stone houses and additions quickly replacing log. (Ill. 12) These buildings are still locally referred to as "rock" houses. According to Alvin Bronstad, "the rock house movement seemed to quickly gain momentum and spread over the county" beginning in the late 1860s. "Not only were there rock schools built, but rock became the common construction material in the county for fences, dwellings, mills, etc."[27] As Charlie Knudson would later note: "Stone houses weren't expensive. Everything needed was right at hand. [The early settlers] dug white rock out of the hills and hauled it home while it was fresh and soft and could be sawed. After the rock had been out in the air a while it became hard. The same limestone produced mortar they needed to hold the stones together. A hole dug into the hillside and lined with hard blue stone made a serviceable kiln. Chunks of limestone were placed on a grate in the kiln and wood burned under it. The resulting powder was mixed with sand and water for mortar and after the house was erected was used to plaster the inside walls."[28]

Reiersen, in his *Veiviser,* recommended that immigrants construct their first houses of sun-dried adobe bricks. A house of this material was preferable, he argued, to "a damp log cabin made of raw timber," which was one of "the most important causes of the ague," an ailment he not only found common among the northern colonists he had visited, but one that would severely afflict the first Norwegian settlers in East Texas. The soft caliche limestone which these immigrants found in the hills of the Bosque River Valley was almost as easily worked as adobe, and when it hardened with age, was much more durable. Like sun-dried brick houses described by Reiersen, a limestone home was "dry, warm in the winter, cool in summer, and completely free from vermin. It [could] be built by an ordinary workman, with only a little help from a carpenter or cabinetmaker, in a very short time. It cost . . . virtually nothing for material except what was needed for doors, floors, windows, and roof. And most important, it [was] just as durable as the best baked-brick building."[29]

While many of the stone buildings that characterize the Norwegian settlement area of Bosque county appear to have been erected largely by their owners, some, like their log counterparts, may have resulted from a more cooperative effort. The exceptionally high quality of the workmanship exhibited by many of them, however, would seem to betray the hand of professional, or at least well-trained, stonemasons. According to Johanna Rogstad, at least one immigrant, her grandfather Berger Rogstad, had indeed practiced as a "rock mason" in Norway before coming to Texas in 1853. In an account which she gave a century later she noted that "he helped to build many of the old rock houses in the community, some of them still standing—such as the rock building on the Questad place and an old rock building in Meridian." Around 1855, "Grandpa purchased some land on the mountain, now known as the 'Rogstad Mountain,' where he built a nice little rock home for his family."[30]

Although the Rogstad house no longer stands, several stone buildings survive on the Questad farm, at least one of which may be the "rock building" that Berger helped to build (Ill. 5). This may have been the main house, which, according to Karl Questad's grandson, Lloyd Swenson, was constructed between 1856 and 1858. In addition to being remembered as a skilled blacksmith and prosperous farmer, Karl Questad is also still often referred to as a skilled "rock mason" as well, raising the possibility that Berger and Karl worked together on at least one of the Questad farm buildings. Although Karl Questad is not listed as such, Berger Rogstad (enumerated as Berry Rochester), John Johnson, and Eric Linberg are all also identified as rock masons in the 1860 U. S. Census. While Johnson remains elusive, Eric Linberg's farm has survived in a state of partial ruin directly across the creek from the Questad place.[31] Both the house and an impressive bank barn have been built into the side of the ridge that faces this farmstead.

An early photograph of the Linberg house shows that it once possessed a striking symmetrical facade marked by a central gable with scalloped bargeboards and an intricate, open-work porch (Ill. 13) that recalls the ornamented gables, galleries, and porches of Norway. A 1954 newspaper illustration (not shown) of the Ringness facade depicts a similar entryway that once

Ill. 13 (right). Eric and Martha Linberg House, c. 1861, Bosque county, Texas. *Courtesy of Alvin and Ibrey Linberg, Clifton, Texas*

Ill. 14a (above). Jens and Kari Ringness House with the Blacksmith Shop in the background, c. 1860, Bosque county, Texas. *Courtesy of Kenneth Breisch, The Texas Historical Commission*

Ill. 14b (right). Plan of the Jens and Kari Ringness House, c. 1860, Bosque county, Texas. *Courtesy of Kenneth Breisch, The Texas Historical Commission*

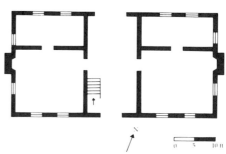

Kenneth A. Breisch

graced this house (Ill. 14a). As in Norway during this period, decorated central gables and porches continued to be popular in the Bosque county settlement until the end of the century, even after milled lumber had replaced stone as the preferred building material in the late 1880s.[32] While similar to those of the often sod-roofed houses in their homeland, the proportions and pitch of the gables of several early residences in Bosque county, such as that of Jens and Kari Ringness (Ill. 14a), also recall the form of the numerous one-story Greek Revival homes that these new immigrants would likely have seen in New Orleans or East Texas, the residences of prosperous merchants, lawyers, and plantation owners on the new frontier.

Although it lacks the end chimneys that are such a prominent feature of many of the early stone houses in Bosque county, such as the Ringness house, the plan of the entry-level floor of the Linberg home (Ill. 13) was probably symmetrically arranged with a central passage or chamber flanked by rooms to either side. The standard disposition of rooms found among the half dozen early Norwegian homes in Bosque county which display a symmetrical order is a central passage plan with a single room to either side. This type of arrangement can be fouænd at the Kittle and Liv Grimland house, which was erected about 1868 (Ills. 15 a-b). In contrast, the disposition of the Ringness house, which is said to have been erected in the late 1850s, is more complex, with two rooms set to either side of the central space (Ill. 14b). These central passage plans may be related in some way to the Scandinavian *dobbelthus* (double-house or pair-house) tradition. By the mid-eighteenth century the double-house had become a common type of residence for upper middle-class landowners in all parts of Scandinavia. Like the symmetrical houses of Bosque county, they are characterized by a tripartite plan.[33]

A parallel configuration can be observed, of course, in southern American dogtrot and I-houses of the type which many of the Norwegian immigrants would have seen, and lived in, in East Texas before moving to Bosque county. As was noted above, the first house raised by the Reiersens at Brownsboro, which was described by Johan as "two log rooms 16 feet square, with a 10-foot hallway between them and porches on both sides" and erected by an American builder, may, in fact, have been derived from this tradition. Elise Wæren-skjold and her husband seem to have had a similar type of residence constructed by Norwegian carpenters at Four Mile Prairie in the late 1840s (Ill. 2). With its wide central breezeway and massive stone end-chimneys, the Wærenskjold house in Four Mile Prairie, indeed, appears to be a good example of the southern "dogtrot" type. In all of these homes the Norwegian immigrants appear to have abandoned the more traditional corner hearths, and often even the tile or iron stoves, of their homeland for the much less efficient Anglo-American end-chimneys. "For many years, even after they had built their stone houses," noted Charlie Knudson, "the Knudsons," for example, "continued to use an open fireplace for cooking and heating." Wærenskjold,

Ill. 15a. Kittle and Liv Grimland House, c. 1870–1875, Bosque county, Texas. *Courtesy of Daniel Hardy, The Texas Historical Commission*

Ill. 15b. Plan of Kittle and Liv Grimland House, c. 1870–1875, Bosque county, Texas. *Courtesy of Kenneth Breisch, The Texas Historical Commission*

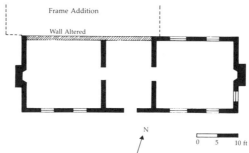

Frame Addition

Wall Altered

N

0   5   10 ft

Kenneth A. Breisch

on the other hand, had by 1870 installed both a stove and a kitchen range in her Four Mile Prairie home.[34]

Previous familiarity with double-houses in Norway, reinforced by their exposure to similarly planned residences in East Texas, might well have encouraged Norwegian immigrants to adopt a comparable form in Bosque county, as not only a reflection of their new agrarian prosperity, for which both Norwegian and Anglo-American precedents could serve as models, but also in response to the intense summer heat which they encountered in Texas, a circumstance which itself had contributed to the rise of the dogtrot form in the American South in the first place.

In addition to the more imposing centrally planned houses of Bosque county, a dozen smaller, one and two-room stone dwellings were constructed by Norwegian immigrants to this area during this same period (Ills. 3, 4a-b, 16 a-b). These typically incorporated a single room similar in form to the larger flanking rooms of the symmetrical buildings. If a second room was added to this configuration, it was typically narrower and appended to the gable-end of the house opposite the hearth. The arrangement of doors and windows in all of these houses varied greatly, with entries commonly placed in the long elevations, but occasionally in the gable end. In the latter case exterior doors might give access to one or both of the rooms. In single-room houses, such as that of Andreas and Olia Alfie (Ill. 12), doorways were placed either in the longer elevations or in the gable end opposite the chimney and hearth. The chimney-end elevations of these houses were typically like those of the central passage houses, with low pitched roofs and massive exterior chimneys flanked by one or two small square attic windows (Ill. 14a). Most

Ill. 16a (left). Gunsten and Lofise Grimland House, c. 1870–1875, Bosque county, Texas. *Courtesy of Daniel Hardy, The Texas Historical Commission*

Ill. 16b (right). Plan of the Gunsten and Lofise Grimland House, c. 1870–1875, Bosque county, Texas. *Courtesy of Kenneth Breisch, The Texas Historical Commission*

characteristic is the ubiquitous first-floor living space, measuring somewhere between seventeen and twenty feet on a side, with the hearth set into an outside wall. As was common in Norway, but in Texas typical only among German immigrants, an external wooden stairway was often erected along one of the end-walls to give access to a half-story loft. This attic space was traditionally reserved as a sleeping area for the children or visitors.[35] In the symmetrical homes, as at the Ringness house (Ill. 14a-b), stairways to these attics seem to have been located in the central passage near the front door.

The two-room houses with entries on their long side in Bosque county (Ills. 4b, 16b) may be related to the traditional Norwegian *Akershus* type, whose two-room configuration was composed of a larger *stue*, or hall (living room) flanked on one end by a much narrower bedchamber (Ill. 17). As Darrell Henning has noted, Norwegian immigrants erected similarly planned log-houses in the Midwest during the same period that likewise seem to betray an affinity with homeland forms.[36] At the same time, the two-room houses, with their massive end chimneys, could also reflect the influence of the Anglo-American hall and parlor house, for which there was ample precedent in East Texas. In several cases the smaller rooms, as at the Gunston and Lofise Grimland house (Ill. 15a-b), are much narrower than the "parlor" in a traditional hall and parlor house, although in other examples they are closer to the Anglo-American model (Ill. 4b), leaving the impression again that the Bosque county plans represent a conflation of several traditions based on need and experience.[37]

The introduction of milled lumber, along with the arrival of the railroad to nearby Clifton in the late 1880s, the telephone, and eventually the automobile, ultimately introduced more Anglo-American cultural forms into the Norwegian-American community in Bosque county. By the first decade of the twentieth century, for example, it appears that most children were speaking both Norwegian and English in the home, while communicating in only their newly adopted language in school. The architecture of this period reflects a parallel assimilation of Anglo-American cultural models. During the late 1880s, Norwegians in Bosque county—even recent immigrants—appear to have almost entirely abandoned stone as a primary building material, constructing instead two-story wood frame houses of the type built by Tobias and Wilhelmina Schultz about 1895 (Ill. 18). When in 1926 the congregation of Our Savior's Lutheran Church erected a new parsonage, it was in the same bungalow style then being promoted in countless builders' manuals and mail order catalogues all across the country. Significantly, perhaps, this was only one year after the final entry in the Norwegian language appears in the parish minutes.[38]

Kenneth A. Breisch

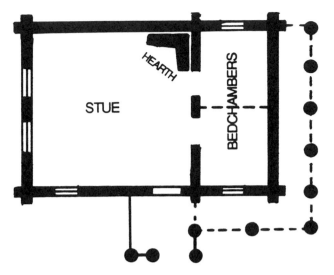

Ill. 17 (top). Norwegian *Akershus* Plan, (Drawn by Kenneth Breisch after Jerri Holan, *Norwegian Wood: A Tradition of Building,* New York, 1990, figs.3, 11).

Ill. 18 (bottom). Tobias and Wilhelmina Schultz House, c. 1895, Bosque county, Texas. *Courtesy of Daniel Hardy, The Texas Historical Commission*

1. Much of the field work for this study was undertaken by myself and David Moore in 1982 and 1983 in preparation for a National Register nomination written for the Texas Historical Commission. I would like to thank David Moore and Marion J. Nelson for their helpful suggestions regarding this work, as well as Judy Mataya for her assistance with the architectural plans reproduced here. This work identified more than one hundred Norwegian-Texan homesteads constructed in Bosque county between 1855 and about 1910. A brief assessment of some two dozen stone houses constructed between 1855 and 1880 was published in 1986. See Kenneth A. Breisch and David Moore, "The Norwegian 'Rock' Houses of Bosque County, Texas: Some Observations on a Nineteenth Century Vernacular Building Type," in *Perspectives in Vernacular Architecture*, 2 (Columbia, Missouri, 1986), 64–71. The standard historical accounts of Norwegian immigration into Texas and especially Bosque county include Axel Arneson, "Norwegian Settlements in Texas," in *The Southwestern Historical Quarterly*, 45(1941), 125-135; Lyder L. Unstad, "The First Norwegian Migration into Texas," in *Norwegian-American Studies and Records*, 8(1934), 39–57; Oris E. Pierson, *Norwegian Settlements in Bosque County, Texas* (Clifton, Texas, 1947); William C. Pool, *Bosque County, Texas* (San Marcos, Texas, 1954); and Odd Magnar Syversen and Derwood Johnson, *Norge i Texas. Et bidrag til norsk emigrasjonshistorie* (Stange, Norway, 1982).

2. Translated by Theodore C. Blegen in "Behind the Scenes of Emigration," in *Norwegian-American Studies and Records* 14(1944), 90–91. Like Cleng Peerson, who had prepared the way for the arrival of the first group of Norwegian settlers to the United States in 1825, Reiersen was a vocal advocate for Norwegian emigration. A liberal newspaper editor from Kristiansand in southern Norway, Reiersen summarized his own populist views and many of the most common reasons he thought people were leaving Norway in the Foreword to his 1844 pamphlet, *Veiviser for norske emigranter til de forenede nordamerikanske stater og Texas.* See Johan Reinert Reiersen, *Pathfinder for Norwegian Emigrants*, trans. and intro., Frank G. Nelson (Northfield, Minnesota, 1981), 3–39 and 60–61. For a general introduction to Norwegian immigration to the United States see Odd S. Lovoll, *The Promise of America: A History of the Norwegian-American People* (Minneapolis, 1984).

3. Reiersen, *Pathfinder for Norwegian Emigrants*, 208.

4. Elise Waerenskjold in a letter which was published in the Chicago weekly, *Amerika,* in 1894. Reprinted in C. A. Clausen, ed. and trans., *The Lady with the Pen: Elise Wærenskjold in Texas* (Northfield, 1961), 159, reprinted by the Memorial Museum (Clifton, Texas, 1976).

5. Reiersen, *Pathfinder for Norwegian Emigrants*, 37, 192. For the Fischer-Miller Land Grant see Walter Prescott Webb, ed., *The Texas Handbook,* I (Austin, 1952), 604.

6. Reiersen, *Pathfinder for Norwegian Emigrants*, 209.

7. Reiersen, *Pathfinder for Norwegian Emigrants*, 209.

8. See Headright Certificate #143, on file with the Texas General Land Office, Austin, Texas. This transaction was witnessed in New Orleans by Edward Hall, business associate and vice-consul to William Bryan, the man who had initially convinced Reiersen to visit Texas in 1843. A major factor in their decision, according to Wærenskjold, was the news, which they learned upon their arrival, that Texas was soon to be admitted to the Union.

Clausen, *The Lady with the Pen,* 78; and Reiersen, *Pathfinder for Norwegian Emigrants,* 43–44. For more on Hall and Bryan and their activities in New Orleans, see Alma Howell Brown, "The Consular Service of the Republic of Texas," in *Southwestern Historical Quarterly,* 33 (1929), 104–189, 207–214. In 1846 the Reiersen claims would become part of the newly created Henderson county.

9. Clausen, *The Lady with the Pen,* 80. See also the letter from Reiersen to his brother Christian, an excerpt from which appeared in *Norge og Amerika. Et Maanedligt Flyveblad,* Arendal, Norway, January, 1847. Reprinted and translated in Reiersen, *Pathfinder for Norwegian Emigrants,* 217–225.

10. Reiersen, *Pathfinder for Norwegian Emigrants,* 221; and Clausen, *The Lady with the Pen,* 160. For the dogtrot house see Henry Glassie, *Pattern in the Material Folk Culture of the Eastern United States* (first paperback edition, Philadelphia, 1971), 89–98.

11. For typical Norwegian log construction see Jerri Holan, *Norwegian Wood: A Tradition of Building* (New York, 1990), 147–166; and John Lloyd, "The Norwegian Laftehus," in *Shelter and Society,* ed. Paul Oliver (New York, 1969), 33–34. Although dovetail corner-notching of the type exhibited by the Reiersen cabin appears to be rare in Norway, Terry Jordan claims to have found significant examples of this type of joining throughout Scandinavia. See Jordan, *American Log Buildings: An Old World Heritage* (Chapel Hill, North Carolina, 1985), 51–59. For examples of Anglo-American and other log construction in Texas see Jordan, *Texas Log Buildings: A Folk Architecture* (Austin, Texas, 1978), 31–81. For a similar and almost contemporary house constructed in the Norwegian settlement at Muskego, Wisconsin, see Richard W. E. Perrin, "An Architectural Remnant of Old Muskego: John Bergen's Log House," in *Wisconsin Magazine of History,* 44 (1960), 1–14.

12. Clausen, *The Lady with the Pen,* 83.

13. Clausen, "Recollections of a Norwegian Pioneer in Texas," in *Norwegian-American Studies and Records,* 12 (1941), 103.

14. Clausen, *The Lady with the Pen,* 92.

15. Clausen, "Recollections of a Norwegian Pioneer," 103.

16. See for example the letters from J. Bronstad of July 20, 1852, and J. R. Reiersen of July 27, 1852 in Unstad, "The First Norwegian Migration into Texas," 45–48, 51–57.

17. Pierson, *Norwegian Settlements in Bosque County,* 14–16.

18. Arneson, "Norwegian Settlements in Texas," 128.

19. See State Patent Records and the U.S. Census and Special Farm Schedule for Bosque county for 1860 and 1870.

20. Holan, *Norwegian Wood,* 27–35; and Lloyd, "The Norwegian Laftehus," 33-48. For the early settlement pattern in Bosque county see Pierson, *Norwegian Settlements in Bosque County,* 15–20, 24. By 1880 the rural communities in Bosque county included Turkey Creek, Upper Meridian, Norman Hill, and Norway Mills, each of which had its own school. See Alvin Bronstad, "The History of Education in Bosque County, Texas" (MA Thesis, University of Texas, Austin, 1933), 52. That these new immigrants were attracted to an agrarian pattern of settlement, itself, reflects the land they left behind, which in 1801 had less than 9 percent of its population living in cities. See Lovoll, *The Promise of America,* 8–9.

21. Holan, *Norwegian Wood,* 35.

22. See Syversen and Johnson, *Norge i Texas*, 258, and Holan, *Norwegian Wood*, 39–49.

23. Holan, *Norwegian Wood*, 89–101. For Karl Questad's reputation as a blacksmith, for example, see Arneson, "Norwegian Settlements in Texas," 132. His "shop" measures approximately 15 x 19 feet, with a 12 foot lean-to on the long side. The Ringness blacksmith shop measures about 25 x 19 feet with a 7 1/2 foot foundation for a porch along the eastern gable end. Both floors of the building could be entered directly from this end, presumably by way of an exterior stair or ladder built into the porch.

24. *The Clifton Record,* April 30, 1954.

25. Of the earliest pioneers, the Dahl, Ringness, Questad, and Jenson families are all said to have occupied one or two room log cabins during the first years of their stay in Bosque county. In addition to the Godager cabin, later surviving cabins or remnants of them can be found on the Erickson-Amundson, Pederson, Bekken, and Ilseng farms. See sites 19, 20, 27, 44 and 47 in Breisch and Moore, National Register Nomination, "The Norwegian Settlement of Bosque County," prepared for the Texas Historical Commission (Austin, Texas, 1983).

26. *Waco Herald-Tribune,* July 14, 1946. Reiersen in his *Veiviser* noted a similar cooperative approach to raising log cabins. Reiersen, *Pathfinder for Norwegian Emigrants,* 100. See also Jordan, *Texas Log Building,* 31–48. For the Knudsons see also Syversen and Johnson, *Norge i Texas,* 215–219.

27. Bronstad, "The History of Education in Bosque County, Texas," 43.

28. *Waco Herald-Tribune,* July 14, 1946.

29. Reiersen, *Pathfinder for Norwegian Emigrants,* 125–127.

30. *The Clifton Record,* April 30, 1954.

31. According to Alvin and Ibrey Linberg, this large stone house was begun by their grandfather in 1861. It was presumably enlarged during the years following his marriage to Martha Ringness in 1865. Heavy destruction by a tornado makes reconstruction of its early plan impossible. Alvin and Ibrey Linberg in an oral interview with Breisch and Moore (Clifton, Texas, January 18, 1983). Tape on file with the Texas Historical Commission, Austin, Texas.

32. At least four wood-frame houses of a similar configuration survive in Bosque county. Breisch and Moore, National Register Nomination, "The Norwegian Settlement of Bosque County," sites 25, 26, 27 and 36. These are all similar in form and plan to what Fred B. Kniffen has labeled the I-house. See his "Folk Housing: Key to Diffusion," in *Common Places: Readings in American Vernacular Architecture,* eds. Dell Upton and John Michael Vlach (Athens, Georgia, 1986), 4–10; and Glassie, *Pattern in the Material Folk Culture,* 64–69. A number of these wood-frame houses are said to have been constructed by a Norwegian-trained builder, John Nordahl. The original porch configuration of the Ringness house can be made out in an old photograph which was published in the *Clifton Record,* April 30, 1954. The Columbus Cartwright or Stephen Blount houses in San Augustine, which was on the road from New Orleans to Nacagdoches, might serve as good examples of Greek Revival models for the Norwegian houses. Jens Ringness and his wife Kari Jensdatter lived in East Texas for three years before settling in Bosque county in 1854. See Syversen and Johnson, *Norge i Texas,* 262.

Kenneth A. Breisch

33. Breisch and Moore, "The Norwegian 'Rock' Houses of Bosque County, Texas," 68–70. For a variety of double-house plans see Gunnar Jahn, *Byggeskikker på den norske landsbygd* (Oslo, 1925), 57–85.

34. For Knudson's comments see the *Waco Herald-Tribune,* July 14, 1946. Soon after arriving in Texas, Elise Wærenskjold was already criticizing the inefficiency of the open hearth, which, she noted, left you cold on one side and hot on the other, unlike a good tile oven (*kakkelovn*). See Wærenskjold's letter of January 14, 1848, to S. T. Kirkgaard in Syversen and Johnson, *Norge i Texas,* 173. See also Clausen, *The Lady with the Pen,* 92.

35. See, for example, the oral interviews given to Breisch and Moore by Alvin and Ibrey Linberg (Clifton, Texas, January 18, 1983); and by C. Pernell Aars (Bosque county, January 19, 1983). Both tapes on file with the Texas Historical Commission, Austin, Texas.

36. Holan, *Norwegian Wood,* 69–87; and Darrell D. Henning, "The Norwegian Two- and Three-room Traditional House Type in America," in *Perspectives in Vernacular Architecture,* 2 (Columbia, Missouri, 1986), 218.

37. For the Anglo-American hall and parlor tradition see Glassie, *Pattern in the Material Folk Culture,* 64–81. Models for the single-room plan, likewise, can be found in both the Anglo-American and Norwegian building traditions.

38. See Our Savior's Lutheran Church parish minutes for 1926.

"Well, I Wondered When I Saw You, What All These New Clothes Meant": Interpreting the Dress of Norwegian-American Immigrants[*]

by Carol Colburn

NORWEGIAN-AMERICAN IMMIGRANT dress during the period of mass migration to the American Upper Midwest represents the blending of two visual languages. The traditional Norwegian dress was a language understood within a context where society was family-based and community-oriented. By contrast, fashionable dress conveyed individual status within the context of the international European and American economic marketplace. Understanding the dress of the immigrant, who was in transition between these two social contexts, can pose difficulties.

The title of this study is a quotation from Hattie Oleson, a woman who emigrated from Norway to Oshkosh, Wisconsin, in the 1860s. She spoke about a nephew's bride, suggesting that the language of fashionable dress was like a foreign language at first.[1] Traditional Norwegian wedding dress, at least in many areas, included the finest forms of embroidered shirt, skirt, and bodice, with costly accessories of great family significance. Gold and silver, used to decorate the wedding crown, yoke, and belt, and for the accompanying jewelry, indicated the economic status of the bride's family and signified the continued husbandry of family holdings by the two families involved in the marriage. The traditional Norwegian dress would have made a clear and

[*]Research for this article was supported in part by a Summer Fellowship from the University of Northern Iowa. The author wishes to express gratitude to Marion and Lila Nelson and the staff of Vesterheim for assistance throughout this project and to the many families in the Decorah area who shared their family photographs for the study of Norwegian-American dress. For photographic work I wish to thank Richard Colburn; Charles Langton, Vesterheim; and the staff at the Visual and Sound Archives, State Historical Society of Wisconsin.

definite statement about the occasion, family tradition, and a future which referred to the past. The fashionable wedding clothes that Hattie Oleson saw worn by younger relatives posed a question.

This incident indicates that, just as with verbal language, immigrants had to learn the language of American fashionable dress. At first, as in speech, they used a combination of their mother tongue and the language of their adopted land, but eventually they abandoned the vocabulary and even lost the accents that were their heritage from Norway. Indeed, the analogy of visual to verbal language is most apparent when one observes the ease with which children and young people adopted both English and the language of fashionable dress, soon becoming indistinguishable in speech and appearance from their Yankee contemporaries. The older people were often reluctant to use English or to wear fashionable dress, but over time the transition occurred in both language and dress at an almost equal rate.

Throughout this article, the meaning of immigrant dress will be the major concern. Dress, in other words, will be dealt with as a language. Although there are parallels between visual and verbal languages, it is not easy to translate one to the other, or to put into words exactly the message conveyed by dress. In a study of nineteenth-century American dress, sociologists Jeanette and Robert Lauer have established categories of meanings expressed by dress which have been shown to remain constant and to find expression in divergent forms of dress over time and space. They see clothing as expressing personality, moral character, conformity and non-conformity to social norms and roles, social status, and group membership, and finally, as making a general statement about the condition of society.[2]

While all the above categories of meaning conveyed by dress can be discussed in reference to that of Norwegian Americans, two take on special importance in this analysis of immigrant dress: expression of group membership and expression of status. Understanding the dynamics of communication in these categories will be the focus of this article. Broadly speaking, traditional Norwegian dress can be seen as an expression of group membership, where the family, the community, and the Norwegian heritage are clearly identified. Fashionable dress, which communicates the extent to which an individual participates in the international economic marketplace, expresses actual or desired status apart from immediate community or family heritage.

In Norway in the late nineteenth century, the distinction between the professional or upper class and the peasant class was clearly delineated by dress. The professional class wore fashionable clothing, and the peasant class wore traditional folk dress.[3] The following incident related by an educated man of professional background who immigrated to North Dakota demonstrates the confusion which could result from the change of contexts from Norway to America: "As soon as I came into the kitchen . . . I was told that a terribly fine lawyer from Minneapolis had come in. I was very curious to see this fine gentleman, and met him then at the supper table. He condescended to speak to me . . . He had been watching me and wondering what kind of a fellow I was, of the 'better class' and yet wearing working clothes. Since then, Mr. [Alf E.] Boyesen and I have become good comrades. He dupes people with his fine exterior, while I stick to my working costume, though in the evening we discard our masks."[4]

The visual language of dress can be understood only within a social context. The rapid changes in social context experienced by the immigrants must be considered before attempting to deal with the meanings of dress. B. Lindsay Lowell has pointed out that changes in social structure were already in process in Norway during the period of emigration, and that emigration itself resulted from an international economic revolution. In the traditional society, which formed the social environment of most immigrants, the immediate family (the kinship group) and the community formed the dominant social structure.[5] This was true not only among peasants, who comprised the majority of immigrants, but to a degree in other levels of society as well.[6] In Norway, the upper or cultured class consisted of officials, educated professionals, and wealthy merchants. The peasant class consisted of landed farmers and cotters, with trained artisans in the towns and the countryside also loosely associated with it.[7] The families maintained positions within these classes by intermarriage. While a breakdown of this structure was occurring in Norway as a result of industrial and economic developments, the move to America, where these developments had been more rapid, forced individuals to make dramatic adjustments almost immediately. When Norwegian immigrants came to America's Upper Midwest, most areas were already partially settled by a combination of Yankees and immigrants from other countries; therefore they had to interact with a mixed as well as a new society. The dominant society in America had a more cosmopolitan and democratic character with a different industrial and economic base. In the words of an immigrant quoted by Theodore Blegen: "Farmers and artisans are just as good as merchants and officials. They all have practically the same manners, and the appearance and dress of people are usually the same as they are in Norwegian towns."[8]

A Norwegian man who had recently immigrated to North Dakota wrote to a friend in Norway, "You say that you don't like the girls in Vågå, because they are a bunch of dull clotheshorses. I know that you prize simplicity, and so do I. But yet I dare say that you haven't seen anything of clotheshorses, in comparison to me; and here in America it is very difficult to find a girl who according to your definition would not be considered a clotheshorse. Yes, I have often been irritated by all the vanity and pomp, which the girls here are loaded down with. And yet the girl I love is, to this way of thinking, also a clotheshorse. It's just that each one of these poor people wants to be like all the others, and I can only hope that under the fine clothing beats a humble

Carol Colburn

heart."[9] His words demonstrate that the type of dress known from the upper and urban classes in Norway was also by the time of emigration finding its way into smaller rural villages such as Vågå. The reason for it was simply conformity to an expanding and changing society. The principle of conformity, which had led to the standardization of traditional dress, was still at work, but in a new setting.

The wearing of fashionable dress required participation in the international economic system, for it required imported fabric and accessibility to dressmakers and tailors trained in the European sartorial arts. The Norwegian peasantry had developed dress which relied primarily upon materials and skills generated within the family and the local area. While traditional folk dress required great skill to produce and even great expense to the owner, procuring this dress required very little interaction with the international trade community.

The language of Norwegian dress based on family heritage (which included many local dialects and idioms) was still the primary language of dress understood by those who immigrated, although they were already aware of developments that could bring change. Many historians have commented upon the rapidity with which Norwegian immigrants blended into American society.[10] A part of this involved quickly adopting the language of American fashionable dress. Such dress symbolized assimilation into a broader society with the higher economic standing toward which they were aspiring more than it did family, community, or occupational identity. Being aware of fashionable dress in urban and upper-class Norway, but generally not participating in the economic structure on which it was based, the immigrants easily made a change once they entered the new economy. A close look at Norwegian-American immigrant dress, however, indicates that a slight Norwegian accent often remains here as it also does in the use of English. Looking on dress as a language through which the immigrant speaks sheds light on the complexity of the immigrant experience.

The Language of Dress in Photographs, Written Accounts, and Surviving Garments

Photographic portraits are a primary source for the interpretation of immigrant dress. They were an important means of communication among Norwegian families both across the Atlantic and across the American continent as immigrant families and groups divided in their search for new opportunities. Photographic portraiture was relatively new in the mid-nineteenth century when the early wave of migration from Norway to America occurred. Refinements of the positive/negative photographic process, invented in 1839, made portraiture a successful enterprise around the world by 1850. At first using the one-of-a-kind daguerreotype process, photographers had set up businesses in all major cities by 1855 and had by 1860 switched to the cheaper process of albumen printing, using a glass plate negative which produced multiple prints.[11] The availability of multiple prints of photographs meant that immigrants brought photographic portraits along with them, they sent them back to their families, they received them from Norway after they arrived, and they sent them from settlement to settlement within North America.[12] Perhaps the images helped to ease the pain of the separation of friends and families.

The importance placed upon these portraits as a means of communication is attested to by the immigrants' own words:

"I have smartened up the room . . . all my very dear daguerreotypes are hanging, amongst which I miss very much Grandmother and everybody there, besides little Johan and brother Oskar."[13]

"Little Sven is also healthy and growing. . . . In my next letter you will get a picture of him if everything goes as planned, for Uncle Tom has promised to go with us up to a town called Rasjel [Rochelle] as soon as he is through working."[14]

"There is something else that we all want you to do, and that is that you— Father and Mother especially—get your picture taken and send us. We will send you money when you need it, if you will just have your portrait taken. It is difficult to know whether we will ever see you again in person . . . so it will be especially dear to see your picture."[15]

Portraits could be sent with a new immigrant arriving from Norway or with an immigrant who had decided to return. However, they were usually sent through the mail with accompanying letters traveling both directions across the Atlantic:

"Write to me soon, and please, if possible, send me your portrait."[16]

"Sven will soon come sent in a letter, and then you shall see for yourself what a wild American you have for a cousin."[17]

Since photographic portraits were difficult and expensive to have taken, the sitters made every effort to create the images that they wanted their relatives and friends to have of them. Within the convention of using their best clothing, choices in dress were made, and the props and accessories were added to compose a photograph which made a strong and specific statement. The importance of the choices of dress for these portraits is also documented in writing by immigrants themselves:

"Munch and I brought little Else with us to Beloit one day and had ourselves daguerreotyped. . . . It is good of me . . . except that I am equally wide and tall, but that the man [the photographer] certainly could not help; and the bows on my waistband have made me look rather worse than better. I was dressed in my old black costume from Norway, Munch in clerical garb, and Else in a small checkered green woolen dress, indeed, she is so sweet—well, you will be able to judge that for yourself."[18]

"Unfortunately I have no photograph of Ida. She should have had one taken with the little boy, but to tell the truth, she didn't have a decent dress to use, since all her old dresses have become too small and she hasn't had time to

Carol Colburn

sew any new ones. I can't get her to have any made, she wants to do it herself."[19]

Certain occasions precipitated a trip to the photographer; photographic archives attest that confirmations, weddings, family reunions, or occupational achievements were most often commemorated.[20] The usual formal, fashionable American dress associated with these events can be seen in these portraits; but even there personal choice created the individual look and conveyed a carefully composed message to the receiver:

"Many couples of those days had their pictures taken soon after the wedding. But John wouldn't go. . . . It was four months before I could persuade him to do it. By this time he had given me the prettiest present of his life. It was a heavy solid gold chain about one-half inch wide, with little links that were turned on their sides, so that the round part was on top. At the end of the chain was a small fat locket, decorated in blue enamel, which opened up to hold two small pictures. I always thought it set off my outfit very well in the picture."[21] An engagement pendant on a heavy chain was a customary gift from a man to his betrothed in Norway.[22] The pendant became part of the bridal ensemble, so the chain referred to in the above quotation no doubt held special significance beyond the aesthetic effect which Thurine Oleson describes. The chain in her portrait conveyed her Norwegian heritage and the occasion of the wedding in the visual language of dress.

Admittedly, there are certain limitations in using early photographs as documents of communication through dress. First is the lack of color. To our eyes, it appears that everyone wore extremely drab, dark clothing during the entire late nineteenth century. To be sure, it was customary for both women and men to have a best suit and dress of a practical dark color, often black,[23] but these were not always worn for portraits, although the black and white images may suggest that they were. A look at collections of existing clothing from the period dispels the impression that all clothing was dark or black. There is a variety of vivid colors and elaborate patterns, especially in the accessories. Because of the color limitation of the photographs the immigrants often accompanied a portrait with a written description of fabric, as in Caja Munch's letter of October, 1858, quoted above. Even swatches were sent to help the receiver envision dress: "Well, now I must stop, but before I fold the letter up I will ask you for a small gift, and that is a lock of hair from Father and Mother so that I can have a living memory of them, and also a little scrap of cloth from the last dresses you got. I hope to get your portrait sometime."[24]

Another explanation for the drab appearance of clothing in portraits may be advice offered by professional photographers. Edward L. Wilson tells his Philadelphia sitters the following in a pamphlet of 1871 titled "To My Patrons": "A black silk looks nice on almost everybody, and if not bedecked with red ribbons or lace that will take white, generally pleases. . . . striped goods, or goods having bold patterns in them should never be worn for a picture. Avoid anything that will look streaky or spotty."[25]

While the photographs chosen for this article indicate that Wilson's advice was not followed everywhere, one must take into account that such advice could make dress in photographs not necessarily representative of what was generally worn. One could also speculate that the use of distinctive accessories in nineteenth-century portraiture might have been encouraged by such advice, for the dark dresses and suits serve as a fine foil for jewelry and the like.

In addition to the limitations and conventions of photography, one must consider the intended audience of photographs in using them as sources of information on dress. Portraits were made primarily for families or family members who had been separated by migration. Leaving a visual record of oneself for posterity also played a part. Information on intent and the specific audience for photographic portraits is now often lost. Even the precise identification of the subject is often unknown, which significantly reduces the conclusions that can be drawn on the meaning of his or her dress. This accounts for the necessity of supplementing the photographic material with written references to dress and its meaning and with descriptions of actual remaining dress.

The Interpretation of Dress

The dress of the Norwegian Americans tells the story of an evolving society. The change from a family- and community-based social structure to a broader industrial and economic structure required immediate adjustment, and clothing reflected that. "They [Thurine Oleson's parents] had been well supplied with Norwegian clothes when they came here, both for everyday and Sunday. They soon found out, however, that the style and cut of knee breeches with silver buttons, rich embroidered guimpes, and brightly-banded skirts caused laughter wherever they went. So, despite their financial troubles, they had to change over to American style as soon as they could. This was hard, because they had been accustomed to the best, and the best clothes were expensive after the Civil War."[26]

Despite the sweeping changes, some remnants of the dress from Norway were included in portraits, apparently when the sitters wanted to communicate their origin, or when there was still a degree of unselfconscious continuity in dress. The anachronism was probably not detected by most viewers at the time. Sometimes the economic circumstances of peasant class immigrants, or the social structure in which they lived, did not change appreciably in the first years of residence in America. In such cases, the old continued to have a natural place with the new. For whatever reason, examples of women's, men's, and children's dress that recall the old family-based social structure will occasionally appear in immigrant photographs. It was the women's dress which was most likely to contain symbols of continued heritage. Fewer exam-

Carol Colburn

ples of men's clothing reflect this, an indication that men had to find their place in the American economic and occupational system more rapidly than women. Children's clothing depends upon the choices of their parents and is therefore symbolic of their parents' hopes, dreams, and aspirations as Americans.

Elisabeth Koren, whose diaries of the 1850s have been published, refers to two old women from Voss who wore their mountain dress in a remote area of Alamakee county, Iowa, in 1853.[27] Her specific comment on their retention of folk dress indicates that it was a rare sight. Most immigrant women would have known from exposure to international dress among upper-class Norwegians that they would need to transform their appearance to fit their new environment. Judging from both portraits and extant dress, a popular choice of fashionable dress in the early years was the black dress of silk or lightweight wool, often trimmed with bands of velvet at the neckline, cuffs, and hem. While this was considered to be internationally fashionable, actually the manner in which it was worn and the persistence with which it was worn by first generation immigrants often identified them as being from the old country. They had obtained a fashionable dress but then continued to wear it without change just as they had worn the traditional dress. Traditional dress too had undergone slow stylistic evolution but did not change in a constant cycle as is required by definition in fashionable dress. Caja Munch referred to her "old black costume from Norway" in the statement quoted above.[28] It is not clear whether most immigrant women obtained or made their black dresses in Norway or in America. The dresses required skills and materials from the international marketplace, but these were available in most parts of both countries by the second half of the nineteenth century. Examples of this best black dress can be seen in Ills. 1, 2, 3, 13, 17.

Thurine Oleson's description of her mother's dressing for church on Sundays in the 1860s through the 1880s reveals something of the mixed messages of fashionability and retention of old country habits in the dress of immigrant women. "Mother's dressing would go like this: First, next to the skin went a long bandage, wrapped tightly about the abdomen, cotton in summer, wool in winter. This was her corset, and she was never without it. Over that would go a clean white shift of sturdy cloth. Then a full tan cotton petticoat with a border of many colors around the bottom, red and green and brown. This was topped by a pretty white cotton petticoat with lace or embroidery at the bottom, about two or three yards around. Her dress was of black alpaca with tight-fitting waist and full skirt, tight-fitting sleeves, and a little black collar around the high neck, fastened with a black bone pin in the shape of a four-leaf clover. Black jet buttons closed the front and the sleeves. . . . One of us children would be dispatched upstairs for her black cashmere summer shawl, the point of which fell just long enough for her to sit on it. This was fastened

Ill. 1. Ole Halverson and family, the first Norwegians to live in Winneshiek county, Iowa, arriving in 1843. There is a clear distinction in dress between the generations in this portrait. The older immigrant woman is wearing a simple dark dress accessorized with an apron, a scarf at the neck, and a dark cap covering her hair. Her use of these accessories particularly marks her Norwegian habits of dress. The younger women wear dresses which are more fashionable in cut for the 1870s–1880s. The men wear sack jackets, but two have scarves arranged at the neck in an old style. The father has also retained the manner in which he groomed his beard in Norway. *Courtesy of Vesterheim*

Ill. 2. Anonymous couple. The woman's pose with the waist thrust forward is more typical of the stance of a woman in folk dress than the erect posture of a woman wearing fashionable dress of the 1870s. This may be the result of the immigrant woman changing to fashionable dress on the outside, but not adopting fashionable undergarments, including the corset. Her dress is a good example of the dark dress with velvet trim and matching apron which is seen in many immigrant portraits. *Photographer: Slater Sunnes, Iowa. Courtesy of Vesterheim*

Carol Colburn

Ill. 3. Andrew Amundson family near Lodi, Wisconsin, c. 1873.

A family portrait where the ages of the women are well differentiated by their dress. The mother wears the dark dress ubiquitous among first-generation immigrants. Her posture and the manner in which she has belted her dress are reminiscent of women in traditional apparel. The girls are wearing dresses in lighter colors and patterns with a more fashionable cut, the one, however, with a belt identical to the mother's. Like the mother, the father has an old-world appearance, because of the manner in which he grooms his beard. He appears in a well-worn knee-length frock coat, although the details of the waist seam and front closure are obscured by his folded arms. Photographer: Andreas Larsen Dahl, Dane county, Wisconsin. *Courtesy of State Historical Society of Wisconsin WHi (D31)335 detail*

with a long, black-headed pin. In winter, the dark red shawl, being heavier, was held together with two bigger silver pins, hooked together with a chain. These pins were topped by a small silver cup, each filled with a pretty blue stone."[29]

This description indicates that older women adopted the black dress to conform to 'town dress,' which they were already familiar with in Norway. However, they did not always adopt the fashionable corset which provided the body-shaping required to wear truly fashionable dress. They retained their old familiar underwear, the wrapped bandage which provided support for the abdomen but did not give the silhouette one expects to see from corseting. The posture of the women standing in Ills. 2, 3, and 17 is more characteristic of someone wearing the traditional folk dress than the fashionable dress. Even the colorfully bordered petticoat which Thurine Oleson mentions contributes to this bulky silhouette. This stiff petticoat is being used under the more fashionable white embroidered petticoat, again a melding of the two styles of dressing.

The black dress could be used for many occasions. Caja Munch refers to wearing her black silk dress to church in 1855: "On the way home [from church] I wanted to run to keep myself from freezing but tripped in my black silk dress and tore it, but not too much—uh!"[30] Caja Munch, of course, was a minister's wife of upper middle class origin who would have worn a dress of this kind for church even in Norway. Later in the 1880s Berta Serina Kingestad, still a hired woman in other people's houses, has a black dress for formal and important occasions. In a letter to her sister in Stavanger she refers to fabric swatches which she sent back: "The dotted I have for Sundays and the black for a best dress."[31]

If there was a death in the family, the black dress was used for mourning. Berta Serina Kingestad wrote to her family in Norway concerning the use of a black dress for mourning after a sister who remained with her parents in Norway had died: "When you write, you mustn't forget to tell me if you and Mother have black dresses; if not, I shall try to send you a little money when I get my wages here, so you can each get a dress. I will go to town as soon as the weather permits and buy one for myself. I have no black dresses now. I will enclose a little scrap of my collar and mourning band. That is what they use in this country, and you will get a scrap of my dress in my next letter if we live so long."[32]

Her letter provides interesting evidence of influence from immigrant dress back to Norway or, at least, of parallel developments in both countries. A traditional custom of dress for mourning in Norway was to cover ordinary dress with an encompassing white cloth.[33] The American mourning dress Berta describes, consisting of a black dress with mourning bands and collar, documents the increasing dominance of fashionable dress in both Norwegian and Norwegian-American society.

The best black dress did prove to be the dress most often chosen for studio

Carol Colburn

Ill. 4. Wedding party at Old Norway Grove Church near DeForest, Wisconsin, c. 1870.
The bride wears fashionable dress and the bridegroom wears a sack suit. The man to the left of the groom is wearing the longer frock coat that is more closely fitted at the waist. Representing the older generation, parents of the bride or groom stand to the right in the picture, and each is less Americanized than the younger people. The mother, in a plaid dress, has chosen to wear her apron, a hold-over from the Norwegian custom. The father, like many of his generation, has all the elements of American men's wear except the necktie. Some of the guests in the back wear boldly striped shawls which are likely to have been brought from Norway. *Photographer: Andreas Larsen Dahl, Dane county, Wisconsin. Courtesy of State Historical Society of Wisconsin WHi(D3)71*

portraits, but some photographs show women in variously colored and patterned dresses. The woman in a plaid dress in the foreground of Ill. 4 must also be wearing her 'best' dress, as her placement in the wedding photograph implies that she is the mother of the bride or the groom. A striped dress was chosen for a formal portrait in Ill. 10. Plaid and striped fabrics such as these could have been purchased or handwoven by the immigrant women either in Norway or after immigration.[34]

Although the exception rather than the rule, the specific style of the fashionable dress chosen by immigrant women could reflect characteristics of traditional dress. This is seen on five portraits known to me from the 1880–1890s, one of which is included here (Ill. 5). The division of the bodice into side panels and a center plastron with lacing up the center creates a style reminiscent of traditional bodices. Other styles seen on Norwegian-American portraits incorporate rows of brilliant buttons used to divide the bodice in a similar fashion, or arranged in a circular manner as on the traditional bodices of Flesberg or Numedal.

Using a shawl over her Sunday dress both winter and summer also marked

Ill. 5. Anonymous couple. The woman's dress, though of fashionable cut of the 1880s, reflects a characteristic of traditional dress. The bodice is divided into side and center panels and includes the detail of lacing from the bottom edge to under the bust, recalling the structure of the traditional bodice laced over the blouse. The man's clothing is typical of most immigrant men who acquired fashionable dress—the sack suit with jacket, vest, and pants of dark wool. *Photographer: Evans & Norcott, Madison, South Dakota. Courtesy of Vesterheim*

Carol Colburn

Thurine Oleson as retaining an old custom.[35] Although large wool shawls were used throughout the period by old stock Americans as well, fashionable options in the 1860s also included cloaks or sleeved coats, cut wide to be worn over fashionable hooped skirts.[36]

Plaid, striped, plain, and paisley shawls appeared on immigrant women from any country in this period, as they were an item imported worldwide, used with fashionable dress and traditional dress (Ill. 6). Caja Munch probably wore fashionable Norwegian dress before arriving in America, so she was fully prepared to conform to fashionable American dress; yet her comment on a new shawl purchased in America indicates her preference for it over other options for outerwear. Her sister Nanna remained in Norway and had a shawl exactly like the one Caja purchased in America. "Last time Munch returned from Chicago, he brought me a very big, nice and warm plaid exactly like Nanna's, so I must think of you, dear sister, every time I use it, and Munch says the same."[37]

Although the use of shawls was international, with some of the regional Norwegian traditional dress certain patterns and colors of shawls were distinctive. The striped shawl is typically worn as an outer garment with the Setesdal folk dress.[38] Numerous examples of this type of prized colorful shawl appear on portraits of Norwegian Americans, and an actual shawl of this type is in the Vesterheim collection. In Ill. 7, the anonymous woman is wearing a striped shawl folded parallel to the length of the shawl as it was worn particularly in Setesdal, not in the triangular manner which would have been the common method of folding a shawl when worn with fashionable dress. These boldly striped shawls also were worn by a number of the women attending the wedding recorded in Ill. 4.

With the traditional Norwegian folk costume, women in most areas wore aprons. It was a custom to cover the skirt with a functional apron for everyday and a decorative one for Sundays or whenever best dress was required.[39] Hav-

Ill. 6. Fremad Läseselskab (reading society), Moscow, Iowa county, Wisconsin, 1875. (opposite page)
On this chilly day a group of Norwegian women display a variety of shawls, which were prized possessions even if they did tend to mark one's immigrant status in America. Some of the younger women wear the more fashionable capes with hoods, and many wear fashionable hats or the less fashionable sunbonnets associated with rural work dress. The woman on the right in a striped apron is continuing the old-country habit of wearing the apron for all occasions, not just for housework as was the American habit. The men wear a variety of suits with vests, most of which would be considered fashionable with the exception of the lack of neckwear on many. The man whom we can see full-figure standing in the center has a morning coat which is knee-length and has an angled center front edge which is not designed to close. *Photographer: Andreas Larsen Dahl, Dane county, Wisconsin.* *Courtesy of State Historical Society of Wisconsin WHi(D3)54*

Ill. 7. Anonymous young
woman. c. 1870.
The brocade and fringed
silk scarf and striped shawl
are indications of this
young woman's Norwegian
heritage. Two portraits
were taken at the same time,
one with the distinctive
striped shawl and one
without, perhaps for
Norwegian and American
audiences respectively.
*Photographer: Andreas
Larsen Dahl, Dane county,
Wisconsin. Courtesy of
Historical Society of
Wisconsin WHi(D31)748*

ing habitually worn an apron, many first generation immigrants retained it even for formal situations such as sitting for a studio portrait. It can appear even over the best black dress. For such formal wear the apron too was black, often coordinated with the dress through the addition of bands of velvet trim near the bottom edge.[40] Ill. 2 shows this arrangement clearly.

When the Hardanger costume gained ground as the national costume of Norway in the late nineteenth century, a white apron with an insert of open-work embroidery became standard for traditional Norwegian dress. Ill. 8 shows the older women wearing the white apron with their fashionable dress. Ole E. Rølvaag gives us the most dramatic statement of the retention of the white apron for formal dress among the immigrants and of its emotional significance in *Giants in the Earth*. He described Beret as wearing her Sunday clothes to meet the American Indians on the prairie for the first time. Here Per asked her to sacrifice her very best white Sunday apron to bandage an injured Indian's hand: "She hesitated for an instant, then untied her apron and handed it over to him. He knew that it was her very best apron. He could not bear to take it, but he did not say so. 'That's just it, Beret-girl—the very thing! If that doesn't help him, I don't know anything in the wide world that would cure his hand!'"[41]

Not only black or white aprons are used in provincial Norwegian folk dress. Woven striped, checked, plaid, printed floral, and embroidered patterns are also found. Aprons of these types appear in Norwegian-American portraits with a regularity that indicates that this prominent accessory prevailed even when the rest of the traditional folk dress was abandoned. The older women in several multi-generational portraits wear their aprons while the younger do not (Ills. 1, 4, 6).

Other provincial Norwegian accessories that reveal continuity in dress among immigrant women include colorful, often fringed silk neck and head scarves.[42] As part of the folk costume, they were highly prized and were presented as gifts on important occasions such as birthdays, confirmations, and weddings, thus becoming symbolic of the family heritage. The patterned silk scarves were one of the few items of the folk dress that were not produced locally in Norway. Called 'fortune scarves' in Hallingdal, the scarves carried connotations of economic status throughout many districts in Norway and were handed down from generation to generation.[43] Having a large collection

Ill. 8. Detail of a wedding party at the Rue home in Ridgeway, Iowa, c. 1905. White aprons with openwork borders such as those on the older women were part of traditional folk dress used for festive occasions. In the larger photograph, of which this is a detail, the rest of the wedding party appear in fashionable dress. Courtesy of Norma Wangsness, Decorah, Iowa

of silk scarves would allow a woman to choose a favorite for every important occasion. By this means she personalized the folk costume that otherwise allowed her little variation.

Both a heritage of the use of silk patterned scarves and the knowledge that these represented a product of international trade if not necessarily high fashion induced immigrants to bring these scarves with them.[44] They were small and light and were easy to pack among their other belongings. Once in America, they provided a means of embellishing an otherwise simple neckline of a fashionable dress. The manner in which these fringed brocade or plaid scarves were used and the frequency with which they appear in Norwegian-American portraits indicate that they retained some of the significance they once had in Norway even among women who had otherwise adopted fashionable dress (Ills. 7, 9).

Traditional folk costume always included a headdress for the married woman, which was distinctive as to region and often also indicated age and community standing. While the distinctive headdress of regional folk costumes does not appear on Norwegian-American portraits, older immigrant women did continue to wear caps or head scarves to cover their hair for portraits years after this practice had gone out of general fashion in America.

In her diary, Mrs. Koren refers to a woman she visited in the countryside as habitually using a white cap: "Ingeborg [Vold, a native of Voss, Norway], the lady of the house, a handsome, attractive woman who always goes about with a nice white cap on her head, is busy preparing dinner. . . . "[45] Thurine Oleson says of a fellow immigrant woman: "As her hair whitened, she took to black caps with lace on them."[46]

A variety of black and white caps covering the hair are seen on older women in the portraits studied (Ills. 1, 4, 10, 13, 17). On some of these caps wide ribbons tied in a bow beneath the chin held the headdress in place and at the same time provided a decorative finish to the neckline. These caps worn by older women were used indoors and outdoors in a different manner than hats with fashionable dress. By contrast, a variety of fashionable hats designed for outdoor wear and more functional sunbonnets and hooded capes can be seen on the Norwegian-American women in Ill. 6. Although most of the women depicted seem to have adopted a form of fashionable headgear, some wear these fashionable bonnets and hats in a manner which is reminiscent of traditional headdresses, their sunbonnets encircling the face as would head scarves, or their hats planted directly on top of the head in a way that brings to mind the traditional headdresses in such areas as Hallingdal.

Elisabeth Koren was of the educated professional class in Norway before coming to America, so she did not wear folk dress even before emigration. As she aged, however, she habitually wore a small white cap of a type also seen on other older immigrant women of her class. Distinguished by their size and their placement on the crown of the head, these headcoverings used by older

Ill. 9. Anonymous family group.

Note the women's neckwear of brocade and fringe of silk used with fashionable dress of the 1870s. The scarves have thick chains arranged over them, which may have been retained from their folk dress when chains were presented to a woman at the time of her engagement. The younger woman also has a belt with broad metal plates resembling the belts used for high festive occasions in several areas of Norway. *Photographer: N.S. Hassel, Decorah, Iowa. Courtesy of Vesterheim*

Ill. 10. Anonymous couple. 1870s (right).

The husband is wearing a Norwegian vest, prominently displaying metal buttons. The vest is also cut very high at the neck, as opposed to the typical fashionable vest which would show more of the front of the shirt. He also continues old Norwegian grooming habits, with long hair and beard allowed to grow under the chin but shaven from the face. The woman wears a striped dress of lightweight fabric which was probably factory-made. She apparently has not adopted the American corset. The cap (usually white or black) was used by first-generation immigrants from many countries but not by later generations in America. This type, which covers the back and sides of the head, is distinct from the small lace cap worn on the crown of the head by ladies of distinction. *Photographer: Andreas Larsen Dahl, Dane county, Wisconsin. Courtesy of Wisconsin State Historical Society WHi(D3)92*

Ill. 11. Mrs. Elisabeth Koren, née Else Elisabeth Hysing, wife of the Reverend Vilhelm Koren, Decorah, Iowa. Mrs. Koren customarily wore a small lace cap, typical of immigrant women of distinction. Here she wears it with a dress of c. 1900–1905. Preus Collection, Courtesy of Vesterheim

women of standing seem to have served the same symbolic function as the larger traditional headdresses (Ill. 11).

Shoes are another accessory item in which some continuity is revealed but which also seems to have presented a dilemma for the Norwegian immigrant. Although seldom seen clearly in portraits, they are often mentioned in letters, because they were expensive, difficult to obtain, and of as much functional as symbolic or esthetic significance considering the rugged conditions of the American Midwest. They were among items which were requested to be sent from Norway. Caja Munch makes references to shoes sent from there to her brother, her child, and herself.

"Is the old shoemaker still with you? Ask him if he doesn't want to come over here and make me a pair of boots. I can't get any I really like in this country."[47]

A conflicting opinion comes from Berta Serina Kingestad, a woman brought up with traditional rather than upper class dress, when giving advice on what her parents should send with her sister if she emigrates:

"You don't need to rig her out much with clothing and shoes. If she has one pair of shoes then that is absolutely enough for I will tell you that Norwegian shoes aren't worth much over here. They are usually too heavy as it is so hot here and the air so dry in the summer that they go to pieces."[48] Berta Kingestad was then working as a house servant. Later, when she went to work for a man who required that she do farmyard chores as well as housework, she remembered the practical wooden shoes that she wore in Norway for such work, and wrote to request some: "Father, you must make a pair of wooden shoes and send them with Marta when she comes. You know that Mother's shoes will fit me."[49] The quotations demonstrate that both good traditional boots and wooden shoes were still in Norway often produced in the home, and that they were not available everywhere in America. Kingestad's letter also suggests that wooden shoes were used by immigrant women when doing farm work. Wooden shoes are documented as having been worn among immigrants in Willmar, Minnesota, and they are known to have been made at Houston, Minnesota.[50] Wooden-shoe-making equipment is common among the tools that have found their way from immigrant farms to Vesterheim. There is little documentation of the extent to which they were used by women, but they were made for farm work and were therefore undoubtedly used for this by both sexes. One girl is wearing wooden shoes as part of her everyday dress in the school picture in Ill. 21.

Stockings rarely if ever show in portrait photographs. In first person accounts, however, they are mentioned frequently. Norwegian immigrants appear to have continued the tradition of knitting stockings at home even after commercially produced stockings became available. Berta Serina Kingestad's letters make this clear. As an unmarried woman working as a servant in the homes of others, she did not have the means to raise sheep or purchase wool in America, so she requested materials from her family in Norway in order to knit stockings for herself and her son: " . . . there is one thing I would like to have her bring me if she comes [her sister]. That is a little bit of black wool and a pair of carding combs. I have been able to borrow a spinning wheel, but there are so few combs here. I have gotten a little white wool . . . and when Soffia comes with black wool and combs, then I will spin gray yarn and knit gray socks."[51] Later, when her mother sent her some handspun yarn for knitting, Berta reveals the significance placed upon handmade goods: "I could not hold back my tears when I saw all the wonderful yarn and thought that each strand had gone through your hands . . . I must not forget to thank you for the carding combs. No one will ever take them from me. I will borrow Marta's spinning wheel soon, and then I will both card and spin."[52]

Many handknit stockings are found in a collection of textiles at Vesterheim made by three generations of immigrant women, beginning with Kari Iverson Staarvig from Vågå, Gudbrandsdalen, who immigrated to western Minnesota in the 1860s. Several examples that appear to have been made by Kari herself

have a tie-dye (ikat) pattern that research by Marion Nelson has shown to have been common in the area from which she came. There is reason to believe that the transfer of a tradition in handknit stockings documented by this family collection was typical.

Traditional jewelry was the Norwegian accessory most commonly incorporated into fashionable dress. Featured alone on the neckline or on top of silk scarves, Norwegian silver brooches, or *søljer*, appear frequently in Norwegian-American women's portraits. Like the scarves, brooches were easy to transport, were symbolic of social standing, and already had a place in fashionable dress. Originally used as both a decorative and a functional piece to close the neckline of the shirt, the styles of traditional Norwegian *søljer* are distinctive enough to show up very clearly on photographic portraits. Used by the immigrants as decorative jewelry on fitted bodices in the early years, and later on the more loosely fitted shirtwaists, they carried the message of common heritage to others in the group and of distinctive elegance to people outside. In fact, the *sølje* is the one item of dress which has had almost continuous use by women in many Norwegian families ever since immigration. Portraits of women from each decade since immigration can be found in which the *sølje* is prominently displayed on the fashionable dress of the time (Ill. 12). Imported *søljer* remain a staple in Norwegian-American gift shops.

Other items of silver which might have been retained from traditional dress are not as easy to identify as the *sølje*. The silver chain with clasps used to close a shawl and described by Thurine Oleson may have been a jacket chain used as part of the silver belonging to the traditional folk dress in her mother's home region of Telemark.[53] Eight women's portraits have come to light which feature a long chain looped around the neck often arranged over a silk neckscarf. This may be a new way of displaying the chain which was often presented to a bride as part of the traditional folk wedding ensemble (Ill. 9). Silver on women's belts also was typical of Norwegian traditional dress. The younger woman, presumably the daughter, in Ill. 9 is wearing a belt which resembles the distinctive Norwegian belt featuring rectangular metal plates, typical of festive folk dress in Hardanger and other districts.[54] The manner in which identical belts are worn by the mother and daughter in Ill. 3 also recalls the use of the belt as an accessory in Norwegian traditional dress.

Men also retained some of their Norwegian habits of dress in America, though fewer obvious indications can be found in portraits. As with the women, Norwegian accessories used with American clothing are the most common, although a few actual clothing items associated with Norwegian dress do appear. The men's traditional dress of many districts was influenced by Norwegian urban dress to a greater extent than women's traditional dress, so in many instances the distinctions are quite subtle. The traditionally styled jackets and coats usually retained some aspects of the cut and details of late-eighteenth to early-nineteenth century men's wear. For example, the standing collar found on many of the traditional men's coats and jackets had been retained from men's fashions of around 1800. It was perceived as incorrect in America, as shown by a statement made in an immigrant's letter sent home to Valdres. The immigrant's advice to his brother was: "You should have flat-collared jackets or vests."[55]

Men's Dress

The directive meant that the brother need not bring the jackets and vests with standing collars used traditionally in Valdres. The collar should fold and lie flat against the neck, like the collar still used on men's suit jackets today. Other distinguishing features might also mark a jacket or coat to be of Norwegian origin. Many districts had their own distinctive fabrics, cut, and trim. Because of these differences, the men, like the women, invested in one fashionably-styled set of clothing to serve for all occasions requiring one to be dressed well in America. Thurine Oleson says of her father, "He had one best Sunday suit, of the finest black wool; this was seldom pressed but was brushed carefully after each wearing, folded in the original creases, and laid away in a trunk upstairs."[56]

The suit was perhaps purchased, like the woman's black dress, as the man's preparation for becoming American. If brought from Norway, it was probably made by a tailor. If purchased in America, it could have been either ready-to-wear or tailor-made because both options existed here.[57] Judging from photographs, the style chosen was usually the sack suit, which through the decades of the great emigration was fast becoming the international symbol of the businessman.[58] Familiar to us all today, it includes a loose-fitting hip-length jacket with no seam division at the waistline (Ills. 1, 5). This style of suit is actually called the business suit, and it still connotes the wearer's participation in the international economic structure.

Other choices might have been occasion-specific coats which carried more connotations of the old class structure, such as the longer frock coat (Ills. 3, 4), or the morning coat (Ill. 6). Both these coats can be distinguished from the sack jacket by their longer length, falling approximately to the knee, and by a horizontal waist seam serving to give the coat a more fitted look when closed. The distinguishing feature between the frock coat and the morning coat is the shaping of the center front edge. The frock coat closes along a straight center front edge, while the morning coat is cut away at an angle which reveals the bottom edge of the vest. By the 1870s, both the longer coats were considered to be old-fashioned except when worn by men of professional standing or for formal occasions. Most Norwegian-American men in portraits have chosen sack suits even for their wedding portrait, which denotes their interest in appearing 'democratic' as well as moderately fashionable. Many look somewhat uncomfortable in their suits, as if their physiques were more suited to farm clothes that allowed greater physical movement.[59]

Regardless of what fashionable suit they chose, men sometimes retained the vests which they had worn with their Norwegian traditional dress. While Norwegian vests varied from district to district, they usually differed from fashionable men's vests in the following ways. First, the buttons of traditional vests were of silver, brass, or pewter, making a bold statement about position and heritage, not unlike the silver jewelry on women's traditional dress (Ills. 10, 13). The buttons highlighted a closure which might be either single or double breasted depending on the district of origin, creating a neckline usually falling higher on the chest than fashionably styled vests. The lengths of traditional vests also provided more variations. Some ended above the waistline; others continued below the waistline, terminating in a straight edge or in a single point at the center front. The short vest in Ill. 14 is distinctive and might have been retained from traditional dress. The traditional vests were often brightly colored, either solid colors (red was common to many districts) or multicolored stripes, plaids, or brocade patterns (Ill. 16). Few of the traditional vests in portraits reveal these patterns. This may have been the choice for the occasion of the portrait. One suspects that some vests which record black in the photographs were indeed of a bright solid hue because colorful vests were generally worn by Norwegian men.

The American suit was completed with long trousers, which many Norwegian men wore in Norway before emigration. In Norway, however, rural dress of many districts offered the option of knickers for both everyday working clothing and Sunday dress. These were immediately abandoned in America where only young boys wore short pants.

When men did give up their traditional coats, vests, and knickers, they apparently did not discard the silver, brass, or pewter buttons which had

Carol Colburn

Ill. 13. Anonymous couple, c. 1870.

The man is wearing a Norwegian-style double-breasted vest with silver buttons. The ends of his silk neckscarf appear from under his beard. The rest of his dress is American, although with his old style grooming habits and his pose with hands on knees he appears to be of the old school. The woman wears the plain dark dress typical of many first-generation immigrants who did not follow changing styles after their initial adoption of fashionable dress upon arrival. Finishing the neckline of her dress, she is wearing a collar seen on many of the Dahl photographs of Norwegian immigrants taken in the 1870s. With tatting on the edge, it is similar to the turned-down collar of the traditional woman's blouse of some Norwegian provinces. Her headdress is very distinctive. Fur edging trims the bonnet, while a ruffled band frames the face. Though it is not clearly identifiable as a holdover of a particular Norwegian style, a bonnet of this shape would be considered out of fashion in the 1870s in America. *Photographer: Andreas Larsen Dahl, Dane county, Wisconsin. State Historical Society of Wisconsin WHi(D31)751 detail*

Ill. 14. Anonymous family group, c. 1870.

It is rare to find a family group in work clothing rather than in more formal wear. The woman is wearing a fashionably cut dress of a lightweight fabric. Her posture implies that she is not wearing a corset. The men all wear variations on work clothing which mark their transition between Norwegian rural dress and American styles. The checked shirt with asymmetrical placket for the front closure is cut in a style of rural Norwegian origin. The short vest on the other son might also have been retained from folk dress. It is unusual to see a sweater as worn by the father used as outerwear by an American man in the 1870s. Although it does not display the distinctive Norwegian two color patterning, it does feature the contrasting edging like Norwegian sweaters, and might be in the Norwegian tradition. It could have been made either before immigration or after, as many Norwegians continued spinning and knitting in America. *Photographer: Andreas Larsen Dahl, Dane county, Wisconsin. Courtesy of State Historical Society of Wisconsin WHi(D31)393*

embellished them. Numerous buttons which were removed and saved are found in the Vesterheim collection and in private families. The valuable buttons might also have been recycled for use on hand-knit sweaters and other home-produced items.

Formal American neckwear for men required an adjustment which some men were not willing to make. The man in Ill. 15 stands out among men in most conventional Norwegian-American portraits who, at least for formal pictures, did wear the stiff detachable collar and tie. Dr. J. C. Gronvold chose to wear neither collar nor tie. One might consider his shirt a medical gown, but immigrants in other professions also rebelled against the uncomfortable stiff neckwear of fashion (Ills. 4, 6). Thurine Oleson described her father's Sunday clothing in this way: "By the time I was old enough to take notice of things, Father had two elegant boughten shirts, of the purest fine white cloth and American make. They were used only for church, funerals, weddings, and other special events. . . . The shirt was full and wide and long, buttoned down the back. Father never wore an American collar with these shirts, but tied around his neck instead a fine brownish silk neck scarf, knotted in front. They were kept in a special *skuff* [drawer] in the *dragkiste* [chest of drawers]."[60]

Like the women, men too had worn colorful silk scarves with their traditional Norwegian dress. As a portion of dress which cannot escape notice by the viewer, a man's choice of tie was (and is) a crucial decision. As Thurine Oleson wrote, some men continued to use the scarf instead of the more conventional necktie. This could be worn with or without the stiff collar. While a scarf worn at the neck had been part of fashionable men's attire in the 1840s–1850s, its use waned in the 1860s when shirt collars became narrower.[61] The use of the scarf as part of traditional dress may account for its continued use well beyond this time both in Norway and subsequently in America (Ills. 1, 13, 16).

One can generally not see much of the shirt in portraits, as it is usually covered up by the vest or the suit coat. Yet, in a few portraits of men in their work clothing, we can see shirts of traditional Norwegian cut (Ills. 14 and 17). The checked shirt on the man to the left in Ill. 14 has a placket closure much like the traditional *busserull* or Norwegian workshirt. Likewise, the shirt worn by the mason in Ill. 17 displays a cut which was not conventional for American men; it appears to have a center-front buttoned closure, but the square-cut bottom edge, the yoke extending over the shoulder, and the fullness in the sleeve relate it to a Norwegian workshirt. Both of these photographs were made by Andreas Dahl, an itinerant Norwegian-American photographer who loaded his photographs with messages about the immigrants' lives in Wisconsin during the 1870s.[62] They proudly display the immigrants' lives against a setting of material achievements revealed by their homesteads. The clothing is as telling of merging traditions as are the props and settings.

In most occupations other than farming, men were required to make a

Ill. 15. Dr. J. C. Gronvold, Goodhue county, Minnesota. Choosing to wear neither collar nor necktie for a formal portrait would be very unusual for an American man but appears to have been the choice of a number of Norwegian-American men who otherwise adopted American suits and shirts. With the traditional Norwegian dress of many districts, no tie was worn, but a silver neckpin closed the shirt at the neck. In America, such jewelry was not worn by men, so the shirt button sufficed for a closure if no scarf or tie was worn. *Courtesy of Vesterheim*

Ill. 16. Dr. Hans Christian Brandt, said to be the first Norwegian doctor in Iowa.
The professional standing of a medical doctor could be indicated by the choice of a double-breasted frock coat instead of the more common sack coat, although the fit of the coat is not fine. He wears a patterned brocade vest and a silk neck scarf, both of which are typical of many Norwegian folk-dress styles. *Courtesy of Vesterheim*

Ill. 17. Anonymous family group, c. 1870.
Three generations mark different degrees of Americanization in dress. The men display the props of stonemason and blacksmith. The older stonemason wears a style of workshirt reminiscent of the *busserull,* with short square bottom edge and full sleeves. The younger blacksmith is wearing a vest which is of fashionable cut, although it is worn over a workshirt cut in an old style with the yoke falling low on the arm. His work requires a large leather apron. The two oldest women on the right wear the black dress adopted soon after immigrating and retained in spite of changing fashions. The seated pregnant woman and three young daughters all wear more fashionable dress of the 1870s. *Photographer: Andreas Larsen Dahl, Dane county, Wisconsin. Courtesy of State Historical Society of Wisconsin (D31)45388*

rapid change in dress. The clergy who came to perpetuate the state church of Norway among the immigrants, however, needed to retain the dress by which their position was identified in the mother country. Their black cassock, black stole, and white fluted collar constituted a highly visible example of Norwegian occupational dress in at least one segment of the immigrant church. During the emigration period, the Lutheran state church in Norway was facing challenges from the followers of Hans Nielsen Hauge, a dynamic lay preacher, as well as representatives of non-Lutheran denominations. These challenges were intensified among Norwegians who found themselves in the United States, which from the beginning accepted freedom of religion. Dress became a symbolic dividing line between members of opposing factions. The lay preachers or preachers linked with denominations or theological directions other than the high-church Norwegian state Lutheranism showed their differences by wearing no clerical garb. The first constitution of any Norwegian-American church body, written by the Hauge-oriented Elling Eielsen in 1846, condemned the use of state church clerical gowns with a quotation from

Carol Colburn

Luke 20:46, referring to "scribes which desire to walk in long robes and love greetings in the markets, to be seen of men."[63] The lay element among the Norwegian Americans associated state church clerical dress with the oppression from which they had supposedly departed. Peter A. Munch comments: "Typically, the clergy is often singled out as the prime obstacle to social freedom and equality in the old country, and it shows considerable sensitivity on this point when even the clerical garb becomes a symbol of 'oppression.'"[64]

The more liberal elements in the Norwegian peasant class were naturally dismayed to find this symbol of oppression following them to the new land. It was, however, not only the clerical garb of the pastor that aroused resentment. It was the whole set of upper class symbols that characterized even his personal life: " . . . the very presence in the settlement of a Norwegian professional minister and his family, with their refined manners, speech, and dress, seems to have been a constant source of irritation and it was even felt by some to be a threat to their newly won freedom. Obviously, it was a constant reminder of the settlers' own lowly origin, a thing that they had hoped to leave behind and forget about in the new country."[65]

The retention into the 1920s[66] of the clerical garb of Norway by pastors in the Norwegian Synod may seem surprising in the land of the free, but it is also most understandable. With the competition for souls in the New World, the immigrant pastors who looked on themselves as representatives of the official church of Norway had to muster all forces possible to retain their position among disbanded Norwegians who had crossed the Atlantic. Visual symbols of authority are more persuasive than theological arguments in keeping the faith of the simple.

The two images in Ill. 18 demonstrate the imposingly bold sartorial statement made by the clerical dress, as well as the intimidatingly sophisticated and refined impression made by the dress worn by the clergy when not preaching. The impression was not made without cost. Preachers' wives had to devote a great deal of time to maintaining their husbands' symbolic dress and had to acquire skills which in Norway would have been supplied by specialists. Caja Munch describes her struggles in a letter dated February 1857: "You can imagine, it is a laborious task to set up these ruffs for Munch; last time, I was at it for almost two days to get one of them fluted for him, but then it did turn out rather nice except for a little burn here and there. If it is possible to get some sent to him next spring with one of the seven ministers for whom there are vacant charges here, you would do us a great favor."[67]

Male Norwegian-American headdress may not be as revealing of ethnicity as female, but interesting examples exist. In the image of an anonymous young man in Ill. 19, the message of hyphenated culture carries well across time. He is blatantly telling us that he is Norwegian American, as he has chosen to wear the soft "farmer's cap," typical of traditional rural dress in Norway, together with the suit and tie of fashionable American dress.

Ill. 18. Reverend H. Halvorson. Wearing correct fashionable dress in one photo and in another the complete clerical garments of the Norwegian state church, the status and beliefs of this man are apparent. *Courtesy of Vesterheim*

Ill. 19. Anonymous man
In what might be a whimsical combination of a Norwegian "farmer's cap" and fashionable suit and shirt, this man declares his hyphenated culture. *Courtesy of Vesterheim*
Ill. 20. Hans Johnson, lay leader
The black cap was worn by clergymen and other professional, educated men in Norway. In America it was sometimes called the 'preacher's cap,' but was used by older men in other professions here as well. *Courtesy of Vesterheim*

Carol Colburn

Another unusual headdress used by Norwegian-American men was a small black cap which consisted of a soft crown with no brim (Ill. 20). Formal portraits have been found of three pastors, a lay leader, a medical doctor, a skilled clockmaker/carpenter, and a publisher wearing this cap, an indication that it was associated with professional standing. The term "preacher's cap," which was sometimes used for it among the immigrants, reveals which profession they most closely associated it with. In Norway the cap appears to have been used only by some clergymen and other professionals. It has no association with traditional folk dress.[68] Beside declaring the professional status of the wearer, it may have functioned much like the previously mentioned small cap worn by older women, covering gray or thinning hair while also adding an air of distinction. To us it has interest as a distinctive element in the Norwegian language of dress that lingered among the immigrants for at least a generation.

Children's Dress

Children were not hampered by habit in dress, and it would appear that parents recognized early in choosing dress for them that they belonged to the New World. "I have made two woolen swaddling clothes, but they will not at all allow me to use swathe; here they mostly use little woolen skirts [shirts?] of which I have made three; and a thing they use much here is a small woolen bodice directly on the body, later on they wear woolen undershirts, which are used regularly both by women and by children; I will also do likewise, although not for my own person, but for the little one in case God is gracious enough to grant me a child."[69] So Caja Munch wrote in 1856. Three decades later Berta Serina Kingestad still explains the different practices in clothing babies in America to her family in Norway. "Yes, people here are far different than in Norway. People that I had never seen came and looked after me and I can tell you, for example, that I have gotten thirteen pieces of cloth for clothing for the little one. You see, they don't swaddle the babies here in this country."[70]

As the children grew, they required new clothes. Ready-to-wear clothing reduced the effort involved in keeping apace of the situation. Making them American as soon as possible may also have been looked on as giving the greatest benefit of the move to America. Judging from photographs, they were almost always dressed in American fashionable dress according to the financial capability of the parents (Ills. 21, 22). In their dress they were largely indistinguishable from Yankee children or children of immigrant families at the same economic level from other countries. Yet in formal portraits these Americanized children were sometimes given items of dress which bore messages of their Norwegian heritage. Norwegian immigrant parents probably did not want their children to look too foreign to their grandparents, aunts, uncles, and cousins in the homeland or elsewhere in America. Some symbol worn in a portrait would make the lineage as clear as inherited facial features.

Ill. 21. Children at Kjomme School. Highland Township north of Highlandville, Winneshiek county, Iowa, c. 1912. This photograph provides an unusual opportunity to see children's everyday clothing where function is more important than style. The children are all wearing clothing which is predominantly American though most appears to be homemade, consisting of sweaters, simple jackets, and dresses of plain fabrics. The third girl from the left in the front row appears to be wearing wooden shoes, which would have been practical in the grass and dirt of the schoolyard. Wooden shoes were worn for farmyard work on some Norwegian-American farms, as they had been in Norway.

Collection of Mildred Kjome, Decorah, Iowa

Silver jewelry, especially the *sølje,* used as a brooch on girls' fashionable dress, became the most commonly retained item of this kind (Ill. 23).

Woven or braided bands which had previously added pattern and color to traditional costume as belts, headdresses, and garters were in America sometimes used as neckties in portraits of boys and girls (Ill. 24), and as trim on children's clothing. The transformed use of these bands provided a touch of ethnicity that was not too incongruent with otherwise fashionable children's clothing. The bands themselves might have been made in America, either braided or woven on small rigid-heddle looms. Perhaps they had been saved from the traditional dress of the mothers and fathers who were proud to use them on their children consciously or unconsciously as symbols of their heritage.[71]

O. E. Rølvaag reveals the significance of these bands for traditional women's dress in the previously mentioned story about Beret and the injured Indian man. What takes place in the episode below, apart from the touch of humor in it, is one in a series of small rites during which remnants from the familiar language of dress are sacrificed to survival on the prairie:

Carol Colburn

Ill. 22. Picnic at Kjomme School. Highland Township north of Highlandville, Winneshiek county, Iowa, c. 1912.
In their best clothes for their school picnic, many of the same children from Figure 21 appear here in more fashionable dress. The boys wear suits, which were available ready-made, or might have been homemade. The girls wear elaborate dresses of light summer cloth and lace. *Courtesy of Mildred Kjome, Decorah, Iowa*

"'If you had a string to tie around the rags, so that they wouldn't loosen when they got dry, they would keep the heat longer', she said in a low voice, but calm and clear.

"'Oh yes! . . . If I only had it!'

"She turned away for a moment and began fumbling at her clothes; then, with a bashful but determined air, she handed him one of her home-braided garters . . . 'Will this do?' she asked.

"'Do? . . . My God! Beret, that's exactly what we need!' . . . He bound up the sick hand tightly, and tied the garter around the bandage . . . 'The fellow's better already!'"[72]

Conclusion

A language of dress that may have been as precise as verbal language existed in rural Norway almost to the time of emigration. In the late nineteenth and early twentieth centuries, however, it was losing definition through contact with a different and far less articulate international language of dress reaching Norway by way of its ever-increasing upper- and middle-class urban population. The language of this so-called fashionable dress had early become the vernacular in America. The rural immigrant from Norway was therefore forced to make a sudden adjustment to a type of dress with which he had only

Ill. 23. Anonymous girl.
Neck pins such as this were originally used to pin together the collar at the front neckline of the folk dress blouse. The cross dangles on this pin are distinctively Norwegian. This young girl wears the pin as a brooch to display her Norwegian family heritage on her fashionably styled dress of c. 1900. *Courtesy of Carol Colburn, Cedar Falls, Iowa*

Ill. 24. Anonymous family group.
The three children are wearing simply cut dresses of fashionable origin c. 1860. However, the decorative woven or braided bands added to each neckline reflects the Norwegian heritage of the family.
Mrs. Wm. H. Young Collection, Courtesy of Vesterheim

Carol Colburn

slight familiarity. This article has dealt with how the challenge of that adjustment was met.

Both photographic and written documents indicate that the transition from traditional Norwegian to fashionable American dress occurred about as rapidly as economics would allow but that an understanding of the new language of dress came more slowly. One gets, therefore, the question in the title of this article asked by an immigrant woman looking at the wedding attire of her own relative, "I wondered when I saw you what all these new clothes meant."

The shock of adjustment appears to have been eased by retaining bits of the old vocabulary while accepting the basic structure of the new language. These bits now have scarcely more significance than simple familiarity while they originally would have contained precise meaning. That familiarity alone, however, gave comfort. These bits were primarily very personal things, such as a wrapping rather than a corset for the body, or such incidentals as jewelry, aprons, kerchiefs, woven or braided bands, and the like. Children were the first to lose even these except when special circumstances called for them. Mixed language in immigrant dress was therefore largely a first-generation phenomenon.

While significant elements of traditional dress disappeared from use, they did not totally disappear from immigrant consciousness. Parts of early costumes are among the more common treasures of Norwegian-American families[73] and have come in great numbers recently to Vesterheim, the Norwegian-American Museum, as changing life styles make family retention of heirlooms difficult. The reverence for traditional objects of dress is beautifully expressed in the memoirs of Thurine Oleson, who tells of dividing mementoes among her children on her fiftieth wedding anniversary:

"The choicest piece of the whole chest, of course, was the heavy gold wedding chain. It had been settled long ago that that should go to the oldest daughter, Clara . . . the wedding guimpe that had been made and worn by my grandmother, Signe, in 1810, the strips of ceremonial belt that all the grandmothers had worn for generations back. There were silver buttons from my father's coats and trousers . . . "[74]

The lingering respect for the messages of traditional Norwegian dress led eventually to a new chapter in its use among the immigrants. As early as the 1890s, when the last remnants of such dress were still in the process of disappearing from unselfconscious use, a revival of it as an expression of individual identity and ethnic pride began occurring, primarily in cities and towns. The quite different story of this rich and century-long revival is yet to be told.

1. Erna Oleson Xan, *Wisconsin, My Home: The Story of Thurine Oleson as told to her Daughter* (Madison, Wisconsin, 1950), 155.

2. Jeanette Lauer and Robert H. Lauer, *Fashion Power: The Meaning of Fashion in American Society* (Englewood Cliffs, New Jersey, 1981), 36. I tested the applicability of the authors' categories to the study of dress in the Midwest during the late nineteenth century in "The Dress of the James J. Hill Family 1863–1916" (Ph.D. dissertation, University of Minnesota, 1989).

3. Aagot Noss, "From Norwegian Folk Costumes to American Dress," in *The Viking*, 84:5 (1987), 178.

4. Letter from Gunnar Høst to Agnes Hansen, November 13, 1884, Grand Forks, North Dakota, in Solveig Zempel, ed., *In Their Own Words: Letters from Norwegian Immigrants* (Minneapolis, 1991), 63.

5. B. Lindsay Lowell, "Sociological Theories and the Great Immigration," in *Norwegian-American Studies,* 32 (Northfield, Minnesota, 1989), 59.

6. Peter Munch, ed., *The Strange American Way* (Carbondale, Illinois, 1970), 199.

7. Theodore Blegen, *Land of Their Choice: The Immigrants Write Home* (St. Paul, Minnesota, 1955), 199.

8. Blegen, *Land of Their Choice,* 199.

9. Letter from Andreas Hjerpeland to Ivar Kleiven, July 24, 1878, Lanesboro, Minnesota, in Zempel, *In Their Own Words,* 15.

10. Noss, "From Norwegian Folk Costume to American Dress," 180.

11. Naomi Rosenblum, *A World History of Photography* (New York, 1984), 62.

12. This is borne out by the collections at the Norwegian-American Historical Association, Vesterheim, the Norwegian-American Museum, and the state historical societies of Wisconsin and Minnesota.

13. Letter from Caja Munch to her parents, November 25, 1855, describing her first home in Wiota, Wisconsin, in Munch, *The Strange American Way,* 15.

14. Letter from Berta Serina Kingestad to her parents, brothers, and sisters, November 11, 1888, Lee, Illinois, in Zempel, *In Their Own Words,* 38.

15. Letter from Berta Serina Kingestad to her parents, brothers, and sisters, September 18, 1889, Malta, Illinois, in Zempel, *In Their Own Words,* 45.

16. Letter from Andreas Hjerpeland to Ivan Kleiven, June 29, 1889, Daily, North Dakota, in Zempel, *In Their Own Words,* 20.

17. Letter from Berta Serina Kingestad to her parents, brothers, and sisters, November 11, 1888, Lee, Illinois, in Zempel, *In Their Own Words,* 38.

18. Letter from Caja Munch to her parents, Wiota, Wisconsin, October 1858, in Munch, *The Strange American Way,* 149.

19. Letter from Gunnar Høst to Agnes Hansen, December 4, 1893, McIntosh, Minnesota, in Zempel, *In Their Own Words,* 74.

20. For the purpose of this study, portraits were first studied in the public collection of Vesterheim, the Norwegian-American Museum, in Decorah, Iowa, the largest collection of

Norwegian-American portraits in America. The museum has been a primary repository for photographs of Norwegian Americans, and the collection included many portraits of prominent Norwegian Americans, as well as some specific family collections. The Iconographic Collections of the State Historical Society of Wisconsin hold a unique collection of Norwegian-American immigrant portraits made by Andreas Dahl in Dane county, Wisconsin. His carefully composed portraits, many of which document the immigrants' material gains in America, made this source particularly rich for examples of immigrant dress. A collection of photographs was also used which belongs to the author. The photographs were collected by Ole Rood, an editor of the publication *Samband*. The photographs were to be used for publication with the purpose of recording the lives of immigrants from the district of Valdres. Other family collections were also sought. Requests for viewing private collections were restricted to Winneshiek county, Iowa, the county surrounding the city of Decorah. The privately held family albums utilized from the Decorah area were well enough documented to ascertain social status and occupation of many of the individuals depicted in portraits. Historical knowledge of the social composition of this largely Norwegian settlement gave these family collections a context which helped in their interpretation. On the basis of them, for example, comparisons could be made between the effect of town and rural settlement on dress. For the photographs chosen, the dates and identification of subject given by the owner, if appearing to be generally accurate, are indicated. Where a photograph has been dated by the dress, an approximate date is given in the caption.

21. Reminiscence by Thurine Oleson of wedding, dated May 26, 1886, Oshkosh, Wisconsin, in Xan, *Wisconsin, My Home*, 154.

22. Janice S. Stewart, *The Folk Arts of Norway* (Madison, Wisconsin, 1953).

23. Xan, *Wisconsin, My Home*, 62.

24. Letter from Berta Serina Kingestad to her sister Anna, September 18, 1889, Malta, Illinois, in Zempel, *In Their Own Words*, 44.

25. Beaumont Newhall, *The History of Photography* (New York, 1982), 129. Although relating to demeanor rather than dress, another deceptive impression made by old photographs comes from the consistently sober faces. This was a convention comparable to the convention of smiling when being photographed today. The long exposure times that were required for portrait photographs are usually blamed for the stern appearances. The state of dental care at the time may also have entered in. Thurine Oleson has the following to say about it: "Our teeth were never filled, and we often pulled them ourselves by wiggling the decayed ones until they were so loose that they could be pulled out with fingers or pliers. If they were too big for this, or got to aching too badly, of course we had to go to a dentist in some nearby town to relieve the misery. It was taken for granted that all old people were almost toothless. I never remember anyone having false teeth until quite a few years after I was married." (Reminiscence of Thurine Oleson, who was married in 1886, in Xan, *Wisconsin, My Home*, 143.)

26. Xan, *Wisconsin, My Home*, 61.

27. Elisabeth Koren, *The Diary of Elisabeth Koren, 1853–1855*, trans. and ed. by David T. Nelson (Northfield, Minnesota, 1955), 113.

28. Munch, *The Strange American Way*, 149.

29. Xan, *Wisconsin, My Home,* 63.

30. Letter from Caja Munch to her parents, December 25, 1855, Wiota, Wisconsin, in Munch, *The Strange American Way,* 27.

31. Berta Serina Kingestad to her sister Anna, April 27, 1890, Malta, Illinois, in Zempel, *In Their Own Words,* 47.

32. Letter from Berta Serina Kingestad to her sister Anna, April 14, 1889, Malta, Illinois, in Zempel, *In Their Own Words,* 46.

33. Gunvor Ingstad Trætteberg, *Folk Costumes of Norway* (Oslo, Norway, 1966), 30.

34. Carol Colburn, "Immigrant Handweaving in the Upper Midwest," in Catherine Cole, ed., *Norwegian Immigrant Clothing and Textiles* (Edmonton, Alberta, 1990), 61.

35. Xan, *Wisconsin, My Home,* 63.

36. Joseph Schroeder, ed., *The Wonderful World of Ladies' Fashion 1850–1920* (Chicago, 1971), 70.

37. Letter from Caja Munch to her parents, March, 1858, Wiota, Wisconsin, in Munch, *The Strange American Way,* 135.

38. Ingeborg Gravjord, *Votten i norsk tradisjon* (Oslo, 1986), 35, and Noss, "Tradition and Transition: Norwegian Costume from Norway to the United States, 1840–1880," in Cole, *Norwegian Immigrant Clothing and Textiles,* 25.

39. Trætteberg, *Folk Costumes of Norway,* 5.

40. Six examples of this form of black apron used over a black dress were found during the course of this study. Other photographs show dark aprons without the velvet trim.

41. Ole E. Rølvaag, *Giants in the Earth* (New York, 1927), 79.

42. The use of colorful silk scarves was also seen in fashionable dress of the late nineteenth century, so the appearance of these scarves on portraits of Norwegian Americans cannot be considered a unique dress feature retained from folk dress. However, the frequency of their appearance on portraits of Norwegian Americans, distinctive methods of tying the scarves in the folk dress tradition, and the use of the scarves in combination with Norwegian jewelry items distinguish their use by Norwegians from the use of similar scarves as part of fashionable dress.

43. Kjersti Skavhaug, *Norwegian Bunads* (Oslo, 1982), 82.

44. Barbara Schweger, "The Farvolden Collection of Norwegian Costume and Textiles," in Cole, *Norwegian Immigrant Clothing and Textiles,* 99.

45. Koren, *The Diary of Elisabeth Koren,* 111.

46. Xan, *Wisconsin, My Home,* 133.

47. Letter from Caja Munch to her parents, June, 1857, Wiota, Wisconsin, in Munch, *The Strange American Way,* 100. Her diary also refers to children's and men's shoes sent from Norway, 108, 138.

48. Letter from Berta Serina Kingestad to her sister Anna, April 14, 1889, Malta, Illinois, in Zempel, *In Their Own Words,* 41.

49. Letter from Berta Serina Kingestad to her sister Anna, February 14, 1890, Malta, Illinois, in Zempel, *In Their Own Words,* 46.

50. The Skree blacksmith shop that was moved to Vesterheim from rural Houston, Minnesota, had a considerable amount of wooden-shoe-making equipment. Marion Nelson of Vesterheim tells of having been given a pair of early "clogs" worn by the Norwegian immi-

grant grandfather of the giver in Willmar, Minnesota.

51. Letter from Berta Serina Kingestad to her sister Anna, April 14, 1889, Malta, Illinois, in Zempel, *In Their Own Words,* 41.

52. Letter from Berta Serina Kingestad to her sister Anna, March 10, 1891, Malta, Illinois, in Zempel, *In Their Own Words,* 50.

53. Stewart, *The Folk Arts of Norway,* 134.

54. Stewart, *The Folk Arts of Norway,* 136.

55. Carlton C. Qualey, "Seven America Letters to Valdres," in *Norwegian-American Studies,* 22 (1965). Quoted in Noss, "Tradition and Transition," 35. A series of photographs in Noss's article serve to demonstrate the differences between traditional and fashionable men's wear.

56. Xan, *Wisconsin, My Home,* 62.

57. Claudia B. Kidwell and Margaret C. Christman, *Suiting Everyone: The Democratization of Clothing in America* (Washington, D.C., 1974), 111.

58. Jo B. Paoletti and Ira Block, "Changes in the Masculine Image in the United States 1880–1900: A Content Analysis of Popular Humor about Dress," in *Association of College Professors of Textiles and Clothing Proceedings* (Burke, Virginia, 1980), 81.

59. John Berger, "The Suit and the Photograph," in *About Looking* (New York, 1980), 27–36.

60. Xan, *Wisconsin, My Home,* 62.

61. Diana de Marly, *Fashion for Men: An Illustrated History* (New York, 1985), 101.

62. David Mandel, *Settlers of Dane County: The Photographs of Andreas Larson Dahl* (Dane county, Wisconsin, 1985), 8.

63. Olaf M. Norlie, *History of the Norwegian People in America* (Minneapolis, 1925), 202.

64. Munch, *The Strange American Way,* 204.

65. Munch, *The Strange American Way,* 210.

66. Pastor Paul Hasvold, Decorah, Iowa. Telephone interview of January 23, 1992.

67. Munch, *The Strange American Way,* 78.

68. Reference to "preacher's cap" is made by the photographer Andreas Larsen Dahl, as reported by Mandel, *Settlers of Dane County,* 78. Aagot Noss, Curator at the Norsk Folkemuseum, Oslo, reported on the use of the cap in Norway in a letter to the author, May 23, 1991.

69. Letter from Caja Munch to her parents, August, 1856, Wiota, Wisconsin, in Munch, *The Strange American Way,* 51.

70. Letter from Berta Serina Kingestad to her sister Anna, June 20, 1887, Norway, Illinois, in Zempel, *In Their Own Words,* 33.

71. The collection at Vesterheim has many woven and braided bands and the looms on which they were made.

72. Rølvaag, *Giants in the Earth,* 81.

73. Heather Prince, "The Tradition in Alberta: A Case Study of Valhalla Centre," in Cole, *Norwegian Immigrant Clothing and Textiles,* 69; and Mary Ann Jacobsen and Ruth E. Gates "Norwegian-American Ethnicity and Ethnic Clothing, Textiles, and Household Objects," in *Ethnicity,* 6 (1979), 218.

74. Xan, *Wisconsin, My Home,* 222.

Vinaigrettes, Little Immigrant Treasures[*]

by M. A. Madson

O BJECTS THAT the immigrants from Norway to the North American continent valued sufficiently to include in the sparse possessions they brought from their homeland can divulge much about who they were and where they came from. One such type of object is the vinaigrette or, in Norwegian, the *lukteflaske*. The prevalence of vinaigrettes among Norwegian immigrants becomes especially telling when compared to their scarcity among immigrants from Denmark, a country in which these objects appear to have been even more common than in Norway.

Lukteflasker (smelling bottles) or *luktevannshus* (smelling-water container or house) or *slavannshus* (smelling-salts container or house) are all Norwegian words for the same type of object, the English for which is *vinaigrette*. In Danish, these curious objects are called *hovedvandsæg* (smelling salts/eggs); in Swedish, *svampdosor* (sponge boxes); in German, *Eicken* (eggs), or *Reichdosen* (scent boxes), to mention but a few of the names by which vinaigrettes are known in the various countries where they are found as relics of the eighteenth and nineteenth centuries.[1] All terms make clear that they are containers and most allude to the pungent liquid contents. While vinaigrettes can be

*The author wishes to thank Vesterheim, the Norwegian-American Museum, and its former director, Marion Nelson, for their considerable assistance in this study. Further, I wish to acknowledge the generosity of the owners of the vinaigrettes who responded to my inquiry, including the Goldstein Gallery of the University of Minnesota, which provided some of the pictures included, and a number of museums in Norway which had vinaigrettes in their collections.

Ill. 1a-b. Heart-shaped vinaigrette for carrying or hanging on the neck viewed from front (left, a) and back (right, b). Silver. H. 2⅜" W. 1⅝" D.⅞". Inscribed "JODF". Probably Norwegian and dating from the early to mid-nineteenth century. Found in Minneapolis area. *Private collection*

of many kinds of material, they are usually two-part, hollow containers made of silver, which open by means of a hinge (Ills. 1, 2). The vinaigrettes used in the illustrations as examples of types are not specifically those that came to light as part of the Norwegian immigrant study. They measure from two to four inches in height and originally contained a small sponge. This sponge was soaked in a strong-scented liquid, either ammonia or vinegar-based smelling salts or, later, perfume.

Vinaigrettes were made in a variety of shapes and changed in both basic outline and decoration in accordance with prevailing fashion. A very few spherical vinaigrettes are known, hence the connection with the term egg, (Ill. 3), but many have the shape of a small vase or urn (Ills. 4, 5, 6, 8). Other forms include rectangular and fish-shaped (Ill. 7) vinaigrettes as well as the very popular heart-shaped examples (Ills. 1, 2, 8). All the known basic shapes from the whole area of Northern Europe where they occur are represented in Norwegian museum and private collections.

The number of vinaigrettes found in Norwegian-American families, as well as in public and private collections in Norway, establish that they were

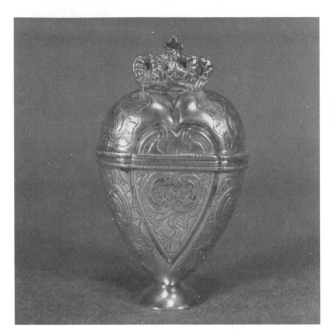

M. A. Madson

Ill. 2. (opposite left) Heart-shaped vinaigrette with attached base. Silver with some gilding. H. 3⅛" W. 2" D. 1". Inscribed on sides "ECDR" "1814" and on base "IJL". Stamped hallmark "AN" on base. The bodies of standing heart-shaped vinaigrettes are almost identical to those without bases (See Ill. 1). The type is most prevalent in Norway. Found in Minneapolis area. *Courtesy of Alice Ross Rogers*

Ill. 3a-b. (opposite right and bottom) Egg-shaped vinaigrette for hanging shown (a) closed and (b) unscrewed to reveal its two compartments and perforated sponge container. Silver with interior gilding. H. 2⅜" Diam. 1⅜". Inscribed with royal Danish monogram and "1726". Thought to be from Norway, which was under the Danish crown. *Courtesy of Vesterheim*

Ill. 4. (top left) Urn-shaped vinaigrette. Silver with clear glass set in finial. H. 3" Diam. 1½". Inscribed "BEK" "DL" on sides. Stamped hallmark "PW" in base. The bodies of urn-shaped vinaigrettes occasionally, like this one, continue the egg-shape of an early hanging type (see Ill. 3) but are more frequently flattened. Possibly west-coast Norwegian. Found in New England. *Courtesy of Alice Ross Rogers*

Ill. 5. (top right) Urn-shaped vinaigrette with extra compartment in base. Silver with glass sets. Gilded interior. H. 3¼" W. 2" D. 1¼". Inscribed "NA" "1803" on base. Photographed with hinged bottom open. This compartment in the base of some vinaigrettes is thought to have been used for a coin but its small size indicates it may rather have been for an additional fragrant substance. *Courtesy of Goldstein Gallery, University of Minnesota*

M. A. Madson

familiar objects within rural Norwegian society in the nineteenth century. Their small size made them easily portable. Made of precious metal, their monetary worth as well as their utilitarian function helped to assure that they would be included in the material possessions transported to North America. As they were usually commemorative or betrothal gifts, passed down within families,[2] their sentimental value would also render them precious reminders of the culture and of loved ones left behind.

Vinaigrettes are primarily a phenomenon of the eighteenth and early nineteenth centuries in Norway. They are, however, part of a much longer tradition of scent containers that dates back several hundred years. Their first purpose was probably medicinal.[3] Some substances were found to relieve certain ailments, such as dizziness, and could perhaps even guard against the dreaded plague.[4] The containers for these substances tended to be named after their contents, rare plant and animal products. Musk and ambergris were stored in a *pomme d'ambre* or *poma de ambra*—ambergris apple—terms which were eventually shortened to *pomander*.[5] These *pomanders*, which are considered to be the predecessors of vinaigrettes, are mentioned as early as 1423 in the inventory of the English King Henry V, although there is no precise information as to when *pomanders* first came into use. They are found in the shape of oranges, apples, heads, skulls, dice, gloves, or small flasks and contained compartments in which were stored solid substances.[6]

With the popularization of liquid scents in the eighteenth century,[7] a different kind of container was needed and the vinaigrettes were developed, coming to Scandinavia in the early eighteenth century.[8] The liquid smelling salts was available in pharmacies in this century and was usually a solution consisting of ammonia and various spices and fragrances, such as lavender, lily of the valley, cloves, sage, and cinnamon, plus animal essences like ambergris or musk.[9] The corrosive nature of ammonia and vinegar required that the silver interior be protected by a thin layer of gold, which is still visible in many examples.

Ill. 6. Vinaigrette of undulating fluted rococo shape. Silver. H. 3" W. 1⅝" D. 1". Inscribed "BLD" in base. Depending on the organic undulations of the shape rather than surface ornament for decoration, this piece related in character to early eighteenth-century serving vessels. Found in Minneapolis area. *Courtesy of Alice Ross Rogers*

Ill. 7. Fish-shaped vinaigrette. Silver and glass. H. 1⅝" L. 4½" W. 1". Stamped hallmark "CC"(?) "S." Possibly Christen Christensen (1830–1885), Copenhagen. *Courtesy of Goldstein Gallery, University of Minnesota*

Ill. 8. A collection of vinaigrettes representing a variety of shapes. The hearts are characteristic for Norway while the urn is more typical of south Denmark. The watch-shaped example has a Swedish hallmark. The book is rare and of unknown provenance. Collected largely in the Twin Cities area of Minnesota. *Donated by Bruce A. Hitman to Vesterheim*

These vinaigrettes were carried by women, although in earlier times there is mention of men using them as well,[10] a practice which continued in England until the middle of the nineteenth century.[11] They could be hand-held, carried in a purse or pocket, or, in Norway, worn on a chain or ribbon about the neck (Ills. 1, 3, 9). Ribbons and chains could be threaded through the finial at the top of the vinaigrette and suspended around the neck. This was most commonly done with heart-shaped vinaigrettes. When the vinaigrette was in the shape of a round pocket watch it was called a *lukteklokke* or *lukteur* (smelling watch) (Ill. 9).[12]

Tradition maintains that during the nineteenth century silver vinaigrettes were often betrothal gifts from a young man to his intended. In the beginning, however, they were simply one of the accessories of the well-dressed woman, like fans, jewelry, and handbags. Portraits from as early as the seventeenth century show the forerunner of the vinaigrette, the pomander, used as a belt ornament by women of the aristocracy.[13] Sigurd Schoubye discusses the transformation of the pomander into the vinaigrette, where it loses its original medicinal function and becomes solely a costume accessory.[14]

The ownership of a vinaigrette seems to have been an accepted part of a well-born lady's toilette. One of the most famous persons known to have owned a vinaigrette was the Danish princess Leonora Christina (1621–1698), a daughter of King Christian IV who detailed her humiliating and lengthy imprisonment in the book *Jammersminde* (Memories of Lamentation) from 1663. In it, she bemoans the loss of many comforts and possessions, among them a fine vinaigrette, for which an inferior lead vinaigrette has been substituted.[15] In a more lighthearted vein, vinaigrettes are mentioned in poetry. In a verse (1728), J. K. Schanderup wrote about "innocent vices," lumping together snuff, scented materials, kissing, and cuddling as temptations one could or perhaps could not avoid:

> *Min Snus Tobach forsvær jeg ey, som har Parfum i Næsen,*
> *En Bidsken af en Balsam-Bys mig ogsaa kan behage,*
> *Men Fafne-Tag og Pige-Kys jeg icke kan fordrage.*
> (I won't give up my snuff, which gives perfume to my nose,
> A 'tasty' morsel from a vinaigrette also pleases me,
> But a hug and a kiss from a girl I cannot stand.)[16]

The Norwegian-Danish playwright Ludvig Holberg uses the vinaigrette in no fewer than three plays as a device to lampoon the attempts of the bourgeoisie to move upward in status by imitating the habits of their social "betters."[17] As time passed and vinaigrettes went out of use among urban residents, their function as a betrothal gift among the landed rural population became more common, which could explain the popularity of heart-shaped vinaigrettes during the nineteenth century (Ills. 1, 2, 8).

M. A. Madson

Because of the expensive material from which many vinaigrettes were made, they were available only to those segments of the population who had some economic means. In most parts of Europe, this would eliminate the rural population. Luxury items, particularly imported wares, were actually forbidden in some places to people not of the upper classes.[18] Sumptuary laws first appeared in France in the sixteenth century, and spread throughout Europe. The first sumptuary law in Denmark-Norway was in 1528 and was directed toward the aristocracy and their consumption of imported goods. Subsequent laws included not only the upper classes but the middle and lower classes as well.[19] Peasants were forbidden to wear imported textiles, and their dress was further restricted in relation to that of the upper classes. In 1783, the King's displeasure at the amount of foreign imports led to one of the final sumptuary laws, which limited not only the dress of the lower classes but even the extent and expense of their celebrations. These laws were never particularly successful and were very difficult to enforce. During the 1790s, there was a continual loosening of such restrictive legislation and it all but disappeared by the nineteenth century.[20]

The regulation of luxury wares applied also to precious metal, which in Denmark was imported. However, in Norway, the availability of native raw silver allowed objects made of precious metal to be more generally accessible to the farming populace.[21] Also, because of the exigencies of climate and the difficulties of farming the rugged landscape, many Norwegian farmers also carried on other occupations, such as logging or fishing, which provided cash income, something otherwise rare in farming communities that depended completely on a barter economy.[22] The accessibility of cash allowed the farm-

Ill. 9. Watch-shaped vinaigrette. Silver. H. 2⅛" W. 1⅜" D.¾". Inscribed "1862" (?). Probably Norwegian. Found in Minneapolis area. *Courtesy of Alice Ross Rogers*

ers to purchase goods that they otherwise could not have afforded such as silver items. Traditionally, the customer either brought silver to the silversmith or paid the smith to acquire the raw material, which was then worked to specifications.

From Viking times and even before, silver jewelry and other decorative objects were part of the Norwegian material culture. Jewelry played an important role in the traditional costumes of many regions of Norway, which might well have made it easier for new forms and types of small, precious objects to gain a foothold among the otherwise conservative rural population. Two well-developed customs made silver objects available to even isolated rural areas. Rural silversmiths, who generally had another primary occupation such as farming, produced silver objects which represented varying degrees of competency but often reflected local tastes.[23] Traveling smiths, who were based in the larger market towns, were able to provide silver objects to even isolated rural areas. These traveling smiths brought not only goods to the provinces but also new fashions and styles from the outside world that were then adapted to local tastes.[24]

The author wrote to a number of museums in Norway for information about Norwegian vinaigrettes in public collections. At the same time, Norwegian-American organizations were contacted in the hope that some of their members might also have such objects in their possession. The response from both groups revealed the existence of a considerable number of vinaigrettes which had traveled to North America in the baggage of Norwegian immigrants. In 1990, Vesterheim, the Norwegian-American Museum, in Decorah, Iowa, offered to sponsor a second notice seeking information from Norwegian Americans as to their possible ownership of vinaigrettes. This was sent to the 7,500 members of Vesterheim. Once more, the response was surprisingly strong; the owners of more than one hundred vinaigrettes responded, either directly to the author or through the museum. While there was some repetition from the initial survey, most were new contacts. The original request was followed by a two-page questionnaire sent to all who answered, asking for a precise description of the object, a history of the family through which it came, and any information they might have on its use. This was done in order to determine what kind of people originally owned these objects: where they came from in Norway, if they were farmers or town dwellers, and when and where they settled in North America. Some open-ended questions were also asked, such as what information or traditional family lore existed regarding the use and previous ownership of the vinaigrettes. A total of 107 vinaigrettes have thus far been identified within this developing effort.

Silver was the most common material (94), with silver plate and pewter also being used (4). Wood, ivory, bone, shell, and glass furnished one example each, and four were made of porcelain. It is possible that wood, ivory, bone, and shell comprised the most numerous categories of vinaigrettes, but, because of the non-precious nature of the material, they were more commonly discarded when they showed wear or when their use went out of fashion.[25] It is more difficult to categorize the containers made of glass and porcelain. While they may have served the same purpose as vinaigrettes, it is also possible that many of them were perfume bottles. A few people noted that the inside of their silver vinaigrettes was gilded, as was the custom, but this thin layer of gilt is often eroded and thus not easy to detect.

While there appears to be a relatively wide variety of vinaigrette shapes found in Norwegian museum collections, the vast majority of vinaigrettes in Norwegian-American hands were heart-shaped.[26] Twenty-six were hearts without a base (Ill. 1), while fifty-four were free-standing on a base (Ill. 2). Of the other more common shapes for Scandinavian vinaigrettes, only one was vase-shaped (Ill. 6), three were covered urns (Ills. 4, 5, 8), four were fish (Ill. 7), and two were in the shape of a pocket watch (Ill. 9). Six were flasks of some kind, usually in another material than silver (probably perfume bottles), and an additional eleven were of more unusual shapes, rectangular, like an egg (Ill. 3), a book (Ill. 8), or a sea shell.[27]

Most terminated in a finial, which in the majority of cases (79) was a crown (Ills. 1, 2, 4, 8). Nine were topped by solid round balls (Ill. 8), and there was one each of hearts, flowers, flowers and balls, scrolls, and compound finials (Ills. 4, 5). Only two vinaigrettes had handles (Ills. 5, 8), and these on both were in the form of the letter C. (The specific examples are not illustrated.) Of the footed variety, forty-six were reported to have closed or solid feet and sixteen hollow. Many of the hollow feet probably opened to reveal a second compartment which was originally designed to contain solid scented material, but in later years it was traditionally said that it held a small coin destined for the church poor box (Ill. 5).[28] This idea may derive from the fact that small coins have been found in vinaigrettes, but a concrete relationship between the coin and the vinaigrette has not been established: it is possible that the coin was placed in the compartment as a keepsake.

Almost all of the vinaigrettes were described as having some type of decoration; only three were reported to be without ornamentation (Ill. 6). This surface embellishment usually took the form of chasing and embossing. Plant motifs in typical rococo (Ills. 1, 2) or neo-classical styles (Ills. 4,5) followed the contours of the vinaigrettes and/or filled the field in the center of the object. In other examples, the entire surface was covered with this type of plant ornamentation. Owners' initials and dates were frequently engraved on the front or foot of the vinaigrettes (Ills. 2, 3, 4). This practice can be misleading in dating the object, however, as they were often engraved or re-engraved to commemorate an event or transfer of ownership years after they were

made. Three vase- or urn-shaped vinaigrettes were reported to have paste "jewels" adorning them (Ills. 4, 5), as did the four fish, where these faceted paste baubles formed the fish's eyes (Ill. 7).

More difficult sometimes to find, and often missing altogether, are hallmarks (Ill. 10). Legally, from the sixteenth century to 1839 when the guilds were disbanded, the guild system in Norway required the marking of each piece of silver with at least the maker's mark, usually the initials. This was to assure the purchaser a minimum level of purity in the silver used and the competence of the smith who made the object.[29] However, small items like vinaigrettes were not always marked. Silver objects under a certain weight could fall outside the marking requirement.[30] Guild regulations were also difficult to enforce in Norway, where the guilds were located only in the larger towns, such as Bergen, Christiania (Oslo), Trondheim, and Kristiansand. Goldsmiths from the towns were known to travel to rural markets to sell their goods.[31] It may be that these silver items were not always marked. There was also the tradition of country goldsmiths, who might or might not have had any formal education in their craft. Many were rural youths who served an apprenticeship in one of the towns for a few years and then returned, sometimes without finishing their apprenticeship, to their original homes.[32] In cases where the apprenticeship was completed, there could be a variety of reasons for the smiths choosing to work outside the guild system.[33] In any case, these craftsmen often did not mark their wares, whether to guard against the guild tracing work back to them or simply because it was not required.[34]

Respondents to the survey mentioned that a total of sixty-five silver vinaigrettes had hallmarks of some kind, twenty-two had none, and for seven there is no information as to hallmarks given. Hallmarks are often found in locations where it is difficult to read them and they are frequently unclear, either because they were stamped indistinctly or, if they are on a more accessible surface, because they have become worn. It can also be difficult for the layperson to identify the sometimes intricate hallmarks used by silversmiths. Identification of specific silversmiths by hallmark must, in most cases, wait for physical examination by a silver specialist.

However, information other than hallmarks was easier to obtain. Fourteen vinaigrettes carried a year mark exclusive of any other engraving done for commemorative purposes. The earliest was an unusually early 1726 and the latest 1841. Seven vinaigrettes were marked with an additional number of some kind, usually 13½ (there was also one 11½). These numbers denote the purity of the silver; 13½ parts out of 16 was one of the most common purity ratios during the seventeenth, eighteenth, and early nineteenth centuries.[35] While the marks of individual smiths can be difficult to decipher, city marks, when they appear, tend to be easily identifiable. Three vinaigrettes carried the mark of Trondheim, four that of Bergen, and one of Stavanger. Three vinaigrettes were marked with the Swedish triple crown.

While the owners of vinaigrettes are proud of their Norwegian heritage, it was none the less difficult to obtain precise information on the original owners of these objects. Of those for which such information was available, southern Norway was the most common origin, with the greatest number coming from the area between Stavanger and Kristiansand (23). The next most represented region is from eastern Telemark up the coast to Oslo (12). Bergen and its environs contributed a smaller number (8),[36] as did Trondheim and its surrounding area (4). Northern Norway, while a large territory, was not known for the making or possession of vinaigrettes, and those few that are identified from that expanse are associated with Mosjøen and Mo i Rana (3).

These numbers tend to correspond with what is known about silver production, both in the towns and by the rural silversmiths, except in the case of Bergen, which was a major silver producer and supplied much silver to the surrounding countryside.[37] In areas such as Telemark, where the Kongsberg mining district was located, raw silver was relatively abundant and was obtainable by town dweller and rural resident alike.[38] The concentration of vinaigrettes originally from southwestern and southeastern coastal areas also agrees with transportation routes, which were least difficult by water.[39] New stylistic impulses and goods themselves flowed along the coasts to the towns and from there to the more accessible of the rural areas. Bergen was a major center of trade and silver production, both for Norway and for as far away as Denmark and Friesland. Whether new stylistic stimuli came directly from Europe or from the capitol in Copenhagen is still under discussion.[40]

The owners of Norwegian vinaigrettes tended to be farmers (37), while only ten were identified as town dwellers. Five were seamen, one a shipbuilder, one worked at farming and logging, and fifty-three were unidentified as to original occupation. One of the seamen's vinaigrettes appears to be an imported Danish *hovedvandsæg*, which is not surprising considering the close maritime connections between coastal Norway and the Danish provinces that produced *hovedvandsæg*. Another, this one in the shape of a fish, was made by the owner's ancestor while he still lived in Norway.[41]

Most respondents, but not all, knew when the family emigrated from Norway. Thirty-four came during the great wave of immigration, between 1850 and the 1890s. One came during the 1850s, five during the 1860s, seven in the 1870s, eleven in the 1880s, and four during the last decade of the nineteenth century. Ten arrived in the first decade of the twentieth century, three during the teens, seven in the 1920s, and one during the 1930s. The owners settled in a variety of places, both urban and rural. As could be expected, most came to the Midwest, with Minnesota (18) and Wisconsin (13) accounting for the greatest numbers. Iowa had six, the Dakotas eight, and other midwestern states five. The Pacific Northwest contributed two, as did Montana, while New York listed four, and central Canada one. The heavy midwestern representation may result in part from the fact that the only personal solicitation went out to the members of an institution, Vesterheim, which is located in the Midwest.

Other family information was more difficult to elicit. Twenty-nine said that their vinaigrettes came from the family of their mother, while twenty-two received them from a paternal family member. Six were gifts, usually from unrelated people, twenty-five were purchased, and for twenty-five no historical information was available. Vinaigrettes have become collectors' items, primarily among Norwegian Americans, for whom they remain objects of ethnic identity. Only twenty-four owners claimed to know the name and dates of the original owner, while the rest evinced uncertainty or had no information.

Most Norwegian-American respondents had general knowledge of what the vinaigrette was used for, at least during its later period. It was called a perfume holder by sixteen respondents, with two alluding to its use as a container for smelling salts, and three mentioning both perfume and smelling salts. One person said the vinaigrette was carried in a handbag. All others who mentioned the method of bearing the object said it was worn "in the bosom" either on a chain or a ribbon, or, apparently, simply tucked into a garment. Of those who spoke of smelling salts, all three referred to a need for refreshment during long church services as an example of how it was used. Five people either said they could remember the fugitive aroma of perfume or maintained that the sponge still carried that scent. Only one individual remembers the vinaigrette being worn by an older relative, although four said that the vinaigrettes were converted into pendants for necklaces by later owners in this country.

The notion that the vinaigrette might have been purchased as a betrothal gift was recognized by five owners, but most knew it only as a treasure in the family that had been passed down through several generations, viewing it as something for which one had considerable affection and respect, but which had little or no meaning above and beyond that of a family keepsake. This is not unexpected, as relatively few people in modern Scandinavia know of these objects, now found mostly in museums. And, as it appears that the purpose of the Norwegian vinaigrette itself may have changed from that of smelling-salts container to perfume holder during the course of its history, it is not strange that there might be some confusion or uncertainty regarding its purpose.

While considerable numbers of vinaigrettes are to be found in Norwegian public and private collections, as well as in the personal possession of Norwegian Americans, the vinaigrette is most commonly known in Denmark. Over 1,000 have been registered in public collections alone, exclusive of large collections in museums in the former Danish-ruled German cities of Flensburg, Altona, and Schleswig, and several hundred in the Nordiska Museet in Stockholm. There are also numerous large private collections of vinaigrettes in Denmark, numbering objects in the hundreds. This would lead one to expect that considerable numbers of vinaigrettes would be found among Danish Americans, even allowing for the lesser number of Danish immigrants and the smaller percentage of the total Danish population that they represent. This has not been the case.

Announcements were sent to large Danish-American organizations and to historical societies in counties with large Danish-American populations. Only three secure examples have been located thus far. On the other hand, these are all well-documented as to owner and when and from where the Danish owner emigrated. The hallmarks are all easily readable and the smiths identified. The latter is, in part, because Danish hallmark study is at a more advanced stage than Norwegian. Comprehensive studies of Norwegian hallmarks are in progress, but are not yet available to the public.

The Goldstein Gallery at the University of Minnesota has a collection of twenty-two silver vinaigrettes, of mainly Danish origin, twenty-one of which were collected by one individual with ethnic ties to Denmark. Approximately half of these vinaigrettes are identifiable as to date and maker; several of them are reproductions. At least one is probably Norwegian. The most recent acquisition, a fine South Jutlandic example, is included in the three previously mentioned Danish immigrant vinaigrettes, as it came well documented from a family of Danish descent and the original owner was known. For the remaining twenty-one vinaigrettes, all information as to provenance has been lost.

The discrepancy between Danish and Norwegian vinaigrettes leads to the question of why, if there were larger numbers of vinaigrettes produced in Denmark, there are not more in Danish-American possession. Ongoing research may support the most obvious explanation that the relevant Danish-American population has not yet been reached. However, since the largest immigrant organizations have been approached, this would not seem to be the case, which leads to the conclusion that the dramatic difference in numbers must have some other cause. One possible reason may be that the Danish immigrants are said by some to assimilate faster into American society than the more numerous Norwegians,[42] retaining fewer ethnic ties. Perhaps they would not preserve objects, such as vinaigrettes, for which the emotional significance had disappeared. On the other hand, it seems unlikely that objects made of precious metal would have been simply disposed of even if they no longer had meaning as ethnic symbols. And this would not explain the relative paucity of examples among those who *did* retain ties to the Danish-American community.

Emigration from Norway was more extensive than that from Denmark, in terms of both real numbers and percentage of the population.[43] In fact, as Norwegian emigration historian Ingrid Semmingsen notes, with approximately 750,000 persons emigrating from Norway between 1825 and the First World War, only Ireland of European countries had a greater proportionate loss of population through emigration.[44] In contrast, there were approximately 309,000 Danish emigrants from a country with a population somewhat larger than that of Norway.[45] The total nineteenth-century movement from Norway equaled 33.6 percent of the 1900 population as opposed to 12.6 percent for Denmark.[46] But even this difference in emigrant numbers and percentages, imperfect as this measuire is, would not entirely explain the much larger numbers of Norwegian-American vinaigrettes.

The lack of Danish vinaigrettes becomes more surprising when looking at emigration from an area traditionally Danish but from 1864–1920 under German rule: the southern part of the Jutland peninsula called North Schleswig or Sønderjylland. Emigration from South Jutland during the time of German rule was about 60,000 out of a population of approximately 150,000 at the beginning of the period.[47] South Jutland was also the site of the last flowering of vinaigrette production in Denmark, which culminated in the 1860s,[48] just as the great waves of emigration were beginning. The precise number of vinaigrettes produced in South Jutland is not known, but several public and private collections exist numbering South Jutlandic examples in the hundreds. There are also certain to be large numbers still in the families of origin, living both in South Jutland and elsewhere. But not even among emigrants from this geographic area is there evidence of vinaigrettes anywhere near the proportionate numbers among Norwegian Americans. Of the three Danish-American vinaigrettes so far located, only one is of documented South Jutland production.

Other factors must enter into the marked difference in numbers of immigrant Norwegian and Danish vinaigrettes. There is a correlation between the classes of people who emigrated and the ownership of vinaigrettes. Emigration out of Norway, particularly in the first years and up to the 1870s, was pre-

M. A. Madson

dominantly emigration by families; and these were primarily land-owning rural families. As Semmingsen says, "it was the farm owners who went to America, while the cotters, who could not afford the trip, ordinarily moved to Møre or to northern Norway."[49] During the period before 1870 when vinaigrettes were still being produced and used, in other words, the people who emigrated from Norway were precisely those who were most likely to have owned them. They were rural and these objects by the nineteenth century had shifted from the urban to the rural population. They were landowners and therefore might be expected to own at least some luxury items. The fact that they emigrated as families added to the likelihood of their including vinaigrettes in their luggage. If a single man brought silver with him at all, it would most likely have been in the form of buttons or pipe decorations. Even single women may not ordinarily have brought vinaigrettes except as heirlooms because at that time they were most commonly used as betrothal gifts.[50]

Statistics show that from 1866 to 1879 emigration from Denmark was 64.3 percent male as compared to only 54.2 percent from Norway at approximately the same time.[51] These figures support Semmingsen's contention that the early emigration from Norway was largely in families while they also show that males, many of them single, made up a large part of the early emigration from Denmark. This would account in part for the smaller number of vinaigrettes among Danish than Norwegian immigrants.

Another contributing factor would have been the higher percentage of urban emigration from Denmark.[52] As previously mentioned, the use of vinaigrettes had become largely a rural phenomenon by the nineteenth century after having originated in the upper classes in the seventeenth and having found its way into the bourgeoisie in the eighteenth.[53] The fact that many of the urban immigrants from Denmark had recently left the countryside would not necessarily change the picture regarding vinaigrettes. Most of these newly urbanized Danes were attempting to find subsistence in the slowly industrializing market towns as ordinary laborers after having difficulty surviving in the farm villages. The decision to emigrate was one of last resort, when everything else had been attempted.[54] If these people had owned vinaigrettes, it is very likely that they would have sold them to realize the cash value of the silver, either for daily living expenses or to help defer the cost of the journey abroad. Sentiment would have had no place under such dire circumstances.

The Danish rural population that existed at little above survival level, even that portion of it that owned land, would in any case have had less opportunity than their Norwegian counterparts to possess vinaigrettes. Denmark did not have the rural silver mining and crafting industry found in Norway.[55] Objects in silver were in Denmark obtained only by the outlay of cash, something uncommon in poorer rural society of the nineteenth century. In Norway, on the other hand, the access to silver through barter as well as purchase made it much easier for the rural population to obtain. Items in silver could easily be turned into cash if necessary, while in the meantime serving aesthetic or other cultural purposes such as contributing to personal status. More research needs to be done on the rural, non-guild silversmiths of Norway and on Norwegian rural economy in general in order to better understand the amount of silver owned by the peasantry.[56]

The material culture brought to this country by the immigrants and preserved or perpetuated by them here is not necessarily representative of material culture in the home country or even in the general socioeconomic group from which the immigrants came. This study shows that a subtle combination of historic, economic, and demographic circumstances determines what elements in the native material culture transfer and retain a place in the immigrant society. While there is considerable evidence that vinaigrettes were more prevalent in the folk culture of Denmark than of Norway, there is equally good evidence that the number of vinaigrettes in the Norwegian-American community today is overwhelmingly greater than in the Danish-American community. The objects that immigrants brought with them and preserved can when used together with other sources of historic information shed new light on just who the immigrants were and how they related to their past after settling in the New World.

NOTES

1. The most comprehensive studies of vinaigrettes to date deal primarily with the Danish variant, the *hovedvandsæg*. These include Chr. A. Bøje, *Balsambøsser og hovedvandsæg* (Copenhagen, 1950); Sigurd Schoubye, *Sønderjysk sølv* (Aabenraa, Denmark. 1982), "The Danish *Hovedvandsæg*," in *Silver Magazine* (January-February and March-April, 1990), and his two studies of South Jutland *hovedvandsæg: Hovedvandsæg fra Vestslesvig* (Tønder, Denmark. 1978) and *Hovedvandsæg fra Østslesvig* (Tønder, 1982); and M. A. Madson "The Social and Artistic Development of *Hovedvandsæg* in Denmark 1720–1860" (Ph. D. dissertation, University of Minnesota, 1990). Norwegian vinaigrettes are discussed most fully in Rikard Berge, *Norskt bondesylv* (Risør, Norway. 1925).

2. Gorm Benzon, *Kjærestegaver* (Copenhagen, 1978), 73–75, 82, 86, sees a continuity among betrothal practices, including the giving of gifts such as vinaigrettes, along the western coast of the North Sea from Holland to Norway, while Schoubye, *Hovedvandsæg fra Østslesvig*, 8, and Bøje, *Balsambøsser*, 17, discuss the vinaigrette as a betrothal gift in Denmark. Weddings, anniversaries, and birthdays were also commemorated by the giving of vinaigrettes. The Goldstein Gallery at the University of Minnesota owns one vinaigrette which was engraved in observance of the owner's eightieth birthday.

3. Bøje, *Balsambøsser*, 10; Schoubye, "The Danish *Hovedvandsæg*," 8. They could also be representative of an ancient Scandinavian tradition of metal scent containers: "Pendant capsules of silver occur sporadically in mid- and late-Viking context. They presumably contained herbs, and one from Birka grave 552 has a runic inscription indicating that is was

used against vermin." Signe Horn Fuglesang, "Viking and Medieval Amulets in Scandinavia", in *Fornvännen*, 1–2 (1989), 16.

4. Schoubye, "The Danish *Hovedvandsæg*," 8; Bøje, *Balsambøsser*, 10–11. In a study by Henrick Smidt of Malmö, *En liden bog om pestelentzis aarsage 1557* (A little book on the cause of the plague, 1557), both the origins of the plague—"bad steam and smoke which are combined with the air" arising from animal and human waste—and preventative herbs are enumerated. Further, recipes for medicinal distillants and containers to hold them are mentioned as early as 1423, in that case a pomander. Bøje, *Balsambøsser*, 12.

5. Bøje, *Balsambøsser*, 9–10

6. Bøje, *Balsambøsser*, 9–12, 13; W. Turner, "Silver and Plated Ware: Pomanders," in *Connoisseur*, 32 (1912), 151–152; Seymour B. Wyler, *The Book of Old Silver* (3rd ed., New York, 1937), 99; Michael Clayton, *The Collector's Dictionary of Silver and Gold of Great Britain and North America* (New York, 1971), 201, 206, 334.

7. Schoubye, "The Danish *Hovedvandsæg*," 2; Turner, "Silver and Plated Ware," 152.

8. Schoubye, "The Danish *Hovedvandsæg*," 7; "Silver and Plated Ware," 152.

9. Bøje, *Balsambøsser*, 9–12, 19–20; Schoubye, "The Danish *Hovedvandsæg*," 2–3.

10. Bøje, *Balsambøsser*,10–12.

11. Bøje, *Balsambøsser*,10–11; Judith Banister, "English Gold and Silver Vinaigrettes of the 19th Century," in *Antique Dealer and Collector's Guide* (June, 1975), 125; Eileen Ellenbogen, *English Vinaigrettes* (Cambridge, England, 1956), 4–5; L. Middleton, "The Vinaigrette," in *Connoisseur*, 90 (1932), 308–315.

12. Berge, *Norskt bondesylv*, 539–540.

13. Bøje, *Balsambøsser*, 16,21.

14. Schoubye, "The Danish *Hovedvandsæg*," 1.

15. Bøje, *Balsambøsser*, 14.

16. Schoubye, "The Danish *Hovedvandsæg*," 3; Bøje, *Balsambøsser*, 14.

17. Schoubye, "The Danish *Hovedvandsæg*," 3; Shoubye, *Hovedvandsæg fra Vestslesvig*, 6–7. The three plays in which vinaigrettes are mentioned are *Den politiske kandestøber*, (1722), *Jacob von Tyboe* (1725), and *Barselstuen* (1731).

18. Frances E. Baldwin, *Sumptuary Legislation and Personal Regulation in England* (Baltimore, 1926), 10.

19. Troels Lund, *Dagligt liv i Norden i det 16de aarhundrede*, 4 (Copenhagen, 1903), 131–132.

20. Erna Lorenzen, *Hvem sagde nationaldragt?* (Højbjerg, Denmark, 1987), 9–10.

21. Thorvald Krohn-Hansen and Robert Kloster, *Bergens gullsmedkunst fra laugstiden* (Bergen, 1957), 12. The Kongsberg mines were opened in 1624, and from that time onward silver was available, although not always through regular channels, to the farming population. See also Berge, *Norskt bondesylv*, 43,55.

22. Andreas Holmsen, "General Survey and Historical Introduction," in "The Old Norwegian Peasant Community," in *Scandinavian Economic History Review*, 4:1 (1956), 18–24; Alan S. Milward and S. B. Saul, *The Development of the Economics of Continental Europe 1850–1914* (Cambridge, Massachusetts, 1977), 519.

23. Berge, *Norskt bondesylv*, 27, 45.

24. Berge, *Norskt bondesylv,* 60. When King Christian II brought miners from Saxony to work the Kongsberg silver mines, they also brought with them new stylistic impulses which were passed on to the populace and adopted into the vocabulary of the silversmiths, both rural and urban. Berge, *Norskt bondesylv,* 34,43.

25. Niels Jørgen Andreasen, "Hovedvandsæg og balsambøsser i træ, ben og horn," in *Købstadsmuseet 'Den Gamle By' Aarbog* (1986), 81–97.

26. Some of the vinaigrettes that were identified for this study were owned by collectors who had no knowledge of their previous ownership. Their identification with Norway was made on the basis of hallmarks and/or decoration or preserved stories relating to the objects. Sometimes it was not possible to associate a vinaigrette with a particular country of manufacture. However, all those that are listed in this study and that could be firmly connected to a family of Norwegian descent represent one of the major types. All known shapes are found to have been, if not produced in Norway, at least known and used there.

27. Some of the more unusually shaped containers might also be snuffboxes, particularly those in which it would be difficult to house a sponge.

28. Bøje, *Balsambøsser,* 17; Schoubye, "The Danish *Hovedvandsæg,*" 10.

29. August Schou, *Håndverk og industri i Oslo 1838–1938* (Oslo, 1938), 16; Krohn-Hansen, *Trondhjems gullsmedkunst 1550–1850* (Oslo, 1963), 14, 16; Berge, *Norskt bondesylv,* 21–22.

30. Berge, *Norskt bondesylv,* 55, 58.

31. Berge, *Norskt bondesylv,* 60.

32. Thor Kielland and Helge Gjessing, *Gammelt sølv i Stavanger amt* (Stavanger, 1918), 18.

33. They might not have completed their Master Piece, which would disqualify them from working as independent smiths, or they might not qualify for guild membership because of illegitimate birth or any number of other reasons. Madson, "The Social and Artistic Development of Hovedvandsæg," 89; Berge, *Norskt bondesylv,* 53,55.

34. The guilds were constantly on guard against silver produced by smiths outside the system. If a piece was not marked it could not be traced conclusively to a specific smith. In Norway it was also possible that the silver had been obtained by means which were not strictly legal, such as private, illicit mining. In such cases, it again would be inadvisable for the wares to be marked. See Berge, *Norskt bondesylv,* 55, for further discussion.

35. Bøje, *Danske gull- og sølvsmedemærker,* Svend Fritz and Finn Grandt-Nielsen, eds., 2 (Copenhagen, 1982), 9–11.

36. This is consistent with the smaller number of immigrants from Bergen proper, although the town was one of the most important ports from which immigrants sailed. See Ingrid Semmingsen, *Veien mot vest* (Oslo, 1942), 100–101, 103–104.

37. See Reidal Guddal, "Gullsmedlauget i Bergen," in *Bergens Historiske Forenings Skrifter,* no.45 (Bergen, 1939).

38. Berge, *Norskt bondesylv,* 43, 49–50.

39. Holmsen, "General Survey," 18.

40. Differing views have been held as to the ultimate origin of stylistic impulses in Norway, but there seems to be general agreement as to how and where such information spread

on reaching Norway. Eivind Englestad, "Hollandere, friser og jyder," in *Vestlandske Kunst-industrimuseum Årbok* (1946–1948), 29–57; Robert Kloster, "Stilspredning i laugstiden," in *Vestlandske Kunstindustrimuseum Årbok* (1949–1950), 111–116.

41. The descendent of the original owner stated that her grandmother came to the United States on the ship *Nymphen* around 1870. The woman's future husband traveled on that same ship. All of them eventually settled in Hawley, Minnesota, on a farm still owned by a descendent. The maker of the vinaigrette was either the grandfather or the great-grandfather of the current owner and the family owns other pieces of silverwork made by that smith.

42. Ann Regan, "The Danes," in June Drenning Holmquist, ed., *They Chose Minnesota* (St. Paul, 1981), 277–278.

43. Andres A. Svalestuen, "Nordisk emigrasjon. En komparativ oversikt," in *Emigrationen fra Norden indtil I verdenskrig* 1 (Copenhagen, 1971), 12, 14.

44. Semmingsen, *Norway to America: A History of the Migration,* trans. by Einar Haugen (Minneapolis, 1978), 99.

45. Kristian Hvidt, *Flugten til Amerika eller drivkræfter i masseudvandringen fra Danmark 1868–1914* (Århus, 1971), 24.

46. Svalestuen, "Nordisk emigrasjon," 12.

47. Leif H. Nielsen, "The Emigration from North Schleswig," in Steffen Elmer Jørgensen, Lars Scheving, and Niels Peter Stilling, eds., *From Scandinavia to America: Proceedings from a Conference held at Gamle Holtegaard* (Odense, 1987), 59.

48. See Schoubye, *Hovedvandsæg fra Østslesvig* and *Hovedvandsæg fra Vestslesvig.*

49. Semmingsen, *Veien mot vest,* 243.

50. Bøje, *Balsambøsser,*17. The most common peasant betrothal gifts in Denmark were, for the man, silver buttons and silver pipe fittings. The young woman would receive a vinaigrette and sometimes a silver-mounted psalm book. The items represented a large portion of the transportable wealth of the peasant and petit bourgeois classes.

51. Svalestuen, "Nordisk emigrasjon," 39. The number of exiting Danish males is even more dramatic for southern Jutland, where emigration was used, in part, to escape conscription into the Prussian army. Farmhands and agricultural workers, many if not most of whom were unmarried, made up 49 percent of those emigrating. Nielsen, "The Emigration from North Schleswig," 70, 73.

52. Hvidt, *Flugten til Amerika,* 122.

53. Schoubye, "The Danish Hovedvandsæg," 10.

54. Regan, "The Danes," 277, 287, note 4. The point is made that the immigrants may have been in a second or even third stage of emigration. They would have been listed as urban in origin, although that would not, strictly speaking, be accurate.

55. Schoubye, "The Danish Hovedsvansæg," 10. Apart from those from southern Jutland, vinaigrettes were always manufactured in towns.

56. Jorunn Fossberg of the Norsk Folkemuseum is currently working on a comprehensive study of silversmiths and silverwork in Norway. When this work is completed, we should have a far better understanding of the nature of rural silver production than is now the case. In her important study, *Draktsølv* (Oslo, 1991), they are not mentioned.

S. O. Lund, A Community Artist from Norway

by Carlin Hibbard

ORIGINAL ART and the presence of artists with professional training and background are commonplace in the Upper Midwest of the United States today. However, outside Milwaukee and Minneapolis such art and artists were a rarity in the area in the latter half of the nineteenth century. It was in a near artistic vacuum that Norwegian immigrant painter Sevald O. Lund (1852–1939) was able to find a place and make his contribution in Eau Claire, Wisconsin.

Eau Claire, situated in the Chippewa River Valley, was a growing city during much of Lund's painting career. It was three separate villages at the time of Lund's arrival from Norway in 1865 and was an impressive young city of over 14,000 by 1890. Located nearly one hundred miles east of Minneapolis, it was a city launched quickly by the burgeoning growth of the lumber industry.[1] However, the history of Eau Claire prior to about 1900 when Lund's career was at its height reveals little else in the way of artistic activity in the area. There were a few itinerant professional artists, as well as artists serving the community from larger urban settlements. These artists had a common agenda: to execute the altar paintings needed for newly founded churches, paint curtains for the local opera houses, or furnish portraits and interior decoration for the more successful members of the community. An example of an altar painting created by such an artist may still be seen in the Spring Brook Lutheran Church just west of Eau Claire. The painting, "Jesus, the Good Shepherd," was executed by Norwegian immigrant August Klagstad (1866–1949), an artist known to have supplied paintings for both small and large communities throughout the Midwest in the late nineteenth and early twentieth centuries.[2]

If one looks, on the other hand, for artists actually in residence in these developing towns, one finds few. Those who advertised in the local newspapers and city directories as being in the business of "fine art" were generally in photography. Photography as a pictorial medium was sweeping the country, and its practitioners apparently were trying to attain artistic respectability by using the vocabulary of the fine arts. A well-known Norwegian example of such a photographer was Andrew Dahl, who worked in the Madison, Wisconsin, area. Dahl left an extensive photographic record of Norwegian immigrants who had settled in south-central Wisconsin.[3]

Newspaper references to painters of the period were, almost without fail, references to painters of carriages, houses, and interior decoration. Those painters who aspired to the painting of "fine art" seem to have found it necessary to leave for the large cities in order to receive training and to find enough work to support themselves.

There were during this time in the Eau Claire region apparently only two "fine art" painters who remained in residence and were of note in their communities. One was the German immigrant Jacob Miller, who had studied in Munich at the Royal Academy before leaving for the United States.[4] Miller lived in Menomonie, Wisconsin, twenty-five miles to the west of Eau Claire, during the latter half of the nineteenth century. He appears to have been known in the Eau Claire area as well as in Menomonie primarily for his painting, but like other artists of his type on the frontier he supplemented this occupation with a variety of other activities.[5] Sevald Olsen Lund of Eau Claire, the other resident "fine art" painter of note in the area, appears to have received his artistic training from Miller while in residence in Menomonie as a young man in the early 1870s.[6]

Norwegian immigrant Sevald Lund holds the apparent distinction of being the first and only truly community artist for the young city of Eau Claire as it progressed from the chaos and the rough ways of its early development as a logging and milling center to a thriving, diversified community of agriculture, commerce, industry, and culture.

Lund's career reached its height in the 1890s at about the same time that his adopted town began to settle into respectability as a place of culture, with frequent lectures, dramatic performances, and concerts, an established library, literary associations, music teachers, and an opera house. During this period he is known to have had a studio in downtown Eau Claire and at least one patron who provided him with a large number of commissions.[7] He painted numerous large pieces that hung on the walls of churches, social organizations, and businesses. His biographical entry in *The History of the Chippewa Valley, Historical and Biographical Album,* published in 1892, describes him as an artist who had already gained "quite a reputation as a scenic painter."[8]

In 1897 Lund's artistry was extensively praised in print by W. K. Atkinson, editor of the local newspaper, the *Eau Claire Leader*. Atkinson declared Lund "an artist of rare ability," giving an expansive description of Lund, his personality, works, and studio. Further, he invited his readers to stop by the newspaper to see a work that Lund had apparently painted for its office. This was a still life of peaches arranged on pages of the *Eau Claire Leader,* a work he described as a "chef d'ouevre . . . so artistically real that one would imagine the sheets of the *Weekly* stood out in relief."[9]

The factors that combined to allow a poor boy from rural Norway to attain such a prestigious position in the Eau Claire community and just what this position actually meant for Lund as an immigrant are the focus of this study.

When young Lund came to the United States from Norway with his family in 1865, he was a shy, innocent country boy of thirteen. He spoke no English. His family came from farm stock in the Gudbrandsdal valley between Skjåk and Lom. Their ancestry indicates no orientation toward the arts, yet from somewhere within his own unique personal resources and experiences young Lund developed a love and talent for painting and drawing, for expressing himself on paper and canvas, and sharing his work with others.[10] This love, manifested in dedication, spanned his lifetime. It can be traced from his early boyhood immigrant days in the 1860s to his late years as a grandfather entertaining his grandchildren with his artistic talents in the late 1930s.

Although no other artistic activity in the Lund family has been documented, the family came from the heart of an area that had one of the most highly developed folk cultures in Norway. In the seventeenth century, women of the region brought pictorial tapestry weaving for coverlets to a level far above comparable efforts in any other part of Norway between the Middle Ages and modern times. As that tradition was declining in the early eighteenth century, men in the area turned to acanthus carving in wood under inspiration from central and southern Europe. They carried that art to a level not matched in quality and variety anywhere else in provincial Europe.[11] Painting and figure carving were also done by the acanthus artists, many of whom remained alive into the generation of Sevald's parents. No child growing up in the Skjåk-Lom area could have escaped being influenced by this activity. The Lom church in Lund's grandparents' time became a virtual showpiece of local folk art through the carving of Jacop Sæterdal.[12] The central Lund farm, in the complex which Lund apparently came from, had a cupboard with carving by Sæterdal and biblical painting by Peder Veggum, a folk painter from the area.[13] The motivation for artistic creation could well have existed in Lund before he left Norway. Some amateur attempts by him at acanthus carving are evidence that he had observed and remembered the art of his childhood environment.[14]

When Lund's parents, Ole Sevaldsen Lund (1828–1908) and Thoro Olsdatter Bruden (1829–1898), came to the United States in 1865, they were joining thousands of other Norwegians looking for land. Norway's population had increased very rapidly and available farm land had become scarce. Farming itself had become unprofitable because of crop failures and falling prices, and the only apparent alternative within Norway itself was a move to the cities.[15] The Lunds, like many Norwegians, apparently saw their move to the United States as one that would allow them to continue their accustomed way of life.

From the time of his arrival in the United States young Lund was different from most immigrant boys, a difference felt by his family. Even though he was the only son among five siblings, he did not stay with his parents to help them clear land for their farm at Meridean, a few miles south of Eau Claire near the Chippewa River in the township of Peru. Instead he stayed in Eau Claire with his mother's brother, Ole Bruden, for three years.[16] Bruden had in a short time developed a successful business as a hotel and saloon owner on the north side of Eau Claire and became something of a community leader.[17] As a result, his young nephew was exposed to the broader world of Eau Claire, an Eau Claire with the atmosphere of a wide-open lumbering community.[18]

This early stay in Eau Claire gave Lund the opportunity to attend school and to become fluent in English. Such would not have been the case if he had lived with his parents in the tightly knit Norwegian immigrant community at Meridean. Lund, however, did not forsake his Norwegian heritage; he became a member of the very first confirmation class in Eau Claire's Norwegian-American First Lutheran Church.[19]

The next indication that Lund was following a different path from most of his countrymen is found in the memoirs of his cousin, Iver Torgerson. Torgerson reported that young Lund, apparently after finishing school in Eau Claire, made a short-lived attempt at studying painting in St. Paul, Minnesota, but that "Sevald being young and lonesome among strangers stayed only a few weeks."[20]

Lund did not give up his desire to become a painter; as later reported in *The History of the Chippewa Valley*, he went to work under "a German painter" in nearby Menomonie.[21] Such a situation would certainly, at least on the surface, have been a more comfortable one for him. Menomonie, though on a smaller scale (only 3,500 in population by 1880), was a lumber town as well. It was a relatively short distance from Meridean and Lund's family. And there were in the area a number of other settlers from Gudbrandsdalen, among whom were the family of his future wife, Emilia Sandvig (1857–1918), who lived in the town of Elk Creek.

Lund appears to have worked in Menomonie under the "German painter," Jacob Miller, from approximately 1869 to 1874.[22] It was undoubtedly during Lund's time with Miller that the seeds for his future as community artist in Eau Claire were planted. Miller was a figure of high visibility in Menomonie. He was a man of recognized abilities who moved freely among the educated and wealthy. Not only was he a painter of talent, he was also a skilled musician, a teacher of music, a photographer, a mapmaker, and an organizer of a local band, as well as a carpenter, house painter, and decorator. He had served as a mapmaker and artist while in the army during the Civil War. As a young man in Bavaria he had received a scholarship at the Royal Academy of Fine Arts in Munich.[23] In his later life Miller is known to have received commissions for work in the Eau Claire area, commissions which included a large altar painting for the First Lutheran Church of Eau Claire. Affiliation with a painter of notable reputation and European academic credentials would certainly have been helpful to Lund in gaining acceptance as an artist in Eau Claire, as well as in acquiring commissions. Although closely tied to his Norwegian background, family, and community, Lund seems to have prepared himself well to mix and move in the greater Eau Claire community.

Unfortunately, no specific records of Lund's connection to Miller have been discovered. The last year of Lund's stay in Menomonie can be documented, however, by his own clearly dated financial account book.[24] Its first year of record, 1874, was Lund's last in Menomonie. Although Lund made detailed recordings of his expenses during that year, he made no direct comments about his occupation. There are, however, hints. One of the most important of these is his purchase of the large and ambitious volume *Picturesque America,* a book full of beautifully engraved plates glorifying American landscape.[25] The significance of this purchase becomes evident when one realizes that Lund paid the huge sum of twenty-four dollars for this book at a time when he paid just three dollars for a pair of shoes and thirty-five cents for suspenders. In later years Lund used the book as a source for some of his paintings. Another indication of Lund's involvement with art at this time is the sketches in his account book, sketches that show, for example, his familiarity with exercises from a penmanship course offered by the Northwestern Business College and Institute of Penmanship in Madison.[26] At this time Lund also purchased "gentlemen's" clothes, pointing again to his probable participation in Miller's world. Lund's grandchildren report that dressing well remained important to Lund throughout his life.[27]

It may have started with great promise but Lund's stay in Menomonie seems to have ended in stress and personal difficulty. The previously mentioned biographical sketch describes Lund as returning to live with his parents after "the condition of his health obliged him" to leave Menomonie.[28] One of Lund's grandsons states that Lund had been painting in the attic of the man in Menomonie for "only a pittance."[29] Miller is described in his obituary as being a man of "genius," yet at the same time "erratic, inconsistent, and impractical."[30] Miller could not have been an easy man to work for. Lund returned to his parents and the Norwegian community where he was apparently able to find the type of support and rest that he needed. This could not have been physical, however, because almost immediately he became involved in the heavy labor of farming.[31] He remained with his family, surrounded by the comfort and succor of his Norwegian heritage, for nearly ten years. His

Carlin Hibbard

account book indicates that during this time he worked extremely hard, first helping his parents on their farm and then clearing, building, and developing his own farm, as he and his wife Emilia, whom he married in 1879, began a family.

Ill. 1. Emilia Sandvig Lund. Pencil sketch. 1882. 4⅛ x 2⅝ inches. *Courtesy of Virginia Lund Fyksen*

Although Lund had not remained with his parents originally as might have been expected, he was able to contribute to their well-being at this time, not only through his labor but also through his knowledge of the English language. He took his parents' goods to market and assisted in their business transactions.[32]

Throughout Lund's period in Meridean there is no indication that he did any painting that might be construed as artwork. His account book shows the buying of no art supplies. Only a very small pencil drawing that reveals his developed skills remains from this time. It is a miniature portrait of his wife proficiently rendered on a small scrap of paper that had at one time been a bill (Ill. 1). Although there is no other indication of artistic activity by Lund during this time, his account book reveals that he was developing skills often

Ill. 2. Lumber camp scene.
Oil. 1896. 41 x 77 inches.
*Courtesy of State Historical
Society of Wisconsin*

employed by artists to supplement their income, namely the more practical skills of house and carriage painting, as well as plastering and paperhanging.

As much as Lund appears to have found comfort and succor with his family and the immigrant community, he found farming, as he stated, "very hard work," and not for him.[33] He left farming and Meridean behind in about 1884 and returned to Eau Claire. There, as Iver Torgerson reported, he "started to do oil painting for wealthy men and worked for jobbers of the trade."[34] Evidently his training, his connections to Jacob Miller, and his own talent gave him entry into art and a career in painting as a community artist.

There are no known extant paintings by Lund dated in the 1880s. However, Torgerson's comments and the 1892 biographical sketch of Lund in *The History of the Chippewa Valley* indicate that he was, indeed, establishing himself as an artist. Some of his extant undated works may be from this period. The biographical sketch, for example, specifically mentions a "camp scene" (5' x 9') on the Flambeau River (Ill. 2) as having hung "on exhibition . . . for a number of years . . . in one of the business houses of Eau Claire."[35]

Lund had come to Eau Claire thirty years before, a frightened boy of thirteen, so shocked by the unbridled raucous revelry of the local Fourth of July celebration that he is said to have wished that his family would turn around and go back home to Norway.[36] Obviously he had made great strides from those young immigrant days to achieve his position as community painter in Eau Claire, the largest city in northwestern Wisconsin in the 1890s. He apparently had little, if any, competition for this position.

He had a talent for creating images. He could do what others wished they could do, he could create art for the pleasure and satisfaction of those around

Ill. 3. Norwegian farm in
winter. Watercolor. 1895.
10½ x 15 inches.

him. There were few, if any, persons of such talent outside the larger cities of
the Upper Midwest in Lund's time. However, photography had become readily available in Eau Claire, as elsewhere, for the reproduction of local scenes
and personages. The colored print, with the development of the chromolitho-
graphic process in the first half of the nineteenth century, had also by the last
half of the century become quite popular, available, and inexpensive for decorating parlor walls.[37] Locally available original art or paintings, however,
remained another matter. Persons of means who traveled to metropolitan
centers in the United States and Europe could afford to obtain artworks from
artists of academic training and national or international repute. For most
residents of Eau Claire, however, original art would have been scarce and
great art unknown.

Lund filled a void because of his ability to reproduce the world around
him. He was apparently quite willing to paint almost anything that was asked
for. His work covered a wide range, from Norwegian farm scenes (Ill. 3) to
midwestern river scenes, nursery rhyme depictions, Indians and cowboys on
horseback, portraits, mural-sized logging camp scenes (Ill. 2), western mountain landscapes, still lifes (Ill. 4), and genre paintings (Ill. 5).[38] The fact that
he did not necessarily follow all the canons of academic art or had not completely digested all its dictates and rules did not bother his Eau Claire patrons.
They found his work pleasing, as was his personality and demeanor. He
enjoyed painting for those around him. He painted what they asked for,
enjoyed, and appreciated; and he gave many paintings away.[39]

Atkinson in his *Eau Claire Leader* article of 1897 gave an extensive account
of Lund's artistic output at that period, and in many cases named the particu-

Carlin Hibbard

lar local residents for whom Lund had painted or was painting. His article was headlined: "An Eau Claire Artist, One who is coming to the front everyday / His works known far and wide / Some rare oil paintings / well worthy of a visit." Atkinson probably set the tone for Lund's place in the life of the city when he addressed him as "friend Lund" and called him "our cheerful and talented townsman." He noted that not only was Lund well known in Eau Claire, but he was also known in Chippewa Falls and Menomonie, as well as in other parts of Wisconsin. Atkinson counted among Lund's patrons, first and most importantly, Kim Rosholt, whom he dubbed "real estate King" of Eau Claire. Rosholt appears to have provided Lund with a centrally located studio in downtown Eau Claire during the 1890s together with commissions for "no fewer than one-hundred-fifty paintings." Atkinson quoted another community leader, businessman and lumber baron H. C. Putnam, as "speaking in high terms of a particular forest scene of the woods in winter." Further indication given by Atkinson of Lund's status was reference to a large four-by-seven-foot winter "Pioneer Home" scene painted for Senator George B. Burroughs in Madison (Ill. 6).

Atkinson described many of the paintings found in Lund's studio: paintings ranging from a portrait of an Arctic explorer (probably the Norwegian Roald Amundsen although named by Atkinson as Hanson) to landscape scenes, fruits and flowers, Indians and buffalo, trout and dogs, and a portrait of Ole Bull, "as fine as any we have ever seen" (Ill. 7).[40] Ole Bull and Roald Amundsen were among the Norwegian national heroes who enjoyed general popularity in immigrant painting.[41] Obviously Lund was well respected and

Ill. 4. (opposite top) Still life, trout and creel. Watercolor. Date unknown. 13½ x 20 inches. *Courtesy of Esther Micheels Lyders*

Ill. 5. (opposite bottom) Son reading to mother doing laundry. Oil. Date unknown. 4 x 6 inches. *Courtesy of Virginia Lund Fyksen*

Ill. 6. (above) Pioneer farm scene. Oil. 1894. 5 x 9 feet. *Courtesy of University of Wisconsin-Eau Claire*

known for his work in the Eau Claire area. Atkinson revealed Lund's enjoyment in being a part of the greater Eau Claire community when he concluded his article by stating that "Mr. Lund is always pleased to have visitors call on him in his studio."

An important point made by Atkinson was that, while Lund was well recognized and highly respected, he was not able to gain from his painting the income needed to support himself and his family. Lund's primary trades were house-painting, paperhanging, and decorating, a fact which Atkinson bemoaned, stating that "nature intended him for something higher" and "on hundreds of occasions during the last ten years he has given ample evidence of being an artist of rare ability."[42]

Atkinson's article alludes indirectly to the importance of Lund's Norwegian connections in discussing the patronage that he enjoyed from Kim Rosholt. Norwegian-American patronage is further indicated in Atkinson's mention of "a magnificent oil painting seven and a half feet in height representing the Good Shepherd" (Ill. 8). This painting was created by Lund for

Carlin Hibbard

the altar of the Rock Creek Lutheran Church, a Norwegian-American congregation not far from Meridean.[43] He also executed the altarpiece for the Norwegian-American Cranberry Creek Lutheran Church at Meridean. This painting, lost in a church fire in 1940, was described in Torgerson's memoirs as very similar, if not identical, to the painting done by Jacob Miller for the altar of the First Lutheran Church in Eau Claire.[44]

Lund was fortunate in being part of a strong Norwegian-American community in Eau Claire. In the 1890s Norwegian-American Waldemar Ager took over as editor of the Norwegian publication *Reform* in Eau Claire and began his career as a distinguished author and activist for the temperance movement and the preservation of the Norwegian heritage. Ager appeared in *Who's Who in America* and was twice decorated by the king of Norway for his achievements.[45] Lund's patron, Norwegian immigrant Kim Rosholt, was an extremely successful entrepreneur, widely involved at various stages in major real estate, farming, industry, and banking concerns. He also founded Northwestern Steel and Iron which later became National Presto Industries.[46]

Ill. 8. Christ, the Good Shepherd (altar painting). **Oil. 1890s. C. 8 x 5 feet.** *Courtesy of Rock Creek Lutheran Church*

Ill. 9. Norway, fishing huts
and boats. Watercolor.
1907. 13¼ x 16 inches.
*Courtesy of Margaret Lund
Girnau*

After 1901 there are no large dated oils by Lund, nor does there appear to be further mention in the local press of his works or accomplishments. He was, by this time, nearly fifty years old, and his public painting career seems to have slowed greatly, whether because of his age, the changing times, or the exigencies of family life. Judging from dated works, it was, however, shortly after the turn of the century that Lund did the majority of his paintings of Norwegian subjects (Ill. 3). These paintings were generally executed in watercolor (Ill. 9), although there are a number of Norwegian paintings that he completed in oil as well.

Lund's paintings of Norwegian subjects were generally done for friends and relatives. As they are widespread among Lund's many descendants, they may well have served for many as a sort of bridge to the past—a bridge to relatives and homeland left behind. Whether Lund was working from memory or from photographs, his portrayals of Norwegian farms reveal a high degree of ethnographic accuracy (Ill. 3). In addition to farms, he also painted Norwegian mountain scenes, harbors, and fjords (Ill. 9). He even experimented with rendering the light of the midnight sun.

After Lund had achieved recognition and status essentially as an American in the larger Eau Claire community, and had passed the mid-century point of his own life, he seems to have reestablished closer ties with the Norwegian immigrant community. This is revealed not only in his painting of Norwegian subjects, but also through his personal participation in immigrant organizations such as the Sons of Norway and Gudbrandsdalslaget, an organization made up of immigrants from his home valley in Norway.

Carlin Hibbard

Ill. 10. Sevald O. Lund. Photograph. Date unknown.

Although Lund no longer appeared to be working on a large scale as an artist for the greater Eau Claire community after the turn of the century, he continued to be recognized as an artist in the Norwegian community, both within the Eau Claire area and to a degree beyond it. On the occasion of Lund's eighty-fourth birthday in 1934 the Norwegian-language newspaper *Decorah-Posten* carried a commemorative article which celebrated him as the greatest Norwegian-American artist from Gudbrandsdalen and lauded him for his participation in, and support of, Norwegian-American organizations and preservation activities (Ill. 10). A specific indication of his devotion to the immigrant community was the *Posten*'s report of his donation of paintings for a raffle to raise money for the Sons of Norway. The same article concluded with a request that Lund write the story of his early life.[47] Unfortunately, this had not been done before he died in 1939.

Through much of his later life Lund continued to sell paintings. They were, however, generally relatively small pieces that he is said to have sold for modest prices (Ill. 11). After about 1900, when he apparently no longer had the

Ill. 11. (top) "Old
Ironsides." Oil. 1925. 15 x
20 inches. *Courtesy of
Thomas and Karen Moreley*

Ill. 12. (bottom) Birches and
stream. Watercolor. 1912.
13¾ x 19¾ inches. *Courtesy
of Virginia Lund Fyksen*

　　　　　　　　Carlin Hibbard

downtown studio, he worked out of his home and later at his son Edward's home where he moved in 1922.[48] During these later years, not only did he paint Norwegian homeland subjects, he also executed large numbers of local landscapes and pastoral pieces. There are still extant numbers of his soft watercolors of the rivers and bottomlands around Eau Claire (Ill. 12). Lund seemed during this period also to have enjoyed painting meadow scenes with sheep (Ill. 13), as well as riverbank scenes with birches.

Lund's community circle became smaller as he advanced further in age. He turned more to painting for his personal pleasure and for that of his immediate family (Ill. 14). After trips to the states of Washington and Texas he painted a number of western mountain scenes and landscapes. He had revealed an interest in the West earlier in his career when he painted scenes of covered wagons crossing the plains (Ill. 15), as well as cowboys and Indians in mountain settings. Many of those paintings were reminiscent of the works of the then popular Western artists Frederic Remington and Charles M. Russell. He seems to have felt a romantic attraction to America that equaled any nostalgic attachment he had to Norway. In this later part of his life he painted scenes of particular mountains and areas which he had himself visited in his western travels. He is remembered in these years by his grandchildren for his sketches of animals and birds (sketches which they often requested), and for his wooden toys and other small carvings.

Lund apparently had developed wood carving as a hobby by this period of his life, making, in addition to toys, numerous letter openers and other decorative utensils that he often gave away as gifts. In his turn to carving and the

Ill. 14. (top) Bridge in
winter. Watercolor. 1902. 5
x 9 inches. *Courtesy of
Margaret Lund Girnau*

Ill. 15. (bottom) Western
landscape with covered
wagon. Oil. 1892. 33½ x 47
inches. *Courtesy of
Chippewa Valley Museum*

Carlin Hibbard

use of acanthus designs, one finds Lund reverting to the arts that were part of his Norwegian background.

Lund painted for his own enjoyment, but also with an eye toward the desires and interests of those around him. His works varied according to their use and according to their prospective owners, be they businessmen, Norwegian relatives, or grandchildren.[49] It is, therefore, not surprising that Lund is difficult to describe stylistically. His repetition of motifs and the flat schematic manner in which he painted in some of his large early works, Ill. 2 for example, gave them something of the primitive flavor of work by artists who had developed their own personal techniques and ways of solving pictorial problems. However, Lund can not be classified as a truly naive painter because he, at the same time, showed an acquaintance with such academic techniques as modeling (Ills. 5, 8), perspective (Ills. 11, 12), balance in composition (Ills. 2, 3), coordinated color, and the ability to portray atmospheric light effects (Ill. 9). Furthermore, if one were to look only at his Norwegian farm paintings one would probably classify him as a folk artist nostalgically depicting scenes from his past (Ill. 3). These pieces, painted primarily for friends and relatives, were executed with the sort of straightforward simplicity and sincerity that is typical of folk art while lacking its flat and linear quality.

The only direct comment extant from Lund himself on painting relates to an interest in realism. One of his nieces recalls his instructing another young niece, who was interested in drawing and painting, that she must go outside and actually look, that she should not just paint what was in her mind.[50] The care with which Lund himself observed both the details and the broader aspects of nature can be seen in his still lifes on the one hand (Ill. 4) and in his paintings of the local marshlands on the other (Ill. 12). He must also have been a close observer of animals. His sheep, cattle, and horses are almost always in positions natural to them even when shown from different perspectives (Ills. 2, 3, 6, 13).

In spite of Lund's advice to his niece, he did not always paint directly from nature, although this appears generally to have been his point of departure. He did not see Norway again after emigrating at age thirteen in 1865, and yet he painted Norwegian subjects throughout his life. Most of these works too are marked by calm simplicity and essential realism. They appear to be constructed of carefully observed details that he has retained in a memory bank going back to his childhood in Norway. He did several paintings of farmyard scenes with very similar buildings, but seen from different points of view as if he knew them from all sides (Ill. 3). The grandeur of the landscape is not overblown nor are the peasants clad in their Sunday best as in the romantic Norwegian paintings that one would have expected to be his models.

To what extent photographs might have been used as models for the Norwegian paintings has not been determined, but it is not likely that many would have been available to Lund in the 1890s, when some of these paintings were produced. Their simple and well-composed character also speaks against a slavish use of photographs as models. Lund had, on the other hand, no objection to copying. The portrait of Ole Bull (Ill. 7), for example, is based quite directly on a popular print, of which Vesterheim, the Norwegian-American Museum, in Decorah, Iowa, has an example. Much of the realism in Lund's work, however, appears to be the product of exceptional visual memory and a sober disposition.

Romantic elements are not totally lacking in Lund's painting, but these are less prevalent and extreme than in the work, for example, of the slightly older contemporary Norwegian-American painter, John Olson Hammerstad (1842–1925), who was trained in Norway by the late representative of Düsseldorf romanticism C. F. Eckersberg, and was active in Chicago from about 1870 to his death.[51] The quiet composure in much of Lund's work puts him nearer the almost contemporary Herbjørn Gausta (1854–1924), who worked most of his life in nearby Minneapolis but appears to have had no contact with Lund.[52] The quiet realism of Gausta's work is easily explained by his training. In the 1870s he joined such ultimately famous Norwegian artists as Erik Werenskiold (1855–1935), Theodor Kittelsen (1857–1914), and Eilif Peterssen (1852–1928) at the Art Academy in Munich, where they came under the influence of a budding German realism.[53] Lund was in Menomonie working with Jacob Miller, also a product of the Munich Academy, at precisely the same time Gausta was in Munich itself, but Miller had left the Academy there in 1853, before the new realistic directions had developed. Any stylistic relationship between Lund and Gausta must be merely the result of general tendencies of the time and the fact that Lund was by nature more attuned to the direction art was going than to where it had been.

Certain stylistic parallels can be drawn between Lund and Gausta, but their communities were entirely different. Gausta had full academic credentials as a painter and belonged, largely through altar paintings commissioned by mail, to Norwegian Americans everywhere. A small booklet with reproductions of his work was put out by Augsburg Publishing House, and a number of his paintings appeared as colorplates in the nationally distributed *Jul i Vesterheimen.*

With few exceptions, Lund's community was Eau Claire and its environs. From a social vantage point his standing is nearer to that of early American community painters like Edward Hicks (1780–1849) of rural Bucks county, Pennsylvania. Hicks's career was very much that of a local painter, although his work has since achieved national recognition. He painted subjects of his own choice, from the world around him, as well as subjects that were requested of him. His painting procedures were a mixture of the primitive artist's personally achieved methods and knowledge he had gained in the handling of pictorial space and depiction of figures from his work as a sign painter. Like

Lund he cannot really be classified as a pure primitive or as an academic painter. Additionally, Hicks, as was the case with Lund, pursued other work. He began as a coachmaker; he painted signs and did other decorative painting; he also became a traveling Quaker minister known for his preaching and his published sermons.[54] His painting was very important to him, yet it was not the whole focus of his life.

A major difference between Lund and Hicks, however, is that while Lund painted primarily what he experienced visually in nature or those natural scenes that appealed to his neighbors, Hicks was involved with symbolism and religious subjects. Hicks's many versions of the "Peaceable Kingdom" each had references to religious situations and disputes in his own time. Hicks belonged to a romantic period and a community with deep spiritual concerns, while Lund was more realistically inclined and belonged to a community that was pragmatic and ultimately materialistic. What they have in common is being artists of the people, satisfied with serving their immediate community.

Lund remains an artist of his community, with large numbers of his paintings still gracing the walls of many homes in Eau Claire. His paintings are also found in the collections of the Chippewa Valley Museum in Eau Claire, the University of Wisconsin at Eau Claire, and the State Historical Society of Wisconsin. They are spread as well throughout the Chippewa River basin and have now through the mobility of his original patrons and their descendants found homes as far afield as Texas and California.

As a gifted and devoted artist, content to serve the artistic needs of an immediate community, Lund probably represents a category of immigrant artists who have not yet surfaced because of the limited sphere in which they worked. Belonging to a period when exposure to professional art of some kind, at least through publications or travel, was relatively possible even in small rural communities, the work of these artists did not acquire the individual distinctiveness of the so-called limners in the East during the eighteenth and early nineteenth centuries. Midwestern provincial painters have, therefore, not been sought out like their earlier counterparts in the East by artists and collectors seeking work that is grass-roots American and through which the fine arts might be revitalized and given national character.

Community artists of immigrant origin in the Midwest acquired their position not necessarily because of special training but because they had the drive to create original images in a society where there was still some demand for them. The frontier community in general and the immigrant community in particular had specific needs for pictorial material in their churches, public buildings, and homes that outside suppliers could not completely satisfy. This, for a short time in the history of the Midwest, gave a place to artists of and for the community. They now shed light on a far too neglected subject, the grass-roots culture of the area.

1. *History of Northern Wisconsin* (Chicago, 1881), 302–306.

2. Marion J. Nelson, ed., *Norway in America* (Decorah, Iowa, 1989), 78–79.

3. David Mandel, "The Photographs of Andreas Lars Dahl," in Nelson, *Norway in America*, 85–108.

4. Obituary of Jacob Miller, clipping from *Dunn County News,* 1900, Wisconsin-Stout Area Research Center, Menomonie, Wisconsin.

5. George Forrester, ed., *History of the Chippewa Valley, Historical and Biographical Album* (Chicago, 1891–1892), 602.

6. Sevald O. Lund, account book, 1874–1883. Among the only other possible artists in the area was Thomas Ordeman, who came to Menomonie trained in the painting of frescoes in 1871, but apparently went into the photography business without ever entering into any fine art painting. He died in 1881. *History of Northern Wisconsin,* 286. For a time there was another artist, William McEntee, in Eau Claire. He was recognized for his execution of portraits, advertised himself particularly as a crayon portraitist, and was gone from Eau Claire by 1884. *History of Northern Wisconsin,* 327; *Eau Claire City Directory* (1880–1884).

7. *Eau Claire Leader,* February 25, 1897.

8. *History of the Chippewa Valley,* 695.

9. *Eau Claire Leader,* February 25, 1897.

10. Asbjørn Dagsgard, letter to the author (Lom, Norway, May, 1989).

11. The most complete presentations of early weaving and woodcarving in Gudbrandsdalen are found respectively in Thor Kielland, *Norsk billedvev,* 2 vols. (Oslo, 1953–1955), and Roar Hauglid, *Akantus,* 3 vols. (Oslo, 1950).

12. The Lom Church's pulpit and altar screen were carved by Sæterdal in 1793. Hauglid, *Akantus,* 3:304.

13. This cupboard was presented to the Norwegian-American Museum, now Vesterheim, Decorah, Iowa, by the Anders Sandvig Samlinger about 1927. See also Hauglid, *Akantus,* 3:302.

14. A few small pieces of Lund's wood carving can be found today in the collections of his direct descendants.

15. Theodore C. Blegen, *Norwegian Migration to America,* 2 (Northfield, Minnesota, 1940), 464–465. Ingrid Semmingsen, *Norway to America* (Minneapolis, 1978), 103.

16. Forrester, *History of the Chippewa Valley,* 695.

17. "Names of prominent people in Eau Claire," newspaper clipping, 1910, Chippewa Valley Museum, Eau Claire.

18. Study of early Eau Claire newspapers and city fire maps shows a great number of local saloons and an ongoing presence of local brothels as well. See also Orrie Walz's unpublished manuscript, "A Case Study in Community Organizations and Social Deviance: Research Notes from the Eau Claire *Weekly Free Press,* Sept. 1858–Jan. 1881" (Eau Claire, 1986).

19. William F. Bailey, ed. *History of Eau Claire County* (Chicago, 1914), 522. John Ovren, *Decorah-Posten,* copy of clipping belonging to Charlotte Dahl, c. 1936.

20. Iver Torgerson, unpublished family history.

Carlin Hibbard

21 Forrester, *History of the Chippewa Valley,* 695.

22. Forrester, *History of the Chippewa Valley,* 695. Lund, account book, 1874–1883. The Chippewa Valley Museum has a copy of the account book.

23. Forrester, *History of the Chippewa Valley,* 601. *Dunn County News,* June 1, 1872. Obituary of Jacob Miller, 1900. Information also obtained from Heritage Center exhibit materials, Menomonie, Wisconsin.

24. Lund, account book.

25. William Jennings Bryan, *Picturesque America* (Appleton, Wisconsin, 1872).

26. Lund, account book.

27. Family interviews and correspondence, spring and summer, 1989.

28. Forrester, *History of the Chippewa Valley,* 695.

29. Correspondence with Thomas Lund, spring and summer, 1989.

30. Obituary of Jacob Miller, 1900.

31. Lund, account book.

32. Lund, account book.

33. Lund, account book.

34. Torgerson, family history.

35. Forrester, *History of the Chippewa Valley,* 695. Paintings closely resembling such a description are owned and have been exhibited by the State Historical Society of Wisconsin and the Elks Club of Chippewa Falls, Wisconsin.

36. Family interviews and correspondence, spring and summer, 1989.

37. David F. Burg, *Chicago's White City of 1893* (Lexington, Kentucky, 1976). With the advent of chromolithography Currier and Ives flourished.

38. The author has cataloged over one hundred forty paintings and drawings by Sevald O. Lund.

39. One of Lund's grandchildren, Margaret Girnau, reports that for her seventeenth birthday Lund painted, on her request, a blue pastel fantasy landscape to match the blue decor she wished for her future living room. Family interviews and correspondence, spring and summer, 1989.

40. *Eau Claire Leader,* February 25, 1897.

41. Nelson, *Norway in America,* 76.

42. *Eau Claire Leader,* February 25, 1897.

43. This altar piece is of exactly the same composition as one painted by August Klagstad for the nearby Spring Brook Church. It is, however, very different in style.

44. Torgerson, family history.

45. Einar Haugen, *Immigrant Idealist: A Literary Biography of Waldemar Ager, Norwegian American* (Northfield, Minnesota, 1989), 72, 115, 152.

46. Lois Barland, *The River Flows On* (Stevens Point, Wisconsin, 1965), 449; Chippewa Valley Museum newspaper file, 1897–1914.

47. Ovren, *Decorah-Posten.*

48. Family interviews and correspondence, spring and summer, 1989.

49. Lund painted the hill on a niece's parents' farm as a gift on the occasion of their fifti-eth wedding anniversary. Family interviews and correspondence, spring and summer, 1989.

50. Correspondence with Charlotte Dahl, spring and summer, 1989.

51. Nelson, *Norway in America,* 54–56, 63.

52. Nelson, "Herbjørn Gausta: Norwegian American Painter," in *Americana Norvegica,* 3 (Oslo, 1971), 105–128.

53. Kirk Varnedoe, *Northern Light: Realism and Symbolism in Scandinavian Painting* (New Haven, Connecticut, 1988), 204–252. *Dreams of a Summer Night: Scandinavian Painting at the Turn of the Century* (London, 1986), 162.

54. Jean Lipman and Tom Armstrong, eds., *American Painters of Three Centuries* (New York, 1980), 88–95.

Carlin Hibbard

Altars in the Norwegian-American Church: An Opportunity for Folk Expression

by Kristin M. Anderson

Iɴ 1917, just prior to the merger of the Norwegian Synod, the United Church, and the Hauge Synod, Augsburg Publishing House issued a book titled *Church Designs.* The author was Oluf Glasøe, then home missions superintendent for the United Church. Glasøe's book attempted to address the need for suitable worship space for Norwegian-American congregations. *Church Designs* included plans for a number of church buildings, as well as ideas and instructions about appropriate furnishings. Glasøe addressed the appearance of the altar in this way: "The first piece of furniture needed [in the building] is an altar. In chapels and small churches a temporary altar may be made by anyone having a square, a saw, a hammer, and a few nails. . . . While the altar is the chief piece of furniture in a Lutheran church and hence subject to greater effort at ornamentation than anything else, it must not, in an otherwise plain church, be overloaded with ornaments. Balance and proportion must never be lost sight of.

"Quite generally our people like to have an oil painting in the central niche of the altar. In most cases such painting represents an event in the life of Christ. This way of beautifying the altar and sanctuary is commendable. But such painting must be a work of art, otherwise it will do more harm than good. Frequently one may see terrible travesties on art set up in this most holy place, causing pain and distraction even in the most devout of worshippers. It would be far better to place a plain cross (this may be cut out of gilt paper) where the painting should be until such time when someone in the congregation will donate a real work of art to adorn the altar of the Lord."[1]

Firmly embedded in Glasøe's instructions about the altar is an admonition about the nature of good art. The need for an altar frame was established in the inventory of church furnishings, but it is clear that not every frame met the standards of balance and proportion. Further, since the subjects of the paintings displayed in these frames were essentially fixed, as Glasøe suggests, the range of deviation from the high standard of art would not be iconographical. It would rather be in style or, more specifically, in quality as Glasøe conceived it.

It is quite likely that Glasøe's definition of art excluded some of the objects made by Norwegian-American artists at work in the ethnic community. What one might now identify as the creative expression of woodcarvers coming out of the folk art traditions of Norway, or the paintings made by self-taught artists who worked in the fine arts media without the benefit of fine arts training, Glasøe would probably have dismissed as "painful" and "distracting." Yet the general acceptance of such "folk" artists locally as producers of altar frames and altar paintings indicates that there was more than one opinion on questions of quality, value, and propriety even in the early period. In recent years it has turned out to be the productions of the "folk" rather than of the professionals that have brought Norwegian-American church art to the attention of the larger art world in America.

The hundreds of surviving altar paintings and altar frames, and the evidence of hundreds of others no longer extant, indicate the tremendous demand made by Norwegian-American Lutheran congregations for appropriate furniture and paintings. These demands were filled almost exclusively by Norwegian-American artists. This study will address how altars used in the Norwegian-American churches came into being, focusing on those provided by "folk" or "people's" artists. A small group of these artists will stand for countless others whose identities are not yet adequately established.

The Occasion for Creation

The rapid and widespread building of churches by the Norwegians in America during the last half of the nineteenth and the early twentieth centuries created the opportunity and the necessity for large-scale production of chancel furnishings and altar paintings. As an example of the scale of activity in this area, O. M. Norlie's 1915 survey of churches, recorded in *Norsk lutherske menigheter i Amerika 1843–1916,* shows that in Minneapolis 38 congregations had erected at least 51 buildings. In Winneshiek county, a rural northeastern Iowa county with heavy Norwegian settlement, 28 congregations had constructed at least 45 churches.[2]

While the architectural flurry was partly due to the high concentration of immigration from Norway around the turn of the century, other factors added to the frenetic situation. First, the relatively primitive state of transportation meant that churches had to be rather closely spaced for congregations to thrive. Those with members spread too far afield had problems with participation.[3] A second factor was that with the rapid growth of individual congregations, especially in the towns and cities, new buildings were needed

Kristin M. Anderson

to replace outgrown structures or additional buildings were needed to house "daughter" congregations. A third was the tendency toward theological dissidence among Norwegian Americans. Because of various alignments in the immigrant church, some communities had more congregations and structures for worship than might otherwise have been necessary. Finally, the particular attraction of fire and wind to turn-of-the-century church buildings—and of lightning to church steeples—increased the numbers of churches constructed and decorated.

Regardless of the plan or design of a church, the liturgical and visual focus of the interior of the church building is the altar area. This site is the scene of significant action, it is the place where the leader of the worship stands to preside, and it is the location the worshipers face upon their entrance to the sanctuary and during the service. Liturgical practice dictated that the presider face the congregation at some points in the service and the altar at other points. Since the altar table was nearly always adorned with a large altarpiece and pushed close to or against the chancel wall, this meant that at many points in the service all of the participants faced the altar.[4] Further, the traditional Lutheran understanding of the dominance of word and sacrament helped to identify the physical elements that were most important—the font, the pulpit, and the altar itself.

Given the visual and spiritual focus on this part of the church, it is not surprising that the chancel of the church received the greatest artistic attention in the definition of space, in the furniture, and in the decoration. In immigrant buildings, the altar area was often framed within a series of arches: enclosed by an apse to the rear, by an altar ring to the front, and under an arch dividing the chancel from the nave. The particular configuration of the altars themselves served to focus the attention of the worshiper—not only because of their setting, function, and placement, but because of the construction and decoration of the pieces themselves. As Glasøe indicated in *Church Designs,* there was generally a large retable attached to the altar; this contained an image—generally a painting or a sculpture—and frequently an elaborate frame. The use of elaborate framing elements incorporating one or more paintings or statues constituted the typical pattern of altar decoration throughout Norway (Ill. 1). The use of these standard forms was relatively constant in the Norwegian-American churches. Even disagreements over worship practice did not seem to make themselves visible in the spaces or their decoration.[5] The deep roots of these in Norwegian tradition, a tradition which Glasøe as late as 1916 asks parishioners to remember, surely account for this.[6]

The Paintings and Statues

The two principal ways to decorate the niche in the altar frame were with statues or with paintings. In virtually all cases, the principal subject of the altar image was Christ. The scenes or images favored by the artists and congregations were those with theological significance and visual interest, preferably

Ill. 1. Interior of Fiskum
church, Eiker *prestegjeld*,
from *Norges kirker.
Buskerud,* 2: 381.

combined in a single image. Scenes from the passion of Christ were particularly popular, as were scenes in which Jesus is shown with one or two other figures. Using a limited number of figures allowed for a minimum of difficulty in reading or understanding the image, no matter where one was seated in the nave. The visual orientation and arrangement of the composition was nearly always vertical, to make the most effective use of the available space in the niche, which was almost always taller than it was wide. The range of subjects chosen was remarkably uniform throughout the immigrant community. As the subjects displayed uniformity, so did the theological view of Jesus, who was shown as a calm and serene figure. The stylistic range of the images was also consistent, emerging from a common view of Jesus depicted in the conservative religious art of the nineteenth century.

It is rare to find examples of altar art that were strictly original works in the modern sense. Generally the statues and paintings were copies of the established religious art repertoire of the late nineteenth century. The statues were usually copies of a limited number of models, the most famous of which was Bertel Thorvaldsen's statue of Christ from the Church of Our Lady in Copenhagen. The paintings were made from a greater number of models, but were generally of the same style. Most of these models were nineteenth-century German, or occasionally Scandinavian, works of artists like the Germans Heinrich Hofmann (*Jesus in Gethsemane*), Bernard Plockhorst (*The Good Shepherd,* Ill. 2), and Hans Thoma (*Jesus and Mary at the Tomb,* Ill. 3).

The sources of reproductions for the artists to follow in creating their images for the altar were many. Illustrated bibles were available and frequently represented a variety of styles and compositions for a number of significant

biblical stories. The 1890 Holman Bible, with its amalgam of languages and illustrations, provided Norwegian-American artists with an extensive visual resource for biblical scenes, characters, and events. Other reproductions of popular images were widely available, especially in card or print form, and these too were used by immigrant artists as the basis for their altar paintings.[7] A number of immigrant artists who made altar painting a serious and significant part of their business published catalogs, reproducing the European models they were willing to copy.[8] All of this material was as available to the amateur as to the trained artist, contributing to a consistency in the subject matter and iconography of altar paintings in spite of extreme differences in the execution of the work. Since the congregations also had knowledge of or access to the same black and white images as the artists, it made the process of selection of a scene and negotiation over the treatment of the subject a relatively simple matter.

The common availability of and familiarity with these models helped to establish the artistic preferences of the community and its conception of reli-

Ill. 2. (left) Unknown artist, *The Good Shepherd* (copy after Plockhorst). Altar frame by Knut Lee, about 1890. Aal Lutheran church, Hillsboro, North Dakota. *Courtesy of Vesterheim*

Ill. 3. (right) Minnie Martinson, *Jesus and Mary at the Tomb* (copy after Thoma), 1898. Tolgen Lutheran church, Saum, Minnesota. *Courtesy of Kristin M. Anderson*

gious figures. The models were accepted as accurate pictures of Jesus and examples of appropriate styles for religious art. Artists and patrons were able to converse in the same artistic and theological language because of their common access to the images.

The Altar Frames   While the objects enclosed in the altar frame followed standard patterns, the framing elements themselves provided greater variety. The altar and its retable could be an independent piece of furniture, or it could be a part of a suite or set of furniture for the chancel. Many of the factors determining size, style, surface treatment, and decoration were affected by the association of the frame with other parts of the interior design.

Some of the earliest Norwegian-American altars combined the altar table with the pulpit, which was placed above it in the retable (Ills. 4 and 5). In this economizing of form, the principal pieces of chancel furniture were joined in a single unit, restating in visual terms the traditional Lutheran emphases on word and sacrament. This combined form originated in Germany in the early eighteenth century, and it was used in Denmark by the 1740s, appearing in Lauritz de Thurah's design of the chapel at Hørsholm. The altar-pulpit form also appeared in Norway at this time in the interior furnishings of the Kongsberg church (begun 1739).[9] Further, the use of the altar-pulpit allowed for the continuity of the tradition of the elevated pulpit, seen in many Norwegian buildings. In a small log church, a dramatically raised pulpit in its usual position close to the congregation would have been overwhelming, as it is in some small Norwegian churches. The altar-pulpit alleviates some of the physical and visual oppressiveness that the original type of elevated pulpit might have created in these small buildings.

Most of these pieces were quite simple in their design and were usually left unpainted. It might be said that they were constructed rather than created, and they are associated with the building of the church in their materials and methods of construction. The one in Muskego church from 1844 is a good example. The type was a convenient solution to a proper handling of the chancel before the 1880s, when professional painters first became available and amateur artists first found time to develop skills adequate for church decoration. Many immigrant men already possessed fine carpentry skills from Norway and were quite capable of constructing distinctive altar-pulpits.

It is possible for an altar-pulpit combination of a slightly later date to have a painting or sculpture below the pulpit; however, the preacher remains the visual focus of the retable. When decorated, this type of altar usually received some kind of architectural ornament, like engaged columns under the pulpit space. These columns also provided some of the visual support necessary for the structure to "hold" the preacher. Other altars of a somewhat later date in this tradition, like those at East Koshkonong and Scandinavia, Wisconsin,

Kristin M. Anderson

Ill. 4. (top) Interior of the Muskego church, about 1844. Now at St. Paul, Minnesota. *Courtesy of Vesterheim*

Ill. 5. (bottom) Altar-pulpit of the old Hauge church, south of Mount Horeb, Wisconsin, about 1852. *Courtesy of Kristin M. Anderson*

attempt to combine the older altar-pulpit type with elements of the standard frame (Ills. 6 and 7).

While the altar-pulpit is a fascinating early type used in some Norwegian-American buildings, most of the altar frames were made to accommodate art objects. The sense of the framing function is evident in the placement of ornamentation around the image or object. It is frequently the frame that draws the attention of the viewer, and at times the frame may be so large or so ornate that it becomes more compelling than the central image it houses.

The shape of the frame often resembled architectural forms like the portal, the niche, or the window, providing an entrance or point of access from one realm into another (Ill. 6). The sides of the frame were decorated symmetrically, frequently with variations on architectural elements like columns (Ills. 3, 6), or with small versions of the central niche (Ills. 8, 9), representing respectively Neo-Classic and Gothic approaches to framing, established styles following this chronological sequence in nineteenth-century art. The top of the frame could extend well above the niche, completing the architectural forms and continuing the verticality established in the niche's shape. In the predella, just above the altar table and below the niche, it was common to have a panel with an inscription, often related to the image above. "Herre Frels Mig!" (Lord, save me) was used for many images, including some resurrection scenes; "Det er Fuldbragt!" (It is finished) was used under crucifixion scenes (Ills. 10, 8). In the absence of a standard three-word biblical quotation, this panel could be decorated with marbleizing or wood-graining, demonstrating some of the skills of the maker (Ill. 2).

In frames directly dependent on earlier Norwegian folk traditions, acan-

Kristin M. Anderson

Ill. 8. (above left) John Rein, Crucifixion and altar frame, with inscription painted on the canvas. After 1906. Formerly at Malvik Lutheran church, Guthrie, Minnesota. *Courtesy of Malvik Lutheran church*

Ill. 9. (above right) August Klagstad, *Resurrection.* Altar frame and chancel furniture made by Johan Dalhaug, 1906–1907. Nordland Lutheran church, Paynesville, Minnesota. *Courtesy of Kristin M. Anderson*

Ill. 10. (opposite) August Klagstad, *Resurrection.* Altar frame by Østen Pladson, about 1903. Bethania Lutheran church, Northwood, North Dakota. Church and altar now at Vesterheim, The Norwegian-American Museum. *Courtesy of Vesterheim*

thus decoration was used on the sides of the frames (Ills. 2, 7). The majority of the frames were made in the Victorian Gothic style, reminiscent of elements of the architectural revival which informed many of the buildings. Use of the pointed arch, trefoil or quatrefoil shapes, and multiple spires, and emphasis on the verticality of the frame are among the typical Gothic revival features seen in the altar frames. The finish of the altars could be natural wood, perhaps with some paint, but the Gothic-style altars were typically painted white, with gold details.

The Acquisition of Paintings and Frames

Congregations had a number of options for providing their church buildings with the necessary equipment and furnishings. Since woodworking skills were common among Norwegians of rural or working-class origin, many of the wooden furnishings were made locally. Skill in painting pictures, on the other hand, was not as common, and so it was more likely than not that the congregations would obtain their altar pictures from a source outside the congregation or community.

Most of the chancel furniture, statues, and paintings after about 1890 were supplied by a limited number of companies and individuals who specialized in such materials. Upper midwestern sources included some German-American firms in Milwaukee as well as Norwegian-American sources like Augsburg Publishing House in Minneapolis.

Many of the professional artists who supplied the altar paintings for Norwegian Lutheran churches in the Upper Midwest lived and worked in Minneapolis for the majority of their careers, turning out hundreds of works from their studios there.[10] The earliest in this Minneapolis group was Herbjørn Gausta (1854–1924), a landscape and genre painter who probably made the altars to provide himself with a dependable source of income in a business based on long connections with a number of Norwegian Synod personalities.[11] Another early painter was Sarah Kirkeberg Raugland (1862–1960), who produced altar paintings in her studio in Minneapolis from the early 1890s until the death of her husband in 1918 (Ill. 19). Her paintings were produced in large part for congregations of the United Church. A slightly later Minneapolis professional was August Klagstad (1866–1949), who, unlike Gausta, made the church work his primary concern (Ill. 9). Arne Berger (1872–1951) also did many altar paintings, working out of Northfield, Minneapolis, and Portland, Oregon. These artists are representative of the sources for professional church art that became available toward the turn of the century.

It was undoubtedly during the first forty years of church building among Norwegian Americans, from about 1848 to 1885, that artists and craftsmen either experienced in the folk arts from Norway or self-taught in this country were most used for the production of altars. One example is the already mentioned altar-pulpit produced by a rural carpenter for the Muskego church in about 1844 (Ill. 4). Another example is the now lost altar with acanthus carv-

Kristin M. Anderson

ing for the first Norwegian Grove Lutheran church in DeForest, Wisconsin, made about 1861 by Aasmund Aslakson Nestestu, a folk artist with a reputation in Telemark well before he immigrated to Wisconsin in 1843.[12] A third example was the altar of the Adams church near Argyle, Wisconsin, made by congregation members Lars Dammen and Iver Skindingsrud in 1868.[13] However, since comparatively few churches from this period remain, this study is limited primarily to folk creations from the period after 1880, when professionally produced altar paintings and mass-produced frames were becoming alternatives to folk production.

While the necessity for large quantities of altars around the turn of the century provided the opportunity for professional artists like Gausta to make a successful career of painting for their ethnic group, it also opened doors for others in the Norwegian-American community. These alternate sources included individuals who were on the margin of professional status and others not yet in that category who simply happened to be available, sometimes members of the congregation. This might mean that the congregation could get a better buy or even have the work donated. It might also mean that the work would be judged as "better" by members of the congregation, because it would be nearer their own aesthetic level. In his advertising materials, August Klagstad warned congregations about the potential difficulties of this method of acquisition. In a section of his catalogue called "Procure the Best," Klagstad wrote: "There is usually in all localities, an amateur artist said to be a genius, a second Raphael,—who offers to donate a painting to his home church, or to only charge for bare cost of material. The congregation can do nothing else but accept. After those having some knowledge of art have passed judgment on it the congregation realizes the embarrassing position in which they are placed. A case like the above is near my home. The pastor would like to have a good painting in the altar, but the congregation do not like to offend the artist by discarding his work."[14]

Some of these other individuals who provided church furniture and art works without formal training in the fine arts may be called artists of the people. They undoubtedly included people who could have been fine artists but who were limited by circumstances, occasionally by gender. They usually earned their living doing things outside the fine arts, although they frequently worked in related fields. Most common among these were house building, house and sign painting, or occasionally photography.

Many of the wood-carvers and woodworkers involved in making church furniture, even when not professionals, generally had considerable experience with their craft before taking on church work. Some woodworking and carpentry skills were expected among rural males in Norway, and strong traditions both in the crafts themselves and the means of transmitting them existed among Norwegians. Ties to the folk tradition are seen in the continuation of specific patterns and motifs from Norway, especially in the use of the acanthus. Such carvers as Aasmund Nestestu, Knut Lee, Lars Christenson, Andreas Eriksen, and the unknown maker of the Scandinavia, Wisconsin, altar even continue tradition in the organization of the decoration on the altar frame (Ills. 2, 7). Their carving skills were easily adapted to the Gothic style then pervasive in much of the decoration.

The Artists of the Folk Altars

Three groups will stand as representatives of the types of people's artists encountered in the production of church art for the Norwegian-American community. One type might be called the "would-be professional," who was generally employed in art-related fields, but who created a limited number of examples of fine-arts pieces, like altar paintings and portraits. A second type is the itinerant artist, who made paintings, sculpture, architectural ornaments, and other parts of the church environment in a number of locations but still did not possess the skills or artistic versatility of the professional. A third type is the local or regional artist who was situated in a single community and supplied either a single work or several in his or her area.

Regardless of their settings or the shapes of their careers, the kind of information available about artists of the people is often very sketchy. The house painters and farmers who appear as examples of Norwegian-American folk artists have not left papers, sketchbooks, exhibition histories, or gallery records. Neither did they advertise or receive much press coverage. Their conceptions of self and work were not the same as those of the professional artists, making it difficult to form a complete picture of their careers. Further, without a large creative production, the possibility of drawing general conclusions even regarding their work is difficult.

As a would-be professional, Julius Holm emerges as an interesting example of a people's artist active in an urban setting. His art has received some significant publicity in recent years, including the purchase of his 1893 painting *Tornado Over St. Paul* by the Minneapolis Institute of Arts and the reproduction of the same painting on the cover of an issue of *American Heritage* magazine (Ill. 11).[15] Yet despite this relatively broad exposure, very little is known about Holm.[16] It seems that he attempted to make a career for himself as an artist, but met with limited success. The qualities associated with a self-taught artist—perhaps the very qualities that met with Oluf Glasøe's stern disapproval in his description of "unsuccessful" altar paintings—may have prevented Holm from gaining recognition as a professional artist.

Julius Holm was born near Rødenes, Norway, in 1856.[17] He left home after his confirmation in 1870, and eventually enrolled in a military school in Oslo. He spent about three years in Stockholm as a part of the Norwegian contingent at the royal palace there, and then emigrated in 1880. Holm moved to Minneapolis in 1881, boarding with his siblings and mother for many of the succeeding years in various places in the Cedar-Riverside neighborhood. He eventually found his way to a relatively permanent residence on Sixteenth Avenue in 1903.

Kristin M. Anderson

When Julius Holm moved to Minneapolis he began a lifetime of employment related to painting. Holm's obituary noted that he worked as a painter
for the Milwaukee Road in his first years in Minneapolis; he listed himself as a
painter in the Minneapolis city directories in these years. By the late 1880s,
Holm was employed by the John M. Locke Company, a painting and decorating firm. He continued to identify himself as a painter until 1896, when he
began work at Holm and Snesrud, a photography studio.

This experience in a fine-arts-related field may have provided Julius Holm
the impetus he needed to pursue fine-arts work as his employment, at least
for a time. He listed himself as an artist or portrait artist in the city directories
for the next seven years; in 1902 his sister Sophie is listed in the directory as an
artist employed by Holm. In 1904 Holm's listing returned to the designation
of "painter," and he shifted from self-employment to employment by others.

Ill. 11. Julius Holm,
Tornado Over St. Paul,
1893. *Courtesy of*
Minneapolis Institute
of Arts

Ill. 12. Julius Holm
advertisement,
Lutheraneren, March 22,
1905, 190.

His work from this point seems to have been house painting and decorating, the exception being a listing in 1913 as a waiter. His obituary identifies house painting as his primary form of employment for all of the Minneapolis years.

While the entries in the city directories give some indications of Holm's employment and self-identification, they are not entirely accurate reflections of his artistic activity. Holm's best known painting, the *Tornado over St. Paul,* was painted in 1893, before he is first listed as a photographer, artist, or portrait artist. He advertised in *Lutheraneren* in 1905, declaring his ability to paint altar pictures, portraits, and landscapes (Ill. 12). Two of the three known altar paintings made by Holm were produced in 1904 at Westbrook and 1908 at Erskine after he discontinued the use of the "artist" designation in the directories. Emil Johnson's obituary of Holm suggests that his residence-studio was filled with art.[18] Johnson also mentions that Holm worked on his own art projects in the winters, when the house-painting work slowed. Although Holm was unable to transform his interest in becoming an artist into permanent employment in the field, he seems never to have surrendered his self-identification as an artist.[19]

Like the professional painters who made altars for the churches, Holm made enlarged painted copies of prints and photographs. This would have been a part of his artistic training and background from his work in the Holm and Snesrud company, and he continued this practice as he worked on easel paintings. It has been demonstrated that Holm used a photograph for *Tornado Over St. Paul*[20] and the few identified portraits painted by Holm are also obviously copied from existing prints.[21]

Yet while Holm shared with professionals like Gausta the practice of copying models, Holm's ability to translate these photographic or lithographic images from the small black-and-white prints to the larger scale of an altar painting was not as great as the ability of many of the professional artists. Most obvious in his works is the lack of convincing three-dimensionality in the rounded forms, especially in the human figure and its drapery, which may be seen in the Bellingham altar of 1901 (Ill. 13). This difficulty is less obvious in the rectilinear forms of the buildings in *Tornado Over St. Paul.* It is, however, this lack of proficiency in modeling, combined with the high contrasts of

Kristin M. Anderson

light and dark seen in the Bellingham altar, that give Holm's works much of their current appeal as examples of "naive" painting.

The opportunity of urban artists like Holm to succeed was perhaps more limited than it was for their rural counterparts, who usually had less immediate competition and a closer connection with their patrons and viewers. Characteristics that might be taken as lack of skill in an artist from outside the group might be taken for granted and accepted when the product of a native son or daughter. As a Minneapolis artist, Holm might have been judged as a professional and considered second-rate. A congregation's sensitivity to what it considered quality in the work of an outside artist is revealed in a congregational history from Madelia, Minnesota: "In 1887 they decided to buy an altar painting and have an altar, altar ring, pulpit and baptismal font built. Nels Wick built the altar, altar ring and frame for the picture. The painting, 'The Ascension' was decided on, and it was to be purchased from Askenold in Germany, if it could be gotten as cheaply as one bought here. Where the picture

Ill. 13. Julius Holm,
Resurrection, **1901. St.**
Paul's Lutheran church,
Bellingham, Minnesota.
Courtesy of Kristin M.
Anderson

was finally purchased is not stated in the records, but when it did arrive, it was of such poor workmanship that it was returned. The men of the church could come to no agreement on the purchase of an altar painting, so they asked the young people to take responsibility. The painting was purchased in Milwaukee."[22]

The second type of non-professional providing altars and furniture for Norwegian-American churches was the itinerant artist. John Rein (1858–1916) stands as an excellent example of this type. Rein was born at Ørlandet, near Trondheim, and spent his early years just to the southwest on the island of Hitra. He emigrated in 1878, settling near Hendrum, Minnesota. In the next twenty-five years, he and his family lived, among other places, in the Minnesota communities of Henning, Roseau, and Fisher. According to family histories, as well as the widespread evidence of his work, Rein participated in church building, church decoration, and altar painting wherever he went. He is said to have worked on the construction and decoration of church buildings in Wisconsin, Minnesota, North and South Dakota, Montana, and Washington.[23]

Although Rein is identified as a farmer, his background and activity demonstrate various forms of artistic talent. His family biography indicates that he had "a beautiful scripthand," and that he did sign painting, commercial art, house painting, and woodgraining. He was also skilled in woodworking; his father was a carpenter, and when the family moved to Roseau county, father and son had a carpenter shop. Rein's activities in all aspects of church building indicate that he probably was well trained in carpentry and wood carving, and given the nature of the father's skills, this training would have been of the informal variety typical of the folk art tradition.

The most striking Rein painting to come to light is his *Last Supper* from about 1895, done for a church in Roseau county, Minnesota (Ill. 14).[24] Rein chose a logical but unusual subject for an altar painting: the multi-figure Last Supper scene. It has been demonstrated that Rein made use of a modified version of Leonardo da Vinci's *Last Supper* from the 1890 edition of the Holman Bible, which has the disciples stacked for greater verticality.[25] Rein's expressive outlines, seen in figures, furniture, and shadows, contribute to the vitality of the presentation. The highly original and primitive quality of this painting has helped it to become one of the most celebrated pieces of Norwegian-American church art.[26] Later examples of John Rein's altar paintings indicate a gradual move from the primitive style of the Roseau painting to one of much greater refinement like the work of the Minneapolis professional artists. Practice may account for this, but the development of an original conception of the subject, as opposed to the copying of the standard model, may be a factor in the variety seen in Rein's work. Like the Roseau altar painting, some of Rein's altar frames were highly original. However, the striking naïveté of the Last Supper is replaced by sophisticated design in examples like the

Kristin M. Anderson

Malvik church chancel furniture (Ill. 8). As was the case in the immigrant community as a whole, it seems that the woodworking skills were well grounded in tradition and easily applied and manipulated, while the painting skills presented a greater challenge.

One particularly interesting group within this category of itinerants was pastors and members of their families. On occasion their work can be traced from one congregation to another across the span of their careers. Like the other artists considered here, these clergy or clergy-related artists filled a need in the individual churches; they also had a chance to dictate taste, and leave behind tangible evidence of their presence and service at the congregation.

The probable contributions of Claus L. Clausen to some of his early churches indicate that this pattern of the pastor-carpenter may be seen from the beginning of Norwegian settlement. H. Fred Swanson suggests that there was a wood-carver in Clausen's ancestry; a maternal great grandfather was supposed to have carved the altar frame for the Rise church on Ærø, Denmark.[27] Clausen worked on the construction of the Muskego church in 1844, when he "often assisted the men in the heavy work of cutting and trimming the logs, and in manifold jobs associated with the undertaking."[28] He also helped to construct a sawmill in St. Ansgar, Iowa, in 1853–1854.[29] Beyond his actual participation in the building, he is often credited with the supervision of these major projects and related design work. Luther Valley "church traditions" extended Clausen's responsibility to the making of the interior furnishings of the East Luther Valley church.[30]

Not all pastors who contributed to the decoration of their churches were adept at the task,[31] but some, such as Mathæus Stensen (1870–1942), appear to have been well prepared for their contributions. A number of the congregations he served, including churches in Staples and Menahga, Minnesota, were provided with his paintings.[32] Caja Wulfsberg Thoen's copy of Plockhorst's painting of the Good Shepherd, made for the altar at Our Savior's Lutheran church in Wells, Minnesota, is an example of work by a pastor's wife (Ill. 15). Her artistic bent probably came from her family background; she was the daughter of the printer and publisher Einar Wulfsberg. There might have been more altar paintings from her hand, had her husband, Jacob Ellingsen Thoen, continued in the parish ministry.

The last category of non-professional artists and craftspeople working in the church are those working in a limited area. Some established themselves in the history of their locality by doing a single work for the church building. Others operated more like the semi-professional or itinerant artists, supplying paintings or frames for a number of churches around them, or for more distant congregations with which they had some personal or direct connection.

Of the local or regional artists, the painter Minnie Martinson (1878–circa 1947) is an interesting example. Martinson lived in Lake Park, Minnesota, for much of her life. She was from a family that seemed to those who knew them to be unusually gifted with their hands. Her father was described in a congregational history as a "sort of super-handyman,"[33] and according to conversations with longtime Lake Park residents, it seems that her brothers possessed many of the same abilities. The congregational history describes Martinson as a "talented artist, [who] painted china dishes, portraits, and many altar paintings. The studio, in which she worked, built along the Martinson home . . . had a north skylight and was large enough to house the tall pictures."[34] Martinson's paintings are found in the northwestern area of Minnesota (Ill. 3), and a few have been located in North Dakota. An unusually primitive painting attributed to Martinson is located in the museum in Ulen. Like John Rein, Minnie Martinson evidently was willing to display work that was not entirely refined or polished (Ill. 16).

This category of non-professional artists and craftspeople is responsible for some of the major wood carving and other woodworking done in the immigrant church, much by artisans with some knowledge of their craft from

Norway. The altar carvings of these artists demonstrate a close resemblance to Norwegian prototypes and sometimes continue to use traditional motifs like the acanthus.

The most celebrated carved altar in Norwegian-American church history is the unfinished altar of Lars Christenson (1839–1910) (Ill. 17).[35] While most of the carving on altars was applied to the form and ornamentation of the frames, this altar uses wood carving as the vehicle for the altar imagery. Christenson was born in Sogndal, and before his emigration he learned blacksmithing and wood carving. He immigrated to Iowa in 1864, and eventually settled near Benson, Minnesota. Marion Nelson has thoroughly documented inspirations and influences for Christenson's altar, ranging from the vaguely remembered patterns of Norwegian church art to contemporary bible illustrations in Christenson's possession.[36] As was the case with John Rein's early attempts at figure depictions, Christenson used highly abstracted human forms in the panels of his altar. He incorporated with greater ease the non-figurative elements of the scrolling acanthus plant at the top of the altar, and

Ill. 15. (left) Caja Wulfsberg Thoen, *The Good Shepherd,* **about 1900. Our Savior's Lutheran church (now Good Shepherd Lutheran church), Wells, Minnesota.** *Courtesy of Kristin M. Anderson*

Ill. 16. (right) Minnie Martinson, *Ascension,* **at Ulen Museum, Ulen, Minnesota.** *Courtesy of Philip Thompson*

Kristin M. Anderson

demonstrated a great respect for the wood and its intrinsic beauty. Christenson worked on this altar, intended for his own church, from about 1897 until 1904. It is suggested that he stopped work because it seemed that the congregation was unreceptive.[37] These parishioners probably shared with Oluf Glasøe and August Klagstad traditional ideas about beauty in church art, and according to these standards Christenson's altar was bound to be misunderstood.

Carvers before Christenson had built on the Norwegian acanthus tradition in the making of altars. One of these acanthus carvers was Aasmund Aslakson Nestestu of Telemark (1797–1885). A second altar in a Rococo variant of this style, made by a farmer named Andreas Eriksen of rural Rothsay, Minnesota, is still located in the South Immanuel Lutheran church northeast of Rothsay (Ill. 18). Erikson carved the complex altar frame in 1893, using a typical Norwegian pattern to surround two vertically arranged paintings—the Last Supper and the Ascension—with rocaille formulated to resemble traditional acanthus. In a celestial design reminiscent of the sunburst at the top of Nestes-

Ill. 17. (opposite) Lars Christenson, *Altar,* 1897–1904. *Courtesy of Vesterheim*

Ill. 18. (above) Andreas Eriksen, altar frame, 1893. South Immanuel Lutheran church, Rothsay, Minnesota. *Courtesy of Marion John Nelson*

tu's lost DeForest altar, the peak of Eriksen's altar has an unusual arrangement of volutes surrounding a triangle containing the name *Jehova*. The altar surface was marbled, but repairs to the surface have obliterated that original effect.[38]

Knut O. Lee (or Lie) (1831–1900) also made altars with direct ties to Norwegian altar-carving traditions. Lee's acanthus altar for the Aal church at Hillsboro, North Dakota, is his only extant altar of this type (Ill. 2). Lee was from Øier in Gudbrandsdalen. He emigrated some time before 1870, and lived first in Coon Valley, Wisconsin, where he made some of the furniture for the log church, including the altar frame, the pulpit, and the baptismal font.[39] He moved from Coon Valley to northern Wisconsin, and eventually he settled in Mayville, North Dakota, where he was a miller.[40] Gudbrandsdalen had developed as an important center for the richly scrolled acanthus carving in the eighteenth century. Lee's contact with the tradition is clear in his Aal altar, but he imposed an interesting balance and unusual restraint on the acanthus forms by setting them around the strong architectural elements of columns and portal and by draping the acanthus over a horizontal "rod" at the top of the frame.

While the survival in America of the Gudbrandsdal style carving is remarkable to art historians, the intended viewers of the altar noticed other elements. An anniversary history of the congregation recognizes Lee's ties to tradition and his skill with the material, saying that "he had learned the art of wood carving in the Old Country." The description dwells on a different aspect of the altar, discussing the small religious symbols at the top of the altar frame and suggesting that these are the features of the greatest interest: "In [the altar] can be found the Ark of the Covenant, the Lamb of Sacrifice, the dove of peace, the fruit of the vineyard, and the olive leaf."[41]

The interior of the Lyster Lutheran church near Nelson, Wisconsin, done by congregation member Ole Myren (c. 1831–1908), shows the extension of the acanthus decoration beyond the confines of the furniture (Ill. 19). Myren is described in congregational histories as an expert with wood, being skilled in carpentry, cabinetmaking, and wood carving.[42] He is credited with providing the turned columns used to hold up the gallery in the church.[43] The Lyster altar has sections of acanthus at the crown and upper sides of the frame, while the lower sections of the frame next to the altar table have oval panels with Roman numerals representing the ten commandments. The strong architectural form of Myren's altar and the relatively small acanthus at the sides of the frame are typical of altar frames of the later period, but the spread of the acanthus to the pulpit—and especially to the chancel arch—are reminiscent of the exuberance of earlier Norwegian folk-church interiors. The general appearance of the interior has been changed by the typical but unfortunate practice of painting most of the chancel and its furniture white. The frame originally

contained a painting of the crucifixion, done by Sarah Kirkeberg Raugland in about 1889; the date of Myren's carving, then, appears to be before 1890.[44]

Another exceptional local church carpenter is the Hallingdal-born Østen Pladson of Hatton, North Dakota (1846–1914). Pladson built (and rebuilt, after tornadoes) a number of churches in the Northwood, North Dakota, area in the 1890s and 1900s, providing not only construction expertise but also the cabinetmaking, turning, and carving skills to create the chancel furnishings.[45] His highly ornate altars go beyond the normal exuberance expected in the Victorian Gothic revival styles; they include areas with acanthus scrolls, and call to mind the *horror vacui* of the folk art tradition (Ill. 10).

In the early twentieth-century work of Norwegian-American carvers and painters there is a growing acceptance of the prevailing style of church furnishing and decoration and a shift from obvious Norwegian styles and forms. However, woodworking skills and a continued, although more subtle, use of Norwegian wood-carving styles can be seen in some early twentieth-century folk altars. One example of this type is the work of John Barikmo, who was born in Telemark in 1872 and emigrated in 1893. He farmed near Iola, Wisconsin, and lived until 1965. Local and family sources indicate that he was trained in wood carving before leaving Norway.[46] His American production is largely furniture, and among these pieces are chancel furnishings for Northland Lutheran church in Iola, made by Barikmo in 1907 (Ill. 20). In its general design, the altar frame is very much like the products available through the church supply houses at the time, but Barikmo's treatment of the surface

Ill. 19. Sarah Kirkeberg Raugland, *Crucifixion,* about 1889. Ole Myren, altar and chancel carvings, about 1889. Lyster Lutheran church, Nelson, Wisconsin. *Courtesy of Vesterheim*

Ill. 20. John Barikmo, altar
frame for Northland
Lutheran Church, Iola,
Wisconsin, about 1907.
Courtesy of Vesterheim

reflects his training in Telemark *flatskurd* techniques, in which a flat design is carved in shallow relief against a flat surface.[47]

The altar, altar frame, altar ring, and pulpit of Nordland Lutheran church in rural Paynesville, Minnesota (Ill. 9), demonstrate an awareness of contemporary church design, while maintaining a close connection to Norwegian traditions in wood. The chancel furniture was made by Johan Dalhaug (1865–1909), a Norwegian-trained woodworker who belonged to this congregation. Dalhaug's 1906–1907 frame, which surrounds an August Klagstad *Resurrection,* was made in the Victorian Gothic style, with pointed arches, pinnacles, spires, and tracery. The description of Dalhaug's work in the centennial history of the congregation reads like a hagiography, elevating the production of the artistic material to the level of sacrificial activity: "The work was done in the living room of his home. . . . The oak lumber that Mr. Dalhaug used had been sawed and seasoned for furniture for his home. His turning lathe was of his own making as were also some of his tools. As power for his turning lathe he used a 'horse-power.' A 'horse-power' meant that a horse was hitched near the end of a long pole in such a way that it could walk only in a circle. This set in motion gears near the other end of the pole. A shaft from the gears through the living room window and to the turning lathe set that in motion when the horse walked. When necessary the horse was urged on to more speed by a whip manipulated through the open window. As parts were completed, they were hung from the ceiling of the living room. Can we fully appreciate the skill and patience Johan Dalhaug must have had to complete this work of beauty which we see when we sit in our church? Or, could we match the unselfishness of his wife, Petronelle, who let the living room of

Kristin M. Anderson

her small house be used for a carpenter shop and gave up the lumber which was to have been her furniture?"[48] Quoting this account by no means makes light of Dalhaug or the esteem in which he and his work are held in the congregation, but the story and its retelling indicate an enduring appreciation of the talents and the contributions of local artists to the church, even though the subtle honoring of the Norwegian tradition is not noted.

The presence of examples of various kinds of folk altars in the Norwegian-American church may serve as evidence of acts of kindness or faith on the part of the creators, who sought to contribute to the decoration of one of the most significant spaces in their communities. Since the local church had been a typical site for folk creations in Norway, it is not surprising to find churches continuing to act as an outlet for the work of folk or people's artists. The strong demand for many pieces of chancel furniture and altar art opened windows of opportunity for many Norwegian-American artists. If demand had not been so high, competition with the professional artists might have kept the folk furnishings out of many Norwegian-American churches; however, for some congregations, the relative cost of works was probably a factor in favor of the use of folk artists.

Conclusions

Regardless of the issues of price, competition, and opportunity, the wish to create and express is not exclusive to those who are formally trained or gainfully employed in these areas. The heritage and traditions of the Norwegian Americans stressed an economy of materials and means, favoring the use of skills and materials close at hand, and numerous individuals with significant creative capacities were clearly willing and able to provide art for the church. These circumstances added immeasurably to the richness and ultimate artistic significance of Norwegian-American church art.

NOTES

1. Oluf Glasøe, *Church Designs* (Minneapolis, 1917), 99.

2. O.M. Norlie, *Norsk lutherske menigheter i Amerika, 1843–1916,* 1 (Minneapolis, 1918), 321–331, 539–553.

3. In *Norsk lutherske menigheter,* 925, Norlie indicates that a number of congregations divided or dissolved "*paa grund av for lang kirkevei,*" for example, St. Ansgar's near Colton, South Dakota.

4. This practice was still included in the *Service Book and Hymnal* (Minneapolis, 1958), where the minister is instructed in the rubrics, usually when addressing God instead of the people, to "turn to the Altar" or to pray when "standing before the Altar, and facing it."

5. E. Clifford Nelson, in *The Lutheran Church Among the Norwegian Americans,* 2 (Minneapolis, 1960), 127, states that "if one attended a Haugean service in the late nineteenth or early twentieth century, he would note the traditional Norwegian Lutheran chancel arrange-

ment: a free-standing altar at the center, the pulpit at one side and the baptismal font at the other. . . . However, almost immediately the visitor would note disregard for the usual rubrics of the *Ritual.*"

6. The most obvious examples in Glasøe's plan book are seen in the drawings made by Torgeir Alvsaker, which include a building in the style of a stave church. *Church Designs,* 38–41.

7. The papers of Herbjørn Gausta, at Vesterheim, the Norwegian-American Museum, in Decorah, include many examples of these small reproductions.

8. For example, Sarah Raugland published two catalogs through Augsburg Publishing House (1893 and 1899). Arne Berger and August Klagstad also had catalogs printed.

9. Anders Bugge and Henning Alsvik, eds., *Norges kirker. Kongsberg kirke* (Oslo, 1962), 56. Marion J. Nelson has suggested that the Norwegian-American use of the altar-pulpit can be traced in large part to Danish roots, as Claus L. Clausen, a Dane, made early use of this form at Muskego.

10. In a 1915 article from Marinette, Wisconsin, written at the time of painter August Klagstad's departure from that city, he is said to have chosen Minneapolis "in order to develop the more artistic side of his work . . . and to get in touch with the artistic circles and atmosphere of a larger city." In a 1987 interview, his daughter, Alice Berning, suggested that business opportunities were also a factor.

11. Marion J. Nelson has suggested that Gausta probably would have preferred other types of painting over the relatively static copy work of the altars, but used the altar-painting market to supply himself with reliable business. See Marion J. Nelson, "Herbjørn Gausta, Norwegian-American Painter," in *Americana Norvegica: Studies in Scandinavian-American Interrelations,* 3 (Oslo, 1971), 15–16.

12. George T. Flom, *A History of Norwegian Immigration to The United States: From the Earliest Beginning down to the Year 1848* (Iowa City, 1909), 253; Nelson, "American Woodcarvers from Telemark," in *Telemark Historie,* 8 (1987), 26–28; and Nelson, "Norwegian-American Woodcarving: Historic and Aesthetic Context," in *Norwegian-American Wood Carving of the Upper Midwest* (Decorah, Iowa, 1978), 16.

13. This altar was destroyed in 1990 in a fire which gutted the 1864 church. Parts of the altar are visible in the congregation's centennial publication (1956). Aslak Lie, originally of Perry, Wisconsin, could perhaps be included in this list; but in spite of the extensive research on him by John Holzhueter of the State Historical Society of Wisconsin, it has been difficult to document specifically the nature of his involvement with the altars associated with him.

14. August Klagstad, "Sacred Art for the Church," brochure (Marinette, Wisconsin, 1906), 6.

15. A detail of this painting was used on the cover of the June/July 1978 issue of *American Heritage,* 29:4, to accompany an article called "The Winds of Ruin: Tornadoes on the American Landscape." A small but complete image of the painting is included with the table of contents."

16. The Minneapolis Institute of Arts has no specific information about Holm in its files.

17. Much of the early biographical information about Holm is gleaned from his obituary

in *Skandinaven* (December 23, 1930), written by his friend Emil Johnson Skislet. Johnson was also born in Rødenes, and came to the United States in 1881, a year after Holm's arrival. The two friends stayed in touch, even after Johnson moved to Erskine, Minnesota; the Erskine church has a Holm painting, and Johnson's obituary for his friend describes Holm's residence at the time of his death.

18. "Hans Arbeidsrum var fuldt med all Slags Billeder. . . . Han hadde et vakkert Hjem," in *Skandinaven,* December 23, 1930.

19. Carl G. O. Hansen's *My Minneapolis* (Minneapolis, 1956), 175, mentions another "would-be professional," Olaf H. Aalbu (died 1926). Aalbu was employed as a decorator, but his home was filled with easel paintings on marine themes. Hansen made special note of a painting of the Titanic.

20. Mark Meister, "The Man Who Painted the Lake Gervais Tornado," in *Minnesota History* (Winter, 1977), 329–332.

21. Meister's article mentions two Holm portraits at St. Olaf College, of Martin Luther and Hans Nielsen Hauge, and Timothy Trent Blade has mentioned a Holm portrait of Woodrow Wilson in a private collection.

22. Seventy-fifth anniversary history (1945), Trinity Lutheran Church, Madelia, Minnesota, 11.

23. Factual material on John Rein comes from a ninetieth anniversary history (1987) of Malvik Lutheran church, Guthrie, Minnesota, which reprints information taken from an informal family biography of John Rein. Marion Nelson included additional information on Rein in "The Material Culture and Folk Arts of the Norwegians in America," in Ian M.G. Quimby and Scott T. Swank, eds., *Perspectives on American Folk Art* (New York, 1980), 118–120.

24. In *Painting and Sculpture in Minnesota 1820–1914* (Minneapolis, 1976), 60, Rena Coen identifies the altar's point of origin as the Old Rose church of Greenbush. However, O. M. Norlie's inventory of churches in Roseau county lists John Reien (sic) as the only congregational officer—the secretary—of the Hvidsø church, near Greenbush. This congregation dissolved in 1904. (*Norsk lutherske menigheter,* 796). It is likely that Rein painted the altar for his own church, but that the painting became part of the collection of another congregation after the closing of the Hvidsø church.

25. Nelson, "The Material Culture," 121.

26. The Roseau altar was discussed and reproduced in color in Rena Coen's *Painting and Sculpture in Minnesota;* in addition, it received exposure in a 1980 Winterthur publication in Nelson's essay in *Perspectives on American Folk Art.*

27. H. Fred Swanson, *The Founder of St. Ansgar: The Life Story of Claus Laurits Clausen* (Blair, Nebraska, 1949), 14.

28. Swanson, *The Founder of St. Ansgar,* 51.

29. Swanson, *The Founder of St. Ansgar,* 120.

30. Claire Selkurt, "The Domestic Architecture and Cabinetry of Luther Valley," in *Norwegian-American Studies,* 30 (1985), 268 and 270.

31. The Swedish-American church at Alborn, Minnesota, now abandoned, has a very

primitive painting by its pastor, Carl Pontus Peterson. Peterson's painting is a copy of Plockhorst's Good Shepherd, and although he did his best to simplify the image by leaving out the "excess" flock, his lack of training is evident.

32. Stensen's biography in Norlie, *Who's Who Among Pastors in all the Norwegian Lutheran Synods of America 1843–1927* (Minneapolis, 1928), 549, gives no indication of artistic training.

33. Centennial history (1974), Lake Park Lutheran church, Lake Park, Minnesota, 29.

34. Centennial history, Lake Park church, 30.

35. Erwin Christensen, a former curator at the National Gallery in Washington, D.C., was among the first to identify this altar as a significant piece, in the *Index of American Design* (Washington, D.C., 1930).

36. Nelson, "A Pioneer Artist and His Masterpiece," in *Norwegian-American Studies*, 22 (1965), 3–17.

37. Nelson, "The Material Culture," 118.

38. Conversation with Mrs. Lillian Aas of Rothsay.

39. Hjalmar R. Holand, *En historisk beretning om de norske menighter i Coon Valley* (Minneapolis, 1928), 224. Fragments of Lee's acanthus altar survive and are in private hands.

40. Seventy-fifth anniversary history (1947), Aal Lutheran church, Hillsboro, North Dakota; Nelson, notes on Knut Lee and "*Norwegian-American Wood Carving*," 80.

41. Seventy-fifth anniversary history, Aal Lutheran church, 18.

42. The seventy-fifth anniversary history (1941) of the Lyster congregation also notes that Myren was "also the one people went to when they had broken bones, or teeth to be extracted" (11).

43. The centennial history (1966), Lyster Lutheran church, Nelson, Wisconsin, dates the church building to 1867, but the chancel was an 1883 addition. The history does not give a date for the construction of the gallery.

44. Raugland's 1893 catalog includes a chronological list of works completed. The first painting on the list was done for Pastor Wik of Urne, Wisconsin; this is certainly the same painting. In 1952, the Raugland painting was removed and an image of Jesus knocking at the door was put in its place.

45. Angela Pladson Midbo, "Østen Pladson, Kirkebygger og Alterkunstner," in *Hallingen* (December, 1973), 8–14.

46. Cited in Nelson, "American Woodcarvers from Telemark," and in "*Norwegian-American Wood Carving*."

47. Nelson notes that the realistic quality of Barikmo's plant forms is unlike the traditional Telemark carving. "American Woodcarvers from Telemark," 39.

48. Centennial history (1968), Nordland Lutheran church, Paynesville, Minnesota, 15.

Contributors

M ARION JOHN NELSON is a professor of art history at the University of Minnesota and director emeritus of Vesterheim, the Norwegian-American Museum. He retired from the latter position at the end of 1991 after having served as director for twenty-seven years; during that time he spearheaded fundamental change and impressive growth in the museum collection and its operation to make Vesterheim the premier ethnic museum in the United States. Nelson has specialized in the folk, decorative, and fine arts of Scandinavian Americans, but in addition to American art has lectured and published widely also on Scandinavian art.

Reidar Bakken has an advanced degree in ethnology with supporting studies in art history and Norwegian history from the University of Oslo. He has been director and curator at the Norwegian Emigrant Museum in Hamar and the museums in Upper Gudbrandsdalen. Since 1992 he has been a free-lance ethnologist. Bakken has written a forthcoming book on American immigrants from Valdres.

James Skurdall received his B.A. from Pacific Lutheran University in Tacoma, Washington, and an M.A. in languages and literature from Washington University in St. Louis, Missouri. For twenty years he taught and did translating in Norway and in Bonn, Germany. He now continues to do both in Decorah, Iowa.

Kenneth A. Breisch has a Ph.D. in art history from the University of Michigan. From 1981 until 1986 Breisch was employed as coordinator of the Survey and Planning Division of the Texas Historical Commission and he currently teaches architectural history at the Southern California Institute of Architecture in Los Angeles. Breisch has just completed a book on the libraries of

Henry Hobson Richardson, and is editing a guidebook to the architecture of Texas.

Carol Colburn has a Ph.D. in art history from the University of Minnesota. She teaches costume history and theater costume design at the University of Northern Iowa, Cedar Falls. Currently she is continuing the study of Norwegian-American transitional dress, having received a grant from the Norwegian government to study in photographic and clothing collections in Norwegian museums.

M.A. Madson has a Ph.D. in design, housing, and apparel from the University of Minnesota. She is at present an associate for public programs at the Minneapolis Institute of Art. Madson continues to pursue her professional interests in costume, silverwork, and historic preservation.

Carlin Hibbard has a M.A. in art history from the University of Minnesota. She has done extensive research and recording of the life and works of S.O. Lund for the Chippewa Valley Museum in Eau Claire, Wisconsin, under the direction of Marion Nelson. Hibbard has been a guest curator for an exhibit on this artist titled "Images of Old and New: S.O. Lund, Norwegian-American Artist." She is currently employed as gallery manager and art consultant by Accola Gallery, Durand, Wisconsin.

Kristin M. Anderson has earned master's degrees in art history at the University of Minnesota and in church history at Luther Northwestern Theological Seminary. She is currently chair of the Art Department at Augsburg College. Anderson is continuing her research in Scandinavian-American religious art and architecture.